Vulnerable Subjects

Vulnerable Subjects

Ethics and Life Writing

G. THOMAS COUSER

Cornell University Press / Ithaca and London

First published 2004 by Cornell University Press
First printing, Cornell Paperbacks, 2004

Printed in the United States of America

Library of Congress Cataloging-in-Publication Data

Couser, G. Thomas.
    Vulnerable subjects : ethics and life writing / G. Thomas
Couser.
        p. cm.
Includes bibliographical references and index.
    ISBN 0-8014-4185-4 (cloth : alk. paper) — ISBN 0-8014-8863-X
(pbk. : alk. paper)
    1. Autobiography—Moral and ethical aspects.   2. Ethics.
I. Title.
    CT25.C698 2004
    920'.001—dc21

                                            2003010655

Cornell University Press strives to use environmentally
responsible suppliers and materials to the fullest extent
possible in the publishing of its books. Such materials include
vegetable-based, low-VOC inks and acid-free papers that are
recycled, totally chlorine-free, or partly composed of
nonwood fibers. For further information, visit our website at
www.cornellpress.cornell.edu.

Cloth printing   10 9 8 7 6 5 4 3 2 1
Paperback printing   10 9 8 7 6 5 4 3 2 1

To Jane Couser Barton

Contents

Preface
Auto/Bio/Ethics

THIS IS NOT A BOOK ABOUT BIOETHICS, much less a contribution to that field. Rather, it is about certain connections between life writing, especially contemporary life writing, and bioethics. Encapsulating what I see as vital relations between the two, the term *auto/bio/ethics* fuses the term *auto/biography*—which refers to life writing that focuses on the relation between the writer and a significant other—with *bioethics*.

The first connection that interests me is that contemporary life writing, at least in North America, often deals with conditions that raise questions concerning quality of life. The term "quality of life" is intended to distinguish individuals' sense of the worth of their existence from mere quantity, that is, the duration of their lives. The idea that individuals have an interest in their lives beyond merely extending them seems sound to me, and the question of the value of a life to a particular individual often comes to the fore in contemporary life writing—especially when it concerns disability.[1] A good example of both auto/biography and what I call quality-of-life writing is *Elegy for Iris* (1999), John Bayley's memoir of his life with the late philosopher and novelist Iris Murdoch. What made this book, published while Murdoch was still alive, remarkable was that a considerable portion of it was devoted to the final period of her life, when she had a form of dementia. What surprised and touched many readers was the book's testimony that Bayley and Murdoch continued to enjoy each other's company even after her formidable mental powers had dwindled into senility. The spectacle of the brilliant former don and novelist watching *Teletubbies* without real comprehension is a sad one, and yet, as Bayley tells it, in some ways the life of the couple continued to provide considerable gratification to both of them. This book raises questions such as: When does life cease to be meaningful? When does a human being cease to be a person or lose her identity? Can quality of life be sustained in the face of serious mental impairment?

Iris also exemplifies another, independent and ultimately more important connection between bioethics and contemporary life writing. In depicting his demented wife, Bayley is representing someone I would describe as a vulnerable subject. Indeed, like most of the subjects I discuss in this book, she is doubly vulnerable, or vulnerable in two dimensions. Her impairment makes her subject to harm (abuse and exploitation) in her life; and it also renders her vulnerable to misrepresentation in her husband's writing because it deprives her of the capacity to take part in, examine, respond to, or resist that representation. (Representation of such subjects also has two dimensions: *mimetic,* insofar as it speaks *about* its subject, and *political,* insofar as it speaks *for* its subject.) She is clearly unaware that Bayley is writing about her, and she is without competence to consent to having her dementia so publicly portrayed. (The feature film based on the book, which brought the story to a much larger audience, was produced after Murdoch's death.) Since Murdoch would likely never have wanted to be represented as incompetent, there is some question as to the ethicality of such representation. (I do not propose to adjudicate this question; I confine myself to saying that because the representation is evidently so loving and respectful—because it ascribes value to what seems an inherently undignified condition—I am inclined to think that Bayley does not violate Murdoch's integrity or that of their relationship, although he takes a great liberty with her story.)

The representation of vulnerable subjects in life writing is fraught with questions that bioethics, perhaps the most highly developed form of contemporary ethics, has considered because they often arise in biomedical scenarios. And the cardinal concepts of the approach to biomedical ethics known as "principlism"—respect for autonomy, beneficence, and justice—seem pertinent to the sorts of life writing under consideration here. It is now a critical commonplace that all *auto*biography is necessarily *hetero*biography as well because one can rarely if ever represent one's self without representing others. (Even *Walden,* popularly regarded as an account of a solitary sojourn in the woods, has a surprisingly large cast of characters; that most are anonymous or pseudonymous does not mean that they are entirely beyond harm. Indeed, Thoreau has been criticized for his prejudicial representation of the Irish in "Baker Farm.") Where does the right to express and represent oneself begin to infringe on another's right to privacy? How shall the desires of the self be weighed against the demands of the other, concern for aesthetics with concerns for ethics? Is it necessary, or at least desirable, to obtain consent or permission from those to be represented? When consent cannot be obtained, what constraints, if any, should apply to intimate life writing? What sorts of relationships, if any, confer surrogacy in life writing? Are auto/biographers obliged to "do good"—or at least to do no harm—to those they represent? Can harm to minor characters in one's autobiography be dismissed as unavoidable and trivial? If life writing necessarily involves violating the privacy of others and possibly harming them, what values might offset such ethical liabilities? Further, since published life writing is, after all, a commodity—in today's market, often a valuable one—is it necessary, or at least desirable, to share any proceeds with one's subject? What constitutes appropriation or even expropriation of someone else's story?

Life writing in the professions, such as medicine, is governed by certain ethical principles and procedures. In medicine, of course, the principles are precisely (but not exclusively) those just listed, which govern relationships between physicians and patients. For example, physicians and psychologists must protect the confidentiality of their patients or clients in their case histories or case reports. In contrast, no such regulations constrain lay life writing, and there is no standard procedure for regulating it. Nor am I calling for any such regulations or procedures. But I am interested in whether and when lay life writing raises the sorts of ethical issues that are addressed by professional ethics, and what sort of obligation devolves on life writers—and critics—when such ethical questions arise. Perhaps the question that trumps others is this: To what extent should ethical principles—or other ethical guidelines—be observed in nonprofessional life writing?

The paramount concern here is not the ethics of self-representation, concerning which there have been notable recent "scandals," such as those involving Rigoberta Menchú and "Binjamin Wilkomirski"; such scandals have focused on the truthfulness of their stories and the authenticity of the identities they claim. Rather, it is with the representation of others, in scenarios such as those submitted to Randy Cohen's *New York Times Magazine* feature "The Ethicist":

> I have a really crazy family. . . . I've been reading all these memoirs about people's messed-up childhoods, and even though I'm not a great writer or famous or anything, I though I might try my hand at writing one. Do you

think it's ethical to write a tell-all about your own family while the people in question are still living? (Cohen, "Case Study Study")

Browsing at a bookstore, I came across a book written by my old psychotherapist. To my surprise, I was an (unnamed) case study. Was it ethical to publish that without notifying me or verifying the details? [signed, naturally, "Anonymous"] (Cohen, "A Novel Solution")

My primary concern is with the ethics of representing vulnerable subjects—persons who are liable to exposure by someone with whom they are involved in an intimate or trust-based relationship but are unable to represent themselves in writing or to offer meaningful consent to their representation by someone else. Conditions that render subjects vulnerable range from the age-related (extreme youth or age) and the physiological (illnesses and impairments, physical or mental) to membership in socially or culturally disadvantaged minorities. Of primary importance is intimate life writing—that done within families or couples, close relationships, or quasi-professional relationships that involve trust—rather than conventional biography, which can be written by a stranger. The closer the relationship between writer and subject, and the greater the vulnerability or dependency of the subject, the higher the ethical stakes, and the more urgent the need for ethical scrutiny.

∽

I introduce my concerns about the ethics of life writing in chapter 1, "Consensual Relations: Life Writing and Betrayal," which invokes two life writing scenarios. The first involves the collaboration between Joe McGinniss and Jeffrey MacDonald which produced *Fatal Vision* and was much later the subject of *The Journalist and the Murderer* by Janet Malcolm. McGinniss was hired by MacDonald to write an account of his trial for the murders of his wife and daughters (the "Green Beret murders"). When the account produced was not at all to MacDonald's liking, he sued McGinniss for fraud on the grounds that McGinniss misled him by pretending to believe in his innocence long after he had concluded that MacDonald was guilty. The second involves the poet Patricia Hampl. Hampl's mother objected when Patricia wished to publish a poem that "outed" her as an epileptic. Hampl managed to get her mother's consent to publish the poem, but in an essay written years later, she revisited the incident and impugned her own behavior. Although the scenarios are, on the surface, radically different, both involve betrayals of trust and some degree of vulnerability; thus, they serve to illustrate some of the ethical concerns and concepts that inform the rest of the book.

In chapter 2, "Auto/Biographical, Biomedical, and Ethnographic Ethics," I show how bioethics and anthropology may provide ethical guidance with problematic instances of life writing, such as those involving dependent or vulnerable subjects. In chapter 3, "Making, Taking, and Faking Lives: Voice and Vulnerability in Collaborative Life Writing," I distinguish among circumstances in which cooperative life writing occurs—such as the "celebrity" scenario and the "ethnographic" scenario—and identify ways in which subjects or writers may become vulnerable to exploitation in different situations.

The next several chapters involve cases that raise troubling ethical problems. Chapter 4, "Adoption, Disability, and Surrogacy: The Ethics of Parental Life Writing in *The Broken Cord*," concerns Michael Dorris's account of raising an adopted son whose development was affected by fetal alcohol syndrome. Dorris's book raises difficult questions about a parent's ethical responsibility in portraying a "damaged" child, especially when that child is adopted; it also raises concern about parenthood as the basis for surrogacy in life writing. Chapter 5, "Beyond the Clinic: Oliver Sacks and the Ethics of Neuroanthropology," analyzes Sacks's development as a writer whose practice lies somewhere between biomedicine, ethnography, and biography, and which involves the representation of subjects rendered vulnerable by the neurological conditions that make them candidates for portraiture in the first place. Because Sacks is, first and last, a physician, in this chapter I explore the connection between medical ethics, which governs relations between physicians and patients, and the ethics of lay life writing, which concerns relations between writers and their subjects.

Chapter 6, "Life Writing as Death Writing: Disability and Euthanography," examines the small but growing literature of euthanasia, focusing mainly on narratives by parents of disabled young men; in these narratives, I argue, disability plays a role in life-or-death decisions in ways that are not fully acknowledged. Both the subject matter and the act of representation raise questions of autonomy and surrogacy.

In chapter 7, "Genome and Genre: DNA and Life Writing," I address the relation between the contemporary fascination with genetics—stimulated by the completion in June 2000 of an important phase of the Human Genome Project—and the practice of life writing. I consider DNA as itself a powerful form of life writing, one with the potential to render all of us vulnerable. I consider ways in which a number of life writing genres have been, are being, or may be affected by the emergence of DNA as a unique personal identifier and potential predictor of life course. And I argue that robust life writing may help to contextualize and resolve some of the complex ethical questions raised by DNA research. A short epilogue, "Writing Wrongs: In Defense of Ethical Criticism," addresses the charge that ethical scrutiny of life writing may stifle free expression or function in a discriminatory way.

∽

If even autobiography is inevitably relational, so is scholarship—seemingly a solitary occupation—also necessarily collaborative. I have been blessed with supportive and stimulating colleagues in the two areas in which my work has concentrated, life writing studies and disability studies. Among them, I acknowledge particularly Paul John Eakin, whose work has been a model of excellence, innovation, and clarity, and who has been a source of much personal encouragement. Craig Howes has provided a resonant sounding board, formally and informally. Richard K. Sanderson got me thinking about an odd subgenre, narratives of suicide survivorship, and commented helpfully on my chapter on euthanasia narratives. Colleagues at Hofstra, Sabina Sawhney and Lee Zimmerman, commented instructively on parts of the manuscript. Julie Pedroni offered valuable guidance on some matters of bioethics. Amanda Heller's copyediting was deft and eagle-eyed.

Gratitude for a crucial grant is due to the National Endowment for the Humanities and the Agency for Health Care Research and Quality. Hofstra University generously supplemented that grant to make affordable a year's leave during which I was able to complete the book.

Parts of this book appeared earlier in slightly different form and in some cases with somewhat different titles. Chapter 3, "Making, Taking, and Faking Lives," appeared in *Style* 32.2 (summer 1998): 334–50, and in *Mapping the Ethical Turn: A Reader in Ethics, Culture, and Literary Theory*, ed. Todd F. Davis and Kenneth Womack (Charlottesville: University of Virginia Press, 2001): 209–26. This material is reprinted with permission of *Style* and of the University of Virginia Press. Chapter 4, "Adoption, Disability, and Surrogacy," appeared in *Biography* 21.4 (fall 1998): 421–44; and part of chapter 7, "Genome and Genre," appeared in *Biography* 24.1 (winter 2001): 185–96; this material is reprinted with permission of *Biography*. A portion of Chapter 5, "Beyond the Clinic," appeared as a monograph published in 2001 by the Poynter Center for the Study of Ethics and American Institutions. I am grateful to Alexander Cockburn for permission to quote him in chapter 5.

My sister Jane Barton has displayed a keen interest and pride in my work. My wife, Barbara Zabel, has been most familiar with this book's wellsprings and with its progress. It is hard to imagine having written it without her love and companionship.

Vulnerable Subjects

I

Consensual Relations
Life Writing and Betrayal

_____

> Trust . . . is accepted vulnerability to another's possible but not expected ill
> will (or lack of good will) toward one.
>
> —ANNETTE BAIER, "Trust and Anti-trust"

PROBING THE RELATIONSHIP between Joe Mc-
Ginniss and Jeffrey MacDonald in *The Journalist and the Murderer*, Janet
Malcolm shed some harsh light on the way journalists treat consenting
subjects. In 1970, MacDonald, a U. S. Army physician, was suspected of
murdering his pregnant wife and two young daughters at Fort Bragg,
North Carolina, in the case that became notorious as the "Green Beret
murders." He claimed that his home had been invaded by a group of
Charles Manson–like hippies who stabbed him and slaughtered his wife
and children. Initially investigated and cleared by an army tribunal, he
was much later tried and convicted in a civilian court, in part as a result
of the persistent lobbying of his suspicious father-in-law. On the eve of
this trial, in 1979, MacDonald invited McGinniss to write a book about the
case from the perspective of the defense team, to which he would have
exclusive and privileged access. Indeed, in order to maximize McGinniss's access to confidential material and also bind him by the attorney-
client privilege—that is, to prevent his being called as a witness or having
his notes subpoenaed by the prosecution—MacDonald made McGinniss
an actual member of the defense team. As such, McGinniss lived with
MacDonald and his lawyers during the trial and became a close friend of
MacDonald's. Despite the guilty verdict, MacDonald continued to pro-

claim his innocence, and he clearly expected McGinniss's book to provide a sympathetic narrative of his life and an exculpatory account of the crime. During the trial, however, McGinniss became convinced of Mac-Donald's guilt, and his book, *Fatal Vision*, published in 1983, character-ized MacDonald as a pathological narcissist and murderer (Malcolm, *Journalist* 6–7).

The McGinniss-MacDonald collaboration is an extreme but instructive example of the souring of a relationship between a life writer of sorts—in this case a journalist rather than a biographer—and his subject and prime source. Invited and expected, but not commissioned, to write a de-fense of MacDonald, McGinniss secretly adopted the prosecution view of the crime, and his book not only ratified but justified MacDonald's con-viction. When MacDonald learned of the book's actual gist, shortly before its publication (ironically, in what he regarded as a promotional television interview), he was not only hurt and angry but also shocked, since McGinniss had given no hint of his suspicions during the trial or the sub-sequent four-year period during which the book took shape, even as he audited and edited autobiographical tapes MacDonald had smuggled out of prison and wrote sympathetic letters to MacDonald.[1]

Under the circumstances, MacDonald could not very well sue McGin-niss for libel; he was, after all, a convicted triple murderer.[2] Moreover, he had signed a release protecting McGinniss from any such suit. Although the release took the form of a letter from MacDonald to McGinniss, it was actually written by McGinniss's publisher. (It was thus a ghostwritten document, in which "MacDonald" volunteered his agreement to McGin-niss's conditions.) It read, in part:

> I understand you are writing a book about my life centering on my current trial for murder. . . .
> I realize, of course, that you do not propose to libel me. Nevertheless, in or-der that you may feel free to write the book in any manner that you may deem best, I agree that I will not make or assert against you, the publisher, or its licensees or anyone else involved in the production or distribution of the book, any claim or demand whatsoever based on the ground that any-thing in the book defames me. (Malcolm, *Journalist* 20–21)

When it came time for MacDonald's lawyer, Bernard Segal, to approve this release, however, he added a significant qualifier: "provided that the essential integrity of my life story is maintained" (Malcolm, *Journalist* 21). According to Malcolm, "in the MacDonald-McGinniss suit, it became MacDonald's contention that the 'essential integrity' of his life story had not been maintained in McGinniss's book, and that McGinniss was guilty of a kind of soul murder, for which it was necessary that he be brought to account" (21).

In the event, rather than accuse McGinniss of defamation of character—let alone "soul murder"—MacDonald sued McGinniss for fraud and breach of contract. That is, he accused McGinniss not of misrepresenting him—and thus deceiving his readers by falsely portraying him as a murderer—but of misleading him by concealing his suspicions in order to sustain MacDonald's confidence and cooperation through the long process of post-trial research. (The bulk of the book as life writing, rather than trial coverage—McGinniss's account of MacDonald's pre-trial life—was based on material generated and analyzed after the trial.) MacDonald accused McGinniss, then, essentially of betrayal of trust, of working against him while pretending to work with and for him as a nonlegal advocate. The offense was not so much in the product, *Fatal Vision*, as in the process—manipulation masquerading as collaboration—which licensed its creation.

Of course the product cannot be divorced from the collaboration that produced it; in this case the book bears traces of betrayal despite McGinniss's desire to veil it. The ethical scandal of the book is that it barely acknowledges McGinniss's closeness—physical and emotional—to MacDonald. In the very early pages, he describes meeting MacDonald in 1979 just before the trial, being invited to accompany MacDonald to North Carolina to write about it, and accepting the invitation to live with him for its duration (McGinniss 13, 15). In the section on the trial, however, McGinniss provides a fly-on-the-wall narrative without ever acknowledging how he achieved such a vantage, that is, by joining the defense team and attending its deliberations. Crucially, when he describes the cast of characters living with MacDonald in the Kappa Alpha fraternity house at North Carolina State University during the trial, McGinniss neglects to name himself (485–86), conveniently effacing himself as a member of MacDonald's defense team. Thus, readers may well be surprised when, at trial's end, MacDonald embraces McGinniss as a friend (591). The closest McGinniss comes to acknowledging his deception of MacDonald is when he reports that MacDonald never asked him directly what he thought about his guilt or innocence: "To ask directly would have been to risk getting an answer he did not want. For me, of course, it was easier to let him go right on believing whatever he cared to believe" (602–3). The effect of minimizing his presence in the narrative is to conceal his supportive and friendly relationship with MacDonald. Not incidentally, it makes his narration appear much less ethically problematic than it is. (He might have done better—ethically and aesthetically—to foreground the growing conflict between his loyalty to MacDonald and his increasing suspicions; while none of this would have mollified MacDonald, it would have made for a more candid and compelling narrative.)

McGinniss's defense was that he had continued to express sympathy for MacDonald out of a real, if conflicted, sense of friendship and genuine concern for his plight—a sense that he needed emotional support even if he did not deserve it—rather than out of a desire to keep milking him for material about his earlier life, material he used to create a damning portrait of a pathological narcissist. With one exception, the jury in *MacDonald v. McGinniss* seemed to think that McGinniss's apparent sympathy for MacDonald was utterly dishonest, opportunistic, and exploitative. The gap between McGinniss's scathing published image of MacDonald and the sympathetic tone of his private letters to MacDonald was just too wide for most jurors to account for except as a function of outright duplicity. They sensed that if McGinniss had been candid about his belief in MacDonald's guilt and the direction his book was taking, MacDonald would have ceased cooperating with him and sought out a more sympathetic pen. (He had initially approached the novelist Joseph Wambaugh about writing the book, and other journalists manifested interest in the case even after his contract with McGinniss was made public.) Had subject and writer become alienated, there would have been no ethical dilemma and presumably no lawsuit. But there might have been no *Fatal Vision*, either; or at least, without MacDonald's continuing participation, the book would necessarily have taken a significantly different form. Its substance—and thus its market value—depended in part on McGinniss's exclusive access to MacDonald's first-person account of his early life, which he produced in prison after the verdict.

Malcolm became interested in the lawsuit only in 1987, after it ended. It was settled out of court after the jury deadlocked, with the majority prepared to find for MacDonald, the triple murderer, and against McGinniss, the author of *The Selling of the President* and other best-selling and well-regarded books. The terms of the settlement called for McGinniss to admit no wrong but for MacDonald to receive $325,000, a sum exceeding McGinniss's advance. Malcolm's account opens as follows:

> Every journalist who is not too stupid or full of himself to notice what is going on knows that what he does is morally indefensible. He is a kind of

confidence man, preying on people's vanity, ignorance, or loneliness, gaining their trust and betraying them without remorse. Like the credulous
widow who wakes up one day to find the charming young man and all her
savings gone, so the consenting subject of a piece of nonfiction writing
learns—when the article or book appears—*his* hard lesson. Journalists justify their treachery in various ways according to their temperaments. The
more pompous talk about freedom of speech and "the public's right to
know"; the least talented talk about Art; the seemliest murmur about earning a living. (3)

As a working journalist who has had her own conflicts with subjects—
Jeffrey Masson sued her (unsuccessfully) for libel for fabricating quotes
attributed to him in *In the Freud Archives*—Malcolm readily acknowledges her own complicity in such duplicitous consensual relationships.
But she seems interested finally more in their psychodynamic than their
ethical dimensions. She characterizes journalists and their sources as co-
dependent, although she doesn't use that term. That is, she views their
relationships as pathological romances in which each party is unduly and
anxiously dependent on, and manipulative of, the other: the writer on his
source for material and thus literary capital, the source on the writer for
his attention, and thus a sense of his own significance:

> Subjects do sometimes sue writers, and . . . they do sometimes leave one
> writer for another, or abruptly break off the interviews. It is the latter even-
> tuality, with its immediate disastrous effect on his project, that causes the
> writer the greatest anxiety. . . . But the writer isn't alone in his anxiety. Even
> as he is worriedly striving to keep the subject talking, the subject is wor-
> riedly striving to keep the writer *listening*. The subject is Scheherezade. He
> lives in fear of being found uninteresting, and many of the strange things
> that subjects say to writers—things of almost suicidal rashness—they say
> out of their desperate need to keep the writer's attention riveted. (19–20)

What she says here about journalists and their subjects applies to relationships between life writers—authorized biographers, memoirists, and
collaborative autobiographers—and their willing subjects or collaborators. So could this comment: "The moral ambiguity of journalism lies not
in its texts but in the relationships out of which they arise—relationships
that are invariably and inescapably lopsided [in favor of the journalist]"
(162). In many life writing scenarios, the relationship of the collaborators
is similarly fraught with potential for betrayal and exploitation. A key

word in her indictment, however, is "consenting," which cuts two ways. On the one hand, it demarcates the sorts of relationships in which one kind of ethical conflict arises; as Malcolm notes of her own relationship with McGinniss, who declined further cooperation after an initial interview, "you can't betray someone you barely know" (95). (Which is not to say that you can't inflict harm.) Journalists and biographers are not indebted—and thus are not obliged to be loyal—to nonconsenting subjects. But consensual relationships involving trusting cooperation have unique potential for treachery. At the same time, formalizing consent may insulate against claims of betrayal, depending on the way in which consent is expressed and other aspects of the relationship between the parties.[3] In this case, MacDonald's consent, in the form of a signed release, explicitly absolved McGinniss of any obligation to produce a text that flattered MacDonald, much less one he had a right to preview or censor. The agreement was made between competent and responsible parties, and their consent was informed: both had lawyers or agents to protect their interests. In the form of written legalistic disclaimers or releases, formal consent can be a bulwark against legal charges of betrayal, then, but it is clearly no protection against a sense of betrayal or grievance.

Although the scenario here is not of the sort that interests me most (because of the parity and prominence of the partners), it raises questions and presents issues that are pertinent to my concerns in what follows. Most generally, what ethical rules or principles, if any, should pertain to life writing beyond legal constraints? Should such principles differ from genre to genre? Why and how? Autobiography and biography would seem to be so different as to involve different standards. Indeed, whether a biographical subject is living or dead would seem to change the ethical standards, as it does the legal rules: one cannot libel a dead person, and the right to privacy is also held to terminate with death. The most complex and problematic narratives, and hence the ones that interest me most, are found in a zone between "straight" (i.e., solo) autobiography and "straight" (i.e., unauthorized) biography.

Under what circumstances do life writers have ethical obligations to those they portray? More specifically, how does a cooperative relationship between subject and writer, such as authorization, affect the ethics of the project? What is the nature and extent of those obligations? Is there an obligation to seek consent? Under what circumstances? What constitutes consent? How can it be ensured, and how can it be demonstrated to readers? If all autobiography is also in part biography, what if any con-

straints should there be on our presumed right to write (and copyright)
our own lives? To what extent, that is, is our freedom to narrate our own
lives restricted by the rights of others to privacy? Does the right to commodify one's own life and self entail the right to commodify others'? I am
especially concerned here with the representation of subjects who are vulnerable to misrepresentation or betrayal because of some disadvantageous condition, particularly certain kinds of disability. I do not propose
to answer all of these questions, but I explore some sample texts and cases
in such a way as to move toward an ethics of auto/biographical representation.

The McGinniss-MacDonald situation is revealing because it represents
a worst-case scenario in which a seemingly sympathetic writer produces
not merely an indictment but a post-conviction "sentencing" of its subject. It offers an example of extreme disenchantment leading to an intense
clash between authorial and subjective points of view—and thus a clear
conflict of interests. And yet it represents a scenario involving two parties, initially strangers, who enter into what they conceive of as a mutually beneficial partnership with open eyes and ample protection. The two
parties had a kind of "prenuptial" legal agreement, and both had lawyers
or agents to represent them when they struck that deal. The economic aspect of the transaction was recognized: the arrangement called for Mac-
Donald to be compensated for his cooperation with roughly one-quarter
of the advance and one-third of royalties (Malcolm, *Journalist* 19). The immediate motive for MacDonald's cooperation, ironically, was his press-
ing need for money with which to pay his lawyers; thus, he gave
McGinniss membership in and exclusive access to his defense team in
exchange for money to pay the lawyers on that defense team. When
McGinniss began to disbelieve the defense he was helping to subsidize,
however, he was not, being a journalist rather than an attorney, obliged
to serve as an advocate for MacDonald, nor was he barred by professional
ethics from publishing an account of the case diametrically opposed to
the legal position of the defense, once the trial was over.

The initial arrangement seems to have been a truly and fully consensual relation. The very transparency of the arrangement—even if it
proved somewhat illusory—and the preliminary agreement about control over the text (which was retained by McGinniss) and, especially, distribution of proceeds are highly desirable from an ethical perspective. But
the more or less equal status of the two parties and the release they agreed
on obviously did not preclude ethical problems; whatever exploitation

may have occurred was not a function of the inherently vulnerable status of one or the other. Thus, one lesson to be learned from this case about the ethics of collaborative life writing is that, although equitable contractual arrangements are highly desirable, they are no guarantee against harm or wrong. When both parties are of ethical character, such arrangements prove unnecessary, but when they are not, such arrangements prove insufficient to prevent violation. McGinniss surely took advantage of MacDonald, but just as surely MacDonald attempted to take advantage of McGinniss; his intention from the start was to con him into providing an idealized and exculpatory portrayal. Nevertheless, one could argue that the readiness of life writing partners to commit to reciprocal arrangements beforehand—if not a sign, much less a guarantee, of ethical conduct—is at least a standard against which behavior may be judged and claims of wrongdoing registered. So the MacDonald-McGinniss collaboration is instructive both in its positive features—the spelling out and formalization of the agreement between consenting parties—and in the insufficiency of those features.

Malcolm's book is itself somewhat inconsistent ethically in that it combines repeated indictments of journalistic ethics with multiple reenactments of the very betrayals she finds blameworthy. One of her gifts as a journalist seems to be a talent for eliciting self-condemning testimony from her sources; rather than attacking them, she induces them to indict themselves. The book contains scene after scene in which she leads sources into embarrassing self-exposure. She thus quite self-consciously replicates the behavior she indicts in McGinniss, albeit in subtler forms. Ultimately, she celebrates the conditions that support that behavior: "What gives journalism its authenticity and vitality is the tension between the subject's blind self-absorption and the journalist's skepticism" (144). Similarly, although she describes what journalists do as "morally indefensible" and "treachery" (3), she seems pleased that *MacDonald v. McGinniss* was settled out of court, since she agrees with one of McGinniss's lawyers that the suit was "a threat to journalism" (61). She seems to accept such perfidy as an inherent and necessary part of the job, but she declines to offer the sort of highfalutin, self-serving justification or rationalization she rejects when it comes from McGinniss, who claimed that his only obligation was to the truth (26), or from journalists who invoke the values of art, the right to free speech, or the public's "right to know." Her scorn for McGinniss seems a reaction not to the ethics but to the aesthetics of his exploitation of MacDonald, which she characterizes as "crude and gratuitous" (162), lacking in finesse. What she seems to want from other journalists is not a change in behavior so much as a candid admission of the dirty little secrets of their trade, as well as subtlety and skill in the betrayal of their subjects.

Malcolm's deeply ambivalent account of journalistic ethics isolates issues that also arise in life writing transactions. In addition to providing an extreme instance of conflicting interests, her account of the McGinniss-MacDonald collaboration introduces the phenomenon of competing principles or obligations, which is, after all, the crux of an ethical dilemma.[4] The rights routinely invoked as justifications for journalists' manipulation of their subjects are never absolute; the right to free speech or freedom of expression is limited by libel laws, and the public's "right to know" is limited by privacy protections. From a legal standpoint, as an accused criminal in a high-profile trial, MacDonald qualified as a public figure, and thus his privacy rights were diminished. But legality does not guarantee ethical propriety, and in the case of *Fatal Vision*, McGinniss's deception of MacDonald was arguably not necessary to give the public what it had a "right" to know. Its purpose was simply to elicit material about MacDonald's life and character that McGinniss wanted his readers to know about—some of which he might have got from people other than MacDonald, hence without deceiving him. (What it got him that was not available without MacDonald's cooperation was access to his thoughts and emotions—or at least his account of them, since in one important regard, MacDonald's confidences were not confessional. The first part of McGinniss's overlong book intersperses long chunks of narrative in "The Voice of Jeffrey MacDonald" into McGinniss's third-person reconstruction of MacDonald's early life.)

Despite her skepticism, Malcolm's account of the justifications given by journalists for deceiving their subjects registers the need to vindicate the violation of those subjects' trust by invoking some compensatory gain or value. One implication of her book is that the betrayals characteristic of journalism (and life writing) cry out for justification—or at least rationalization. If journalism necessarily involves treachery, logically Malcolm should condemn the whole enterprise unless it can be justified by some countervailing value. That she doesn't condemn it suggests that despite the sarcasm of her opening passage about the values invoked by journalists (free speech, art), she implicitly endorses some variant of that rationale; and if the inherent treachery of journalism is in conflict with its presumably beneficial purposes, then that is a true ethical dilemma. This raises analogous issues about life writing in situations involving intimacy and trust. If life writing entails potential harms, such as violation of privacy, are they, can they, be offset by countervailing benefits? What good does life writing do, and whose interests does it finally serve—the subjects', the writers', or the readers'?

In addition to illustrating the difference between a practical and an ethical dilemma, Malcolm's book illustrates a fundamental divide in ethical theory—that between deontological (duty-based) approaches, which justify actions by recourse to ethical rules or principles (e.g., the obligation to tell the truth or to live up to one's promises), and teleological approaches, which justify actions by reference to their consequences. Although rule- or principle-based ethicists and consequence-based ethicists will not necessarily reach different conclusions about particular acts, they will reach those conclusions by markedly different routes. (One group considers acts in the light of preexisting principles, the other in the light of the acts' expected results; both are rational and analytical, but one is backward-looking, the other forward-looking.) Utilitarian or consequentialist ethics tends to be inherently less protective of subjects than principlist ethics, since utilitarian calculations of benefits tend to favor majority interests. Thus, in this case, it might be argued that MacDonald's privacy rights—and even his evident trust in McGinniss's belief in his innocence—are outweighed by the value of public knowledge of the truth about the perpetrator of a sensational crime. That is, the end of "knowledge" might be said to justify the deceptive means of acquiring that knowledge.

The case also illustrates the limits of "professional ethics," which can be rather narrow and self-serving codes. One defense strategy in MacDonald's suit against McGinniss was to line up some journalistic heavyweights (the list of potential witnesses included William F. Buckley, Joseph Wambaugh, Tom Wolfe, Jimmy Breslin, and J. Anthony Lukas, although only the first two were called to the stand) to testify that deceiving one's sources was not just standard procedure in professional journalism but ethically justified. One way to think about McGinniss's behavior is to see him as privileging the code that applied to him as a journalist—one whose "only obligation from the beginning was to the truth," as he put it (qtd. in Malcolm, *Journalist* 25)—over the professional code of the other members of MacDonald's defense team, attorneys bound to act on their client's behalf (though restricted in the means of that advocacy). Most members of the jury were not swayed by this argument, however.

For them, the deception of a subject by a journalist was not justified by the invocation of a professional code; rather, it seemed to violate a principle of candor or fidelity embedded in their sense of the common morality. The fact that it might be standard operating procedure in McGinniss's profession did not make it moral; in their view, what was professionally ethical was not necessarily right.

Curiously, from an ethical though not from a legal point of view, Mac-Donald's veracity and candor did not figure prominently in the trial. Called upon to support McGinniss's characterization of MacDonald as a "pathological liar," one of McGinniss's witnesses, the psychiatrist Michael Stone, referred to the tapes MacDonald made while in prison as his "pseudo-autobiography" (Malcolm, *Journalist* 77). This suggests that Stone, at least, saw MacDonald's pathological lying as a violation of his obligation to McGinniss and hence perhaps a justification of McGinniss's deception of him. But it did not seem to matter to the jury that, insofar as MacDonald continued to profess his innocence of a crime he had been convicted of committing, he was guilty of trying to deceive McGinniss. Apparently they did not see the partnership as involving mutual obligation in this respect. All of these considerations—the difference between professional and nonprofessional ethics, the difference between practical and ethical dilemmas, different approaches (duty-based and result-oriented) to resolving ethical conflicts, and especially the notion of mutual obligation—have ramifications in less tightly scripted life writing collaborations.

Patricia Hampl offers a pertinent example from her experience as a poet. The very first poem in her first published book concerns her relationship with her somewhat domineering mother; it includes a crucial reference to her mother's having had a grand mal seizure. Reading the poem before publication, her mother objected vociferously to being "outed" as an epileptic: "You have no right," she insisted (212). Hampl's first response was to justify the revelation by arguing, as she had always felt, that her mother's secrecy about her condition was unnecessary: "She was outraged by my betrayal. I was furious at her theatrical secrecy. Would you feel this way, I asked sensibly, if you had diabetes?" (211). That is, she questioned the premise underlying her mother's objection—her right to privacy—by suggesting that epilepsy was nothing to be ashamed of, and thus not a matter requiring privacy. A second strategy, more consequentialist, was to downplay any possibility of harm from exposure; her mother wasn't likely to be fired as a result of the poem's revelation, she argued, since "no one" reads poetry. Hampl's assertion of her poetic license to expose her mother's condition, then, was opportunistically eclectic.

When her mother proved recalcitrant, however, Hampl offered to cut the poem, even as she proclaimed it the best in the volume, thus playing on her mother's desire to see her succeed. The ploy was successful; conceding the poem's worth, her mother relented. In a gesture similar to that of the journalists who justified their betrayal of sources to Malcolm in terms of high ethical values, Hampl told herself that her victory was just:

> I didn't pause to think she was doing me a favor, that she might be making a terrible sacrifice. This was good for her, I told myself. . . . The wicked witch of secrecy had been vanquished. I hadn't simply won (though that was delicious). I had liberated my mother, unlocked her from the prison of the dank secret where she had been cruelly chained for so long.
>
> I felt heroic in a low-grade literary sort of way. I understood that poetry—my poem!—had performed this liberating deed. My mother had been unable to speak. I had spoken for her. It had been hard for both of us. But this was the whole point of literature, its deepest good, this voicing of the unspoken, the forbidden. And look at the prize we won with our struggle—for doesn't the truth, as John, the beloved apostle promised, set you free? (213)

As Hampl's tone hints, however, her self-congratulatory rationalization was undercut when, years later, she revisited the incident with her mother, only to be told that her mother had always hated the poem and had acquiesced only out of maternal devotion (221–22). Hampl had not liberated her mother; she had not only violated her privacy but also exploited her pride in a talented daughter. Her mother's consent had been a maternal sacrifice, not a concession of Hampl's rights, much less an acknowledgment of the liberating function of art or truth. Hampl comes to see that what she thought she had a right to communicate as belonging to her own life was subject to significant claims on the part of her mother. Hampl helps us see that even poetry with its license can exploit and damage the fragile private relationships that nurture and encourage it.

These two writer-subject relationships are markedly different. One was a temporary, opportunistic, voluntary, contractual partnership entered into by two previously unacquainted men; the other was a permanent, intimate, involuntary blood bond between mother and daughter. In one case, a book contract between strangers led to a mutually instrumental friendship; in the other, poetry grew out of a lifelong kinship. Yet in both, life writing led to, or was perceived as, personal betrayal. These two examples thus illustrate the wide range of life writing scenarios in which ethical questions arise. Indeed, the ethical delicacy of life writing is demonstrated by the fact that in these very different situations, the granting of consent—whether by a murderer or a mother—did not foreclose the possibility of ethical conflict. This is all the truer with more vulnerable subjects. At the same time, as Hampl suggests by revisiting in an autobiographical essay the scene of her poetic betrayal of her mother's secret, life writing can also be the site of ethical self-examination and atonement.[5]

2

Auto/Biographical, Biomedical, and Ethnographic Ethics

Because everyone "has" a memoir, we all have a stake in how such stories are told. For we do not, after all, simply *have* experience; we are entrusted with it. We must do something—make something—with it.

—PATRICIA HAMPL, *I Could Tell You Stories*

Language can never contain a whole person, so every act of writing a person's life is inevitably a violation.

—RUTHELLEN JOSSELSON, *Ethics and Process in the Narrative Study of Lives*

THE DEMOCRACY OR, to put it differently, the catholicity of life writing—its accessibility to "nobodies" (even, in Philippe Lejeune's phrase, "those who do not write") relative to other literary genres—engages subjects who may be especially vulnerable to misrepresentation and exploitation. Today, people with disadvantaging or stigmatizing conditions are increasingly visible in life writing, and those who represent them must take care not to override their interests or over-write their stories. For ethical guidance with life writing projects, especially those involving vulnerable subjects, we may look to the disciplines of bioethics and anthropology.

Biomedicine may seem an odd source for ethical principles pertinent to life writing, for two reasons. First, medicine is a professional field, like law and journalism, and as we have seen, professional ethical codes can be parochial and self-serving. Consider, for example, the notion of "professional courtesy" as preferential treatment for colleagues and hence, in effect, discrimination among clients. But "biomedical ethics" has always meant more than "physician ethics" or even "clinical ethics," and today, as biomedicine attempts to grapple with unprecedented problems and procedures, that is truer than ever.[1] In any case, biomedical ethics is perhaps the most highly developed version of normative ethics available today. Further, according to Tom L. Beauchamp and James F. Childress, the authors of the standard text on the subject, "the common morality contains a set of moral norms that includes principles that are basic for biomedical ethics" (12).[2] If this is correct, then biomedical ethics represents not a set of narrow ethical principles arising from the practice of medicine but rather the invocation in clinical and biomedical contexts of broader, if not universal, principles.

A second reason why biomedicine may seem an odd repository of life writing ethics is that one may not think of it as a site of much life writing, except for the highly specialized clinical genre of the case history (which has generally been ignored as life writing, a neglect I address in chapter 5). A more obvious source would be the social sciences, among which anthropology has been the most concerned with life writing, especially in the form of the ethnographic life history.[3] In fact, anthropology's ethical guidelines are pertinent and useful, and will be invoked later. But because biomedicine involves relationships based on trust, and because patients are by definition vulnerable subjects, biomedical ethics is particularly pertinent to the sorts of circumstances that interest me. Perhaps because of its literally life-and-death concerns, biomedical ethics offers a particularly comprehensive account of ethical principles and reasoning. (And it is doubly pertinent when life writing involves quality-of-life issues, as is commonly—indeed, increasingly—the case. This question will be explored especially in chapter 6 on euthanography.)

Ethical scrutiny is most urgent with regard to subjects who are disadvantaged, disempowered, or marginalized with respect to their partners or collaborators. Beauchamp and Childress's characterization of doctor-patient relations helps to define the sorts of life writing relationships that concern me most: "Both law and medical tradition distinguish the practice of medicine from business practices that rest on contracts and marketplace relationships. The patient-physician relationship is founded on trust and confidence; and the physician is therefore necessarily a trustee for the patient's medical welfare. This model of fidelity relies more on values of loyalty and trust than merely on being true to one's word" (312). Although Jeffrey MacDonald would seem hardly a "vulnerable" subject—except perhaps in his apparent naïveté (which may be the flip side of his narcissism)—any judgment of the ethics of Joe McGinniss would depend in part on the nature of his relationship with MacDonald. And that in turn depends on what one considers the ultimate basis of their partnership, the contractual arrangements made prior to their collaboration or the friendship that developed (or seemed to) during the course of their close contact during MacDonald's seven-week trial. If McGinniss was bound only by the letter of their legal-commercial agreement, then his behavior was proper; if he was bound by the spirit of the trust they seemed to share, then his deception of MacDonald appears ethically problematic.

As Edmund D. Pellegrino and David C. Thomasma point out in a discussion of fidelity to trust in medicine, "trust is most problematic when we are in states of special dependence—in illness, old age, or infancy or when we are in need of healing, justice, spiritual help, or learning. This is the situation in our relationships with the professions that circumstances force us to trust" (65). With life writing, as with some professional practices, persons in states of dependency—such as disability, illiteracy, institutionalization, legal minority, incompetence, or terminal illness—often depend on agents more powerful or privileged than themselves to hear, articulate, and act on their stories. (*Death* would not seem to qualify as a state of dependence; indeed, it might seem to suggest utter invulnerability to harm; but I would argue that it entails maximum vulnerability to posthumous misrepresentation because it precludes self-defense. Thus, we trust that after we die our corpse will be treated with respect, that our "will" will be honored, and that secrets we may have divulged will be respected, either by being kept or by being communicated only to certain parties or in certain ways. In this regard, death may be the state of ultimate vulnerability and dependency.)

But although journalists, doctors, and lawyers may at times function as life writers, journalism, law, and medicine are professions in a way that life writing is not; even for professional biographers, life writing has no official or even consensual professional ethics. Outside the professions, then, with life writing there is no protection for vulnerable subjects in the form of "system trust": trust in the procedures of education, licensing, accreditation, and supervision (Pellegrino and Thomasma 66–67).

As agents, proxies, or collaborators, life writers are rarely selected on the basis of credentials; more often they are chosen (or they nominate themselves, a crucial difference) on the basis of emotional intimacy or relational proximity. The very basis of their qualification—their intimate relationship to their subjects—may reflect their trustworthiness, but when it does not, it places those subjects at high risk of betrayal. Thus, intimacy itself entails a degree of vulnerability.

In life writing scenarios involving particularly vulnerable subjects, such as children, members of disadvantaged minorities, and people with certain kinds of illnesses and disabilities, even when partnerships are formalized, life writing collaborations may be thought of as fiduciary relationships, that is, relationships of trust akin to those between physicians and patients, in which "the benefit to one party is maximized by leaving that party vulnerable to being taken advantage of by the other" (Mehlman 27). (Maxwell J. Mehlman explains this paradox as follows: "The fewer the resources the patient expends to verify the physician's good faith, the more vulnerable the patient is to the risk that the physician will betray the trust" [36n45].) So, too, vulnerable subjects may be inclined and encouraged to rely wholly on trust in their collaborators. In any case, when the relationships between vulnerable subjects and their life writers are roughly analogous to those between patients and physicians, in that the latter have privileged access to and implicit power over the former, then the principles of biomedical ethics may be an appropriate resource for guidance. In what follows, I suggest how these principles may be adapted to inform our consideration of the ethics of life writing.

∞

All four of the major principles of biomedicine that have been virtually canonized—the so-called Georgetown mantra—in the successive editions of the standard text, Beauchamp and Childress's *Principles of Biomedical Ethics*—respect for autonomy, nonmaleficence, beneficence, and justice—seem pertinent to life writing, and all may come into play in different ways. (And as in bioethics, these principles represent only prima facie obligations; that is, they are binding only when no conflicting obligations override them. Thus, they are not absolute and inflexible.) But my focus here is on the relevance of the first three to life writing involving vulnerable subjects. The scenarios examined in this section are generally fiduciary ones. In such relationships, partners whose preexisting characteristics or conditions put them in dependent positions to begin with are at higher-than-usual risk for the exposure inherent in all life writing. (We should not let the acknowledgment of vulnerability in some subjects obscure the fact that even in relationships of unequally powerful partners, each depends on the other for the completion of the project. And we should be alert to ways in which supposedly vulnerable subjects may assert power and agency greater than might be expected.)

A primary principle of ethical representation of vulnerable subjects should be respect for autonomy, which is rooted in a fundamental ethical principle, respect for persons: "Kant argued that respect for autonomy flows from the recognition that all persons have unconditional worth, each having the capacity to determine his or her own moral destiny. To violate a person's autonomy is to treat that person merely as a means, that is, in accordance with others' goals without regard to that person's own goals" (Beauchamp and Childress 63–64). The term "autonomy," whose etymological meaning is "self-rule" or "self-law," is a complex and contested one. To begin with, in reference to individuals, the term has several distinct but related meanings: "The *capacity* to govern oneself, which of course is a matter of degree; . . . the *actual condition* of self-government and its associated virtues; . . . an *ideal of character* derived from that conception; or (on the analogy to a political state) . . . the *sovereign authority* to govern oneself, which is absolute within one's own moral boundaries" (Feinberg, *Harm* 28). Thus, it can apply to the supposed ability of an individual to make meaningful decisions, a particular individual's possession of that ability, the *right* to make such decisions, or the circumstances under which an individual is granted the power to do so. In addition, the notion of autonomy as a character trait has been justly critiqued as reflecting a questionable (and patriarchal) view of individuals as atomistic. As Maeve Cooke has noted, feminists have been concerned that the idea of autonomy as a core cultural value may represent a narrowly gendered and not altogether healthy ideal, since it characterizes the subject as "disembedded," or even disembodied, ignoring the relational and contextual dimensions (258–60).

Believing that ethics requires a notion of autonomy, however, Cooke has suggested that autonomy can be salvaged from its historical interpretations by retaining the ideals of agency, responsibility, accountability, and intentionality while rejecting the notion of selves as atomistic and self-originating. She stresses that individual autonomy cannot flourish under conditions of economic, social, or political oppression (264–69). Hence the principle of autonomy is inseparable from that of justice, broadly conceived. In any case, there is an important distinction between regarding autonomy as an individual characteristic and as a right to be protected, as a capacity to be assumed in competent persons and as a capacity to be nurtured in the vulnerable.

My concern here is mainly with autonomy as a right. Later, in my consideration of ethical cases, especially those involving some form of surrogacy, I will be concerned with autonomy as a transpersonal phenomenon, a capacity not to be found in totally independent individuals but one to be exercised within relationships of interdependency. Indeed, many ethical dilemmas involve our awareness of just those dimensions of the self.

The following statement of the principle of respect for autonomy as a right, devised for biomedical settings, seems to me adaptable to life writing: "The principle . . . includes the right to decide as far as possible what will happen to one's person—to one's body, to information about one's life, to one's secrets, and the like" (Beauchamp and Childress 297). (As I have suggested, in life writing this principle may extend beyond the death of the subject.) By analogy I would argue that, ideally, the subjects of life writing should have the opportunity to exercise some degree of control over what happens to their stories, including secrets and private information.[4] Thus, over-writing their stories—imposing an alien shape on them—would constitute a violation of their autonomy, an overriding of their rights, an appropriation of their literary, moral, and economic property. This principle, however, has to be adapted to different scenarios and the genres characteristic of them. Thus, for example, the subject of an as-told-to autobiography deserves far more consideration and control over the narrative than the subject of an intimate biography, who in turn deserves more consideration than someone who is a secondary or minor character in a memoir or autobiography. The ethical stakes are proportionate to the centrality (and vulnerability) of the figure involved and the intimacy and interdependence between the writer and the subject. The writer's dependence on the subject is proportionate to her need for the subject's cooperation in the form of, say, extended interviews or privileged access; the subject's dependence may be manifest in incapacitating conditions that preclude self-representation or self-defense against misrepresentation.

As Adam Zachary Newton has pointed out, "getting someone else's story is also a way of losing the person as 'real,' as 'what he is'; it is a way of appropriating or allegorizing that endangers both intimacy and ethical duty. . . . [O]ne's responsibility consists of responding to just this paradox" (19). In a biomedical context, one justification of the reduction of personal narratives to medical histories, of persons to patients, is that it serves therapeutic ends. This may be viewed, from a consequentialist viewpoint, as a matter of the end justifying the means, and, from a deon-

tological (duty-based) viewpoint, of favoring the principle of beneficence—doing good—over that of respect for autonomy.

A similar justification might be offered of much social science research
that involves vulnerable human subjects: that it benefits them—or others
like them (an important distinction and a weaker justification). The potential harms of life writing are more akin to those of social research than
to those of biomedicine; the former are not likely to cause physical injury
or death, as medical treatment too often does. But whether and how the
representation of vulnerable subjects in life writing benefits them is also
less clear than with medicine; hence the need for ethical scrutiny.

The psychologist Terri Apter has reflected on unforeseen responses in
her work with adolescent girls:

> One 16-year-old felt that her words had been "stolen": "I see how you got
> what you said. I'm not saying it's wrong, but when you read about your-
> self . . . Well, it's me, but not me. It's really weird."
> Like other psychologists, I would defend my procedures on the grounds
> that good comes from them, too. The changes in perspective that may be
> *forced* on people who read about themselves in someone's rendition of their
> self narratives can be enlightening and validating. (31; emphasis added)

That is, Apter argues that the initial sense of self-alienation, violation, or
appropriation experienced by her subject might be outweighed by the
benefit of the enlightenment or validation it forces on her—an appeal to
the principle of beneficence. Any inquiry into life writing ethics has to acknowledge that life writing can do good for or to its subjects, whether
they seek it or not. Yet, as in medicine, such paternalistic rationales can be
self-serving: note Apter's acknowledgment of force, and note that the hy-
pothetical benefits she cites were not the purpose of the research.

Although the use of composite, altered, or pseudonymically veiled
portraits in much biomedical or social science research shields subjects
from being recognized by others, it does not protect them from the shock
of self-recognition. Thus, the ethics of life writing collaborations can be
tricky even when the subject is anonymous. One of Ruthellen Josselson's
subjects responded to a disguised portrait of her by seeking to revise it,
not because she felt Josselson had misunderstood or misrepresented her
but because she felt she had misrepresented herself: "What she had found
in my report was what she felt was a dishonest version of herself, and this
only increased her shame about the part of herself she regards as a black
spot on her soul. My written account reminded her of the ways in which

she hides from the world. Her stifled narcissistic rage at having partici-pated in my study was about seeing in the textual mirror the 'false self' she presents to the world" ("On Writing" 69).

In this case, while the original report remained unrevised, the dynam-ics of the collaboration became much more complex, as the subject, in a meta-confessional gesture, responded to her veiled public representation by revising her private confidence—and perhaps achieving a new level of self-knowledge. The process of representation became recursive and reflexive to an unexpected and extraordinary degree. Josselson's terms—"dishonest," "shame," "narcissistic rage"—suggest how high the stakes can be for the subject, how emotionally and ethically fraught such inter-actions can become. At the same time, even as the vulnerable subject speaks back to and revises her representation, she is dependent on Jos-selson to validate her self-image.

Josselson concludes with a revealing confession of her own.

I have taken myself out of relationship with my participants (with whom, during the interview, I was in intimate relationship) to be in relationship with my readers. I have, in a sense, been talking about them behind their backs and doing so publicly. Where in the interview I had been responsive to them, now I am using their lives in the service of something else, for my own purposes, to show something to others. I am guilty about being an in-truder and then, to some extent, a betrayer. (70)

This statement nicely isolates one ethical crux: how the life writer nego-tiates between a primary relationship with a subject (which involves self-representation to that subject, usually in person and often over a long period of time) and a secondary relationship with readers (which in-volves a very different sort of self-representation to a very different sort of audience through a very different medium). A host of ethical problems may spring from the divergence between the axes of these relationships and from the displacement of the earlier intimate relationship by the later, distant one. The danger of making one's subjects instrumental to one's own purposes is also clear.

Josselson does not see herself as betraying her subjects by misleading them (as McGinniss misled MacDonald); betrayal comes with her aban-donment of them, her eventual privileging of her relation with anony-mous readers over her prior intimate relation to them. It is a violation not of confidence or privacy but rather of intimacy which she regrets as in-herent in her trade. Like Malcolm and other journalists, she does not forswear what she sees as an act of questionable ethicality; she calls rather for a candid and open acknowledgment of its ethical problematics: "Doing narrative research is an ethically complex undertaking, but I do not advocate that we stop doing it. Rather, I am suggesting here that although this is important work, it is work we must do in anguish" (70). This is of course easy for her to say since it requires mostly a change in consciousness, which is not accessible to inspection, rather than in behavior, which is. Still, the value of such an acknowledgment is considerable, for it supports scrutiny of behavior and of textual products.

The ethical burden of life writing can also be expressed more positively and open-endedly:

> The other does not simply exist; it imposes responsibilities, obligations, constraints, regulations: it claims its rights. . . . Have we attended to the voice, the face, the law, of the other? Have we been faithful to its dictates? Have we permitted the other to be itself, to retain its autonomy? Have we taken proper care, proper responsibility? The answers to such questions form the content of ethical self-awareness. (Harpham 7)

Such self-awareness—that is, acknowledgment of the face and the autonomy of the other even, or especially, when the relationship is consensual—is a characteristic of the most ethically responsible life writing. It is a matter not just of responsibility but of responsiveness. The challenge is to enact or communicate this on the page.

Autonomy is best respected when subjects are granted some control over their stories; this is not inconsistent with what would otherwise be violations of privacy. On the contrary, in this regard the subject of life writing is analogous with the patient:

> When individuals voluntarily grant others some form of access to themselves, their act is an *exercise* of the right to privacy, not a *waiver* of that right. For example, our decision to grant a physician access for diagnostic, prognostic, and therapeutic procedures is an exercise of our right to control access that includes the right to grant as well as to exclude access [whether to the body or to the mind]. . . . In these instances, we exercise the right to privacy by reducing privacy in order to achieve other goals. (Beauchamp and Childress 297)

The agreement of a subject to confide in a collaborator or life writer, then, is not carte blanche, not a waiver of privacy rights, but rather a willing sacrifice of privacy with the goal and expectation of some compensatory benefit. Ethical partnerships, then, especially with vulnerable subjects, would involve respect for the integrity of their stories and for their rights—both authorial and economic—to their own stories. That is, like other collaborators or consensual partners, subjects should have some degree of control over the shape their stories take and, in some cases, an opportunity to share the proceeds from the sale of their stories. Or, if they cede these rights, they should do so only with "informed consent."

Vulnerable subjects are more likely to have their autonomy violated in practice precisely because what makes them vulnerable—whether their extreme youth or age or their physical or mental impairment—may be thought inconsistent with their autonomy; those perceived to have diminished autonomy are often, for that reason, treated in a way that may reduce whatever autonomy they do have. There is a further danger. In some cases, such as those of limited mental capacity or cognition, the very cause of subjects' vulnerability to exploitation may seem to make them invulnerable to certain kinds of harm—such as psychic pain or harm to reputation. (For example, if subjects—Iris Murdoch, for example—are incapable of reading the texts their cooperation or collaboration makes possible, they may be considered beyond being harmed by them.) Ironically, then, the assumption of their invulnerability to harm may make them all the more prone to abuse. Thus, in scenarios involving vulnerable subjects, a kind of legalistic "respect for autonomy" is not always adequate, for that vulnerability affects how their autonomy may be exercised.

The following passage, which expresses an ethical obligation in medicine, might also serve to articulate an ethical ideal in life writing: "Such respect [of doctor for patient] involves respectful *action*, not merely a respectful *attitude*. It also requires more than noninterference in others' personal affairs. It includes, at least in some contexts, obligations to build up or maintain others' capacities for autonomous choice while helping to allay fears and other conditions that destroy or disrupt their autonomous actions" (Beauchamp and Childress 63). Here Beauchamp and Childress recognize that the assumption that individuals are autonomous is not always valid—even among "competent" persons—and that the principle of respect for autonomy requires more than passive, legalistic noninterference. It is not paternalistic to intervene in order to realize or maximize a patient's, or subject's, potential for autonomy. Life writing that is ethically ideal, then, might involve optimizing the autonomy of subjects, not merely "respecting" it.

In medicine, one manifestation of respect for autonomy is the principle of informed consent, which is formalized, quite reductively, in various ways including written permission; medical procedures are authorized only when consent is freely given by an adequately informed, competent patient (Beauchamp and Childress 81). Similar standards apply to all "research involving human subjects"—regardless of discipline—which is governed by uniform protocols and reviewed by institutional review boards (IRBs). Such standards originated with the Nuremberg trials following World War II; the trials of Nazi doctors, who had experimented on unwilling subjects, gave rise to the Nuremberg Code of conditions that distinguish ethical research on human subjects. These in turn inspired codes adopted by the National Institute of Health in 1953 and the Department of Health, Education, and Welfare in 1974 (Shea 28).[5] According to these codes, consenting subjects must be informed of the "risks" and "benefits" of the project, and of their right to withdraw from it.

So, too, I would say, with life writing collaborations, especially those involving vulnerable subjects: they should be apprised ahead of time of the risks and benefits of the project and of their right to withdraw at any point under certain conditions. By benefits, I mean not only the presumed benefits to them, among which the primary one may be the unquantifiable but nevertheless significant value of having their stories told—or even merely listened to—but also the possible benefits to their collaborators and intended benefits to the public. Thus, sources or subjects should be aware of the possibility that others may profit from their stories in tangible or intangible ways. The knowledge that others may profit materially from access to their stories may alert them to mercenary motives in their collaborators and thus protect against economic exploitation. In effect, then, respect for autonomy should include respect for the person not just as "other" but also as a source of literary property with potential market value. As a variant or ramification of the Kantian principle that "one must act to treat every person as an end and never as a means only" (qtd. in Beauchamp and Childress 351), perhaps we can say that, although we have the right to commodify ourselves, we do not have the right to commodify others without their knowledge and permission.

In my ethical calculus, the rights of subjects to proceeds from and control over the text vary with the magnitude of their role in the text and the degree of their involvement in its production—their labor, their time, their granting of access to self and personal information—and with its format, whether biographical ("The Story of X") or autobiographical

("X's Story"). At the same time, the possibility that a wider public may benefit immaterially from subjects' stories may endow cooperation with a desirable and hitherto unsuspected altruistic motive (as when a story of victimization may help to prevent the abuse of others). I am not suggesting, then, that subjects must always be materially rewarded for their stories or their cooperation. They may be sufficiently gratified to know that their otherwise untold stories might have value in the marketplace; thus, the awareness of the potential profit to the writer may provide "psychic income" to the subject.

We cannot expect nor could we require of nonprofessional life writers the sorts of certification that researchers in the medical and social sciences—and even the humanities—are obliged to submit when engaged in research with human subjects. But, in addition to being consensual, their relations with subjects should be characterized by a property I call transactional visibility (or accessibility), which obtains when the partnership's terms and implications are made available for inspection by subjects and, ideally, by consumers of any resulting text. I deliberately avoid the term "contractual," since equitable arrangements can be achieved without written contracts, and as we have already seen, such contracts by no means guarantee equity and justice. (Note, however, that the accessibility of these arrangements to vulnerable subjects can be diminished or compromised by precisely those conditions that render such subjects vulnerable in the first place.) Collaborative transactions too often remain invisible and inaccessible to readers; the arrangements, the negotiations that led to them, and the distribution of proceeds generally occur behind the scenes. Even when they are described or enacted in the narrative, such representations are far from transparent—especially since they are usually controlled by one party. With all of those considerable qualifications, I favor and strongly encourage the inclusion in collaborative narratives of accounts of the transactions and negotiations that produced them—what Paul John Eakin calls "the story of the story." At the very least, this puts on record an account that is subject to verification or challenge by concerned parties.

Some circumstances, such as institutionalization, and some conditions, especially mental illnesses, may compromise, limit, or abrogate autonomy; thus, although all subjects are entitled to respect as persons, not all subjects have autonomy, and the nature of the collaboration—and whether it is in fact permissible—must depend in part on the competence of the subject. In some cases, then, respect for persons will mean honoring autonomous choices, whether they seem wise or not; in others, as noted earlier, it may mean intervening to augment or maximize autonomy where there is some question; in yet others, it may mean recognizing a lack of autonomy sufficient to permit meaningful consent.

In medical contexts, when patients are incompetent, the principle of respect for autonomy is honored by seeking an appropriate decision-making surrogate, according to one or more standards. According to the standard of "pure autonomy," the decision is to be guided by the patient's previously expressed wishes or values, as conveyed by directives such as "living wills" (Beauchamp and Childress 99–100). According to the "substituted judgment standard," a surrogate is asked to make the decision the incompetent person "would have made" if competent. (This requires someone who knows the patient well and has no conflict of interest.) According to the "best interests" standard, the surrogate is to decide which among competing actions or decisions in best overall for the patient, regardless of whether the patient would have made that choice under the circumstances (Beauchamp and Childress 102). This last standard is generally used with children, who may be thought of as not yet having achieved autonomy or having lived long enough to supply meaningful evidence of their ideals and values. Beauchamp and Childress refer to the second of these standards as involving "ghostly autonomy," but that phrase applies more loosely to all of them, since all involve a sort of "ghostwriting" of the life script by a surrogate author (100). These distinctions may help us to parse and resolve the sorts of ethical dilemmas that crop up in life writing collaborations with less than fully autonomous subjects, many of which involve "ghostwriting" not just in the narrowest sense of that term (unacknowledged authorship). That is, these standards may help us assess the conduct of those who write about or for others who are unable to cooperate in a very active or self-protective way, such as subjects with cognitive or psychiatric impairments. Since collaborative writing with, or on behalf of, vulnerable subjects necessarily involves surrogacy, biomedical ethics is a useful reference for analysis and evaluation of such partnerships.

∽

The biomedical principles of nonmaleficence and beneficence are also pertinent to life writing collaborations or partnerships involving vulnerable subjects. Rather than differentiating sharply between these principles, Beauchamp and Childress distinguish among obligations to prevent harm or evil, to remove harm or evil, and to do or promote good (115). This seems a useful approach for life writing ethics as well, especially if we recognize the distinction between ordinary and extraordinary moral standards. According to Beauchamp and Childress:

> The first level [of obligation] is limited to standards in the common moral-ity that pertain to everyone. These standards form the moral minimum. They include obligations specified in moral principles and rules, as well as the virtues that we expect all moral agents to possess. . . . The second level is a morality of aspiration in which individuals adopt moral ideals that do not hold for everyone. . . . Other persons can praise and admire those who fulfill these ideals, but they cannot blame or criticize those who do not pur-sue them. Persons who do not accept these ideals are not bound by them and cannot be criticized for not adopting them. (39–40)

In a biomedical context, of course, beneficence is obligatory; it is, after all, the raison d'être of the profession: "Promoting the welfare of pa-tients—not merely avoiding harm—expresses medicine's goal, rationale, and justification" (Beauchamp and Childress 173). In life writing, by con-trast, beneficence represents an extraordinary standard, at most an ideal rather than an obligation. (We do not expect, and we should not require, biographers to act on behalf of and in the interests of their subjects.) Nev-ertheless, the principle of beneficence may help us to assess the goals and effects of certain life writing projects. And the rules that are obligatory in biomedicine may be desirable in life writing involving vulnerable sub-jects: "1. Protect and defend the rights of others. 2. Prevent harm from oc-curring to others. 3. Remove conditions that will cause harm to others. 4. Help persons with disabilities" (Beauchamp and Childress 167). These rules may be especially pertinent with regard to life writing subjects un-dergoing biomedical procedures or institutionalized in medical or reha-bilitative institutions, as is frequently the case today (as in the work of Oliver Sacks, explored in chapter 5).

Beneficence is also pertinent when life writing partnerships, as sug-gested earlier, constitute fiduciary relationships akin to that between physician and patient. Such relationships, Beauchamp and Childress ar-gue, involve special ethical standards: "When a patient contracts with a physician for services, the latter assumes a role-specific obligation of beneficent treatment that would not be present apart from the relation-ship" (175). Similarly, when writers team up with vulnerable subjects, whether contractually or not, such collaboration entails role-specific obligations. While any partnership—including those between previously unacquainted individuals (like McGinniss and MacDonald)—involves such role-specific obligations, many life writing scenarios involve cooperation with partners who are already embedded in "special moral relationships," such as familial ones (like the Hampls, mother and daughter). In such relationships, the preexisting intimacy raises the stakes, since it creates special liability to exposure and harm. Although it may be unrealistic and inappropriate to require writers to do good to their subjects—and difficult to know how to define and measure that good—it may be proper to expect that writers at least do no harm to consenting vulnerable subjects.

Thus far, I have been invoking biomedical ethics in the form of the somewhat abstract "principlism" of Beauchamp and Childress; at this point, however, I turn to a passage in which they depart from principlism to invoke the ethics of care:

> The ethics of care maintains that many human relationships (e.g., in health care and research) involve persons who are vulnerable, dependent, ill, and frail and that the desirable moral response is attached attentiveness to needs, not detached respect for rights. Feeling for and being immersed in the other person establish vital aspects of the moral relationship. Accordingly, this approach features responsibilities and forms of empathy that a rights-based account may ignore in the attempt to protect persons from invasion by others. (373)

The more intimate the preexisting or collaborative relationship between writer and subject—the more history they have together—the more pertinent the ethics of care is to their life writing partnership, and the more the partners are bound by something greater than mere "detached respect for rights."

Beauchamp and Childress make two further distinctions pertinent to the issue of nonmaleficence. While they define "harm" nonnormatively or nonprejudicially as "thwarting, defeating, or setting back some party's interests," they make a distinction critical to life writing ethics, that between justified and unjustified harm:

> A *harmful* action by one party may not be wrong or unjustified *on balance, although acts of harming in general are prima facie wrong.* The reason for their prima facie wrongness is precisely that they do set back the interests of the

persons affected. Harmful actions that involve *justifiable* setbacks to another's interests are, of course, not wrong. They include cases of justified criminal punishment, justified demotion of an employee for poor performance in a job, and discipline in schools. (116–17)

Thus, in the McGinniss-MacDonald case one could concede that McGinniss had "harmed" MacDonald—by destroying any residual credibility and reputation and undermining his protestations of innocence—but argue that such "harm" was justified by his apparent responsibility for the heinous murder of his family and his stunning lack of remorse.

In this case, the justification would go beyond the defense against libel—that the account was true—to suggest that MacDonald *deserved* to be exposed as narcissistic. That is, the effect of McGinniss's book may not have been beneficial to MacDonald, but it was to the public and his wife's family, removing doubt as to the justice of the verdict and perhaps shedding some light on the genesis of the crime. (In this case, the principle of "justice," which in biomedical ethics usually has to do with the distribution or allocation of scarce resources, would seem to correspond more closely with its conventional legal usage: McGinniss's biographical verdict on MacDonald reinforced the jury's. Justice was done.) Similarly, the exposure of an abuser in a memoir by a victim of child or spouse abuse would qualify as justified harm.

The notion of harm can cover many different sorts of injury relevant to life writing:

> Some definitions of harm are so broad that they include setbacks to interests in reputation, property, privacy, and liberty. So broad is the term *harm* in some writings that it seems to embrace almost every condition that might restrict autonomous action, such as causing discomfort, humiliation, offense, and annoyance. Such a broad conception distinguishes trivial harms from serious harms by the magnitude of the interests affected. (117)

Of course, if we were to adopt a notion of harm so broad that any life writing that caused "discomfort, humiliation, offense, and annoyance" was considered unethical, we would be adopting an inappropriately restrictive standard. Regarding the relations between journalists and their subjects, Janet Malcolm has rightly said: "Journalists who swallow the subject's account whole and publish it are not journalists but publicists. If the lesson of *MacDonald v. McGinniss* were taken to heart by prospective subjects, it could indeed, as [McGinniss's lawyer] maintained, be the end of journalism" (144). Similarly, if life writing were considered unethical whenever it caused its subjects any sort of discomfort or pain, it would be the end of life writing as we know it. But we should remember that the issue is not whether harm is caused but of what kind or order (trivial or serious), and whether any such harm is *justified*. For me the key factor is the degree of vulnerability of the subjects. The more vulnerable the subjects (the less capable of protecting themselves), the more scrupulous life writers must be about avoiding gratuitously harmful representations of them.

A second useful distinction that Beauchamp and Childress make is that between harming and wronging, where harming means adversely affecting someone's interests, while "*wronging* involves violating someone's rights. . . . [H]*arming* need not involve such a violation, or a wrong, or an injustice. To see this distinction, consider that people are harmed without being wronged in circumstances of attack by disease, acts of God, bad luck, and acts by others to which the harmed person has consented" (116).

To rephrase an earlier assessment of the MacDonald-McGinniss relationship, one might concede that while McGinniss had harmed MacDonald, he did not wrong him, insofar as MacDonald's written release constituted consent to McGinniss's act (though one could also argue that McGinniss had wronged as well as harmed MacDonald by violating a trust that transcended a contractual agreement). The point is that whether life writing is ethical or not is not a simple matter of whether it causes harm to its subject; instead the question is whether and how that harm may be justified, and whether it constitutes wrong.

To sum up, I have argued that an approach to the ethics of life writing might look to biomedical ethics for guidance because biomedical ethics today provides a particularly comprehensive account of normative ethics, because life writing partnerships sometimes resemble the sorts of confidential fiduciary relationships that exist between physicians and patients, and also because in some cases the narratives themselves recount scenarios in which more narrowly biomedical issues are the subject. One needs to keep in mind, however, the difference between ethical obligations and ethical ideals, so as not to be hypercritical of life writers.

∽

Although biomedical ethics may be more comprehensive and systematic than anthropological ethics, anthropology is probably the discipline in which life writing has received the most rigorous ethical scrutiny, so it is apt that the ethics of ethnography might also be called upon in formulating an approach to the ethics of life writing, especially when life writing focuses on the "other." Anthropology provides a helpful supplement to the principles of biomedical ethics for two reasons. The first is that its ethical principles and practices have been devised to operate (generally) outside of clinical contexts, which is where most life writing is located. The second is that whereas biomedical ethics tends to focus on one subject at a time, too often in isolation from social, historical, and cultural contexts, anthropology is oriented to communities.[6] According to David M. Fetterman, the ethnographer's ethical code "specifies first and foremost that the ethnographer do no harm to people or the community under study. . . . [T]he ethnographer is careful not to trample the feelings of the natives or desecrate what the culture calls sacred" (120). With the statement that the first principle is the avoidance of harm, we can see the congruence between medical and anthropological ethics, and in fact, there is considerable overlap between the ethical concerns of anthropology and those of medicine; anthropology's concerns with permission (consent), honesty (disclosure), trust (confidence), privacy, and reciprocity (mutual benefit) are also characteristic, as we have seen, of biomedical ethics (Fetterman 130–35). But with the emphasis on respect for the community, we find a dimension lacking in most accounts of biomedical ethics: an overt consideration—indeed, a favoring—of social units rather than mere individual subjects.

Anthropological ethics reminds us that harm can be done to communities as well as to individuals, a realization absent from, or late in coming to, most other academic fields. When life writing has to do with individuals rendered vulnerable by some marginalizing condition, one ethical concern should be with the effect of the project on the community to which such individuals belong—or perhaps to which they may be assigned. Thus, George Rosenwald, a psychologist, reminds us that research that devalues a group can inflict damage on members of that group; there is no protective membrane between individuals and the communities to which they belong:

The *Ethical Standards* ([of the American Psychological Association], 1953) protect individuals only against damage and only against damage inflicted directly and pointedly. On this ethical view, the study of ethnic and gender group differences continues to flourish in human psychology despite the fact that, in addressing issues of social concern, it inevitably produces odious comparisons—odious differences, odious [in]equalities. Because there is nothing in the *Standards* to prevent injuring a tolerant individual through the depreciation of his or her group, there is also little impetus for researchers to exercise their ingenuity in the devising of research that would be beneficial to the groups about whom they are concerned. (258–59)

Increasingly, just as medical patients and disabled people have begun speaking back to physicians and challenging medical narratives about their conditions, members of minority groups are talking back to the social sciences. Sally McBeth, co-author of the life story of an elderly mixed-blood Shoshone woman, notes that "American Indian people no longer tolerate the intrusions of social scientists into their lives without some guarantee that they will not only see the final research project, but also have some control over it. They don't allow anthropologists to conduct research that is not of value to them, that resists their own perception of themselves, or that perpetrates [sic] stereotypes" (153). Through a process of self-examination on the part of social scientists and self-assertion on the part of historically marginalized subjects and groups, the principles and practice of life writing have been subtly but significantly changed.

James Clifford has concisely appraised the predicament of ethnography at the turn of the millennium in ways that are relevant to the representation of vulnerable subjects generally, especially those who are members of distinct communities:

> The writing and reading of ethnography are overdetermined by forces ultimately beyond the control of either an author or an interpretive community. These contingencies—of language, rhetoric, power, and history—must now be openly confronted in the process of writing. They can no longer be evaded. . . . [I]s there not a liberation . . . in recognizing that no one can write about others any longer as if they were discrete objects or texts? ("Partial Truths" 25)

One of the reasons why it is no longer possible—or at least permissible—to objectify others is that those "others" have begun to challenge the cultural, political, and ethical authority of that objectification. As Caroline Brettell notes, one of the factors contributing to anthropology's searching self-examination in the last quarter of the twentieth century was the new phenomenon of ethnography being read and critiqued by its subjects (2–3). For some vulnerable subjects, of course, speaking back is difficult, if not impossible. Notable, however, among hitherto marginalized groups that have begun to respond to their representation, textual or extratextual, by others are people with disabilities, both as individuals and as a community. Indeed, Carol Thomas defines disability as a social construct in terms of the harm it does: "Disability is a form of social oppression involving the social imposition of restrictions of activity on people with impairments and the socially engendered undermining of their psycho-emotional well-being" (3).

What is at stake in the ethics of life writing is the representation of the self and of the other, which is always at once a mimetic and a political act. In the chapters that follow, I invoke principles and distinctions I have introduced here in order to bring to life writing the sort of ethical scrutiny I think it demands and deserves. I use the word "invoke" deliberately. The scenarios that concern me are located neither in the domain of biomedicine nor in that of ethnography but rather in some gray area—but not a no-man's-land—between or adjacent to them. The systematic application of biomedical or ethnographic ethical concepts to these life writing projects would be both tedious and inappropriate. Moreover, as the principles are invoked in particular cases, they may need to be adapted and adjusted. At most, they will serve as guidelines or reference points rather than as rigid rules.

Life writing is far too complex and variable to be subjected to a set of abstract, unvarying, and presumably universal principles. Interesting cases may require the revision, amplification, or qualification of principles, or the invocation of alternative ethical approaches such as the ethics of care. Even though the principles invoked may prove finally inadequate, then, their invocation may be illuminating. Thus, I see the relation between ethical approaches and cases not as a matter of deductive, one-way application but as a recursive and dialectical interaction. Such interaction—the mutual illumination of cases and ethical concepts—may help us negotiate between the two poles represented by the epigraphs to this chapter. Ruthellen Josselson reminds us that the act of writing another's life is inherently partial and thus inadequate, presumptuous, and possibly transgressive. By contrast, Patricia Hampl reminds us of the imperative to make something, through narrative, of the experience—others' as well as our own—with which we are entrusted.

3

Making, Taking, and Faking Lives
Voice and Vulnerability
in Collaborative Life Writing

"Whose book is this?"

—MALCOLM X, in reference to his autobiography

ALTHOUGH ISSUES OF LITERARY ethics may arise in any genre, ethical dilemmas seem to be inherent in collaborative life writing in ways that are peculiar to it.[1] With fiction, drama, and poetry, ethical criticism is usually concerned with questions of meaning and of reception: in the simplest terms, does the text have beneficial or harmful effects on its audience? (Such criticism is thus implicitly consequentialist.) But nonfiction generally, and life writing specifically, raises other concerns. Indeed, although Wayne Booth limits his scope to fiction in *The Company We Keep*, he asks key questions that are perhaps even more compelling for life writing, for example: What are the author's responsibilities to those whose lives are used as "material"? What are the author's responsibilities to others whose labor is exploited to make the work of art possible? What are the responsibilities of the author to truth? (130–32). Especially with collaborative life writing, ethical concerns begin with the production of the narrative and extend to the relation of the text to the historical record of which it forms a part.

Ethical issues are particularly acute in collaborative autobiography because it occupies an awkward niche between more established and prestigious forms of life writing. On one side is solo autobiography, in which the writer, the narrator, and the subject (or protagonist) of the narrative are all the same person; at least, they share the same name. On the other side is biography (or what Philippe Lejeune calls "heterobiography" [190]), in which the writer and narrator are one person while the subject is someone else.[2] In between, combining features of the adjacent forms— and thus challenging the commonsense distinction between them—is as-told-to autobiography, in which the writer is one person but the narrator and subject are someone else. The ethical difficulties of collaborative autobiography are rooted in its nearly oxymoronic status. Although the process by which the text is produced is dialogical, the product is monological; the single narrative voice—a simulation by one person of the voice of another—is always in danger of breaking, exposing conflicts not manifest in solo autobiography.[3] The two voices are permitted to engage in dialogue only in supplementary texts—forewords and afterwords— and even there, the dialogue is managed and presented by one party, the nominal author. Insofar as the process is admitted into the narrative, then, it is generally in supplementary texts, and generally as a chapter of the writer's autobiography. (Exceptions are those narratives, increasingly common, that include what Paul John Eakin calls "the story of the story": an account of the process that produced them.)

Although critics are not in a position to mandate disclosure of the process, fuller divulgence is likely to reflect ethically sound collaboration; in any case, such disclosure can be rhetorically effective insofar as it suggests that the nominal author has nothing to hide. A classic example of a textual supplement that gives access to the backstage negotiation—to the interactive, sometimes competitive process by which a monological text is produced—is Alex Haley's epilogue to *The Autobiography of Malcolm X*. There he recounts moments when he and Malcolm X confronted the divergence between their interests in the book they were making. As Malcolm underwent profound changes in his religious and political perspective, his impulse was to revise parts that had already been "written"; their writer, Haley, had a vested interest in moving forward with the narrative toward the payoff of publication. Clearly, Haley's interest in closure was at odds with Malcolm's openness to new ideas and points of view. Thus, living a life and writing that life may become incompatible, even competing endeavors.

Autobiographical collaborations are rather like marriages and other domestic partnerships: partners enter into a relationship of some duration, they "make life" together, and they produce an offspring that will derive traits from both of them.[4] Both partners have strong interests in the fate of that offspring, which will reflect on each in a different way. Much of this is true of any collaborative authorship, of course; with autobiography, however, the fact that the joint product is a life story raises the stakes, at least for the subject. Perhaps the supreme ethical principle governing the production of collaborative autobiography should be a variant of the Golden Rule: Do unto your partner as you would have your partner do unto you (or the equivalent Kantian imperative, "One must act to treat every person as an end and never as a means only" [qtd. in Beauchamp and Childress 351]). Which is to say that autobiographical collaborations should be mutually gratifying and maximally egalitarian; neither partner should abuse, exploit, or betray the other. Given the subject's special stake in the textual product, a corollary principle might be that the subjects of as-told-to autobiographies, like those of oral history interviews (see chapter 2, n. 4), should have the right to audit and edit manuscripts before publication. As we shall see, however, in some circumstances this is easier said than done.

The vast majority of collaborative life stories involve partnerships that are voluntary, amicable, and mutually beneficial. Still, there are thin and not always clear lines between making, taking, and faking the life of another person in print. Co-authoring another's life can be a creative or a destructive act, a service or a disservice, an homage or an appropriation. The potential for abuse lies partly in something the term itself tends to elide: that is, the process, though cooperative, does not usually involve collaborative *writing* (which can itself be problematic). Rather, ethical difficulties arise from the disparity between the contributions of the two partners. There are, of course, different kinds and degrees of collaboration, but in most cases, one member supplies the "life" while the other provides the "writing."

The extent to which this is an oversimplification of the process depends on a number of factors. I do not mean to endorse a model under which "writing" is taken too literally; as contemporary rhetorical theory insists, in some sense the entire process of composition, from initiation and invention to copyediting, is "writing." Nor do I mean to imply that the "writer" is entirely dependent on the subject for the "story"; most writers are drawn to their subjects by previous knowledge of them, and most supplement interviews with independent research. Nor do I mean to identify "form" exclusively with "writing" and "content" with "life," or to imply that the "writing" does not affect the content; any mediation carries its own messages. Indeed, as we shall see, mediation can be a source of ethical problems, especially in cases of cross-cultural collaboration. For example, when the implications of the narrative form are unavailable to subjects, there is the danger of misrepresentation that will go undetected by them.

Ultimately, no matter how involved the subject is at each stage of the project, the partners bring different skills and contributions to the final product. Their labor is of different kinds, and the wording of the resulting text is largely attributable to the "writer." In the last analysis, then, the partners' contributions are not just different but incommensurate—on the one hand, lived experience mediated by memory; on the other, the work of eliciting, recording, transcribing, organizing, and revising this material.

The inherent disparity between the partners' contributions may be complicated by an imbalance of power between them. Often, collaborations involve partners whose relation is hierarchized by some difference in race, culture, gender, class, age, or (in the case of narratives of illness or disability) somatic, intellectual, or emotional condition that renders them vulnerable to exploitation. Having power or rank over someone else is not the same as overpowering that person, of course. In the scenario typical of what I call ethnographic autobiography, however, subjects may indeed be vulnerable to the writer's domination, in part because they are likely to be among "those who do not write."[5] This has historically been the case with American racial minorities—African Americans in the case of slave narrative and Native Americans in the case of what Arnold Krupat calls Indian autobiography (that which is written in collaboration with a non-Native [30]), and much recent criticism has been devoted to recuperating the point of view of subjects of color.

My work on narratives of illness and disability suggests that, like other marginalized groups, people who are ill or disabled may also be at a disadvantage with respect to their collaborators. The political imbalance latent in collaborative narratives of illness and disability is perhaps most obvious and most problematic in those cases in which the narrative is composed by a surrogate or survivor. For example, I have found that relational (particularly parental) narratives of gay men who die of AIDS are often unwittingly heterosexist to some degree; because they are generally written and published posthumously, the subject has no opportunity to audit them.[6] (In chapter 6, I explore a related concern in euthanasia narratives.) There are circumstances other than terminal disease in which disability or illness may complicate the dynamics of the collaboration; for example, disabilities that make solo autobiography impossible may also make it difficult for the subject to review the manuscript and mandate changes.

Even where such review is possible, the process may involve unintentional misrepresentation. A case in point is that of *I Raise My Eyes to Say Yes*, by Ruth Sienkiewicz-Mercer and Steven B. Kaplan. Sienkiewicz-Mercer was severely disabled at birth by cerebral palsy, and she has never been able to speak or write. Unable to keep her at home when she was a child, her family sent her to a state facility, where she was misdiagnosed and "warehoused" as mentally retarded—supervised rather than educated. She was eventually able to make her abilities known, and partly as a result of the disability rights movement, she was allowed to move out of the state facility. Her story—which, as a story of liberation, is akin to a slave narrative—was written with the collaboration of a lawyer and advocate for disabled people through an extremely labor-intensive process. Sienkiewicz-Mercer would scan customized word-boards to select a category, and through a process of questions and answers she would sketch out a skeletal account of an incident; Kaplan would then flesh this out and read it back to her for corrections.

I see no reason to doubt the factual accuracy of her narrative, which Sienkiewicz-Mercer had the opportunity to review. And there is no question of exploitation: Kaplan seems to have served as her advocate. But there is a discrepancy between Sienkiewicz-Mercer's level of literacy as Kaplan describes it—she reads "at best, at a first-grade level, recognizing only simple words placed before her in a familiar context" (vii)—and the voice of the narrative, which is that of a college graduate and fluent writer. Such discrepancies may be characteristic of many ghostwritten or collaborative narratives, though they may not always be as problematic as academics make them out to be. Certainly a text reflecting her level of literacy might have given a misleading indication of her sensibility and intelligence: simple syntax may connote, but it does not signify, simple-mindedness. One could argue that an account relying on her diction and syntax might have been unpublishable (and virtually unreadable). Is it not better to have a somewhat misrepresentative text written from her point of view than none at all? Is it not ethical to "amplify" her voice by editorial means? After all, is this not done with as-told-to stories of non-disabled people?

The problem is that when mediation is ignored, the resulting text may be (mis)taken for a transparent lens through which we have direct access to its subject (rather than to its author). And it is here that the veracity of the narrative as a first-person account of Sienkiewicz-Mercer's life may be called into question. On the one hand, Kaplan professes his concerns about possible distortions; on the other, he produces a text that Sienkiewicz-Mercer could not have produced even with the aid of some wondrous technology that could transport words directly from her mind to the page. Kaplan's claim that, although "most of the words were not generated by Ruth . . . [,] the thoughts and emotions, the impressions and observations expressed by these words, are Ruth's alone" (xii) assumes too much independence of content from form, message from medium.

The liberties Kaplan takes with "translation" in effect hypernormalize Sienkiewicz-Mercer (if that is not an oxymoron). The monological prose belies the very labor-intensive dialogical process by which it was produced; in fundamental ways, it masks or erases the disability that has so profoundly shaped its subject's life. Here, then, we have an odd ethical phenomenon: the very mediation that seemingly empowers and liberates Sienkiewicz-Mercer drowns out, even as it amplifies, her "voice." Representation in the political sense and representation in the mimetic sense seem somehow at odds. In his role as advocate, speaking for her, Kaplan inevitably mis-speaks her, giving her his voice. In the final analysis, however, I consider this more of an irony than an ethical lapse. Any misrepresentation (in the mimetic sense) involved in this ventriloquism is justified by the value of her story and the desirability of making it accessible to a reading public that requires a fluent, detailed narrative.

Such ventriloquism is also common in collaborative celebrity autobiography, which has far less social value. According to Lejeune, in the scenario typical of celebrity autobiography, "the power connections are inverted: for a star, a hero, or an explorer, who has a life at his disposal to write, there are dozens of ghostwriters in the job market; for an amateur 'ethnobiographer' who wants to capture a life, there are hundreds of thousands of possible models, and the model chosen should consider himself happy to attain a notoriety for which he was in no way destined" (196). As illustration of this disparity between the celebrity and the ethnographic scenarios, consider remarks made in a radio interview by Susan Orlean, author of *The Bullfighter Checks Her Makeup*. She declared her preference for working with non-celebrities because celebrities are always putting up a façade, pursuing an agenda, and staying "on message" in a way that limits her access to them. By contrast, she finds that, although non-celebrities may try to manipulate her, they falter and expose themselves more fully if she spends enough time with them. (Asked whether this made her subjects nervous, she quoted one as saying, when asked if she was apprehensive about a forthcoming story, "No, I'm not; my whole body is covered with hives.")

Rosemary J. Coombe has argued that celebrity identity is authored collaboratively and collectively rather than individually. Nevertheless, in the marketplace, celebrities have the advantage of licensing their replication. And in celebrity autobiography, subjects typically outrank writers in wealth and clout.[7] We might schematize collaborative autobiography, then, as lying somewhere on a continuum ranging from ethnographic autobiography, in which writers outrank subjects, to celebrity autobiography, in which subjects outrank writers. Although I would estimate that most collaborative narratives are situated at the ends of the continuum, significant numbers of texts can be found closer to the middle. At the very center, we would find texts produced by partners who are true peers (e.g., dual autobiographies), in which each partner contributes a separate narrative, and truly co-authored (rather than as-told-to) autobiographies.[8]

Close to the center, but toward the ethnographic end of the continuum, would be found those single-author texts (e.g., Spiegelman's *Maus*) that Paul John Eakin calls relational lives, and that I call auto/biographies, memoirs of proximate others, such as close relatives or partners, which are collaborative in some sense or degree (Eakin, "Relational Selves"). In these texts there is more than one subject, and the process of collaboration may itself be featured in the narrative rather than being consigned to supplementary texts, as is the case at the ends of the continuum. Even in what passes for solo memoir, contemporary authors may acknowledge the extent to which memory is relational; as a result, it may be collaboratively (re)constituted at times and contested at others. In her acknowledgments to *The Liar's Club: A Memoir*, Mary Karr avers, "My sister, Lecia Harmon Scaglione, confirmed the veracity of what I'd written" (n.p.), and yet she sometimes interrupts her narrative to admit that her sister's version of an episode would necessarily be markedly different: "If I gave my big sister a paragraph here, she would correct my memory. . . . I contend that her happy memories are shaped more by convenience than reality" (47). She pays homage, too, to another silent collaborator and vulnerable subject: "My mother didn't read this book until it was complete. However, for two years she freely answered questions by phone and mail, and she did research for me, even when she was ill. She has been unreserved in her encouragement of this work though much in the story pains her" (acknowledgments, n.p.). Here, Karr's admission that her memoir pains her mother is offset by her declaration of her mother's consent and co-operation.

At any point on the continuum, it makes little sense to discuss the "ethics" of collaborative autobiography in isolation from the politics—or, for that matter, the economics—of collaboration, for ethical problems are most likely to occur where there is a substantial differential between part-ners in power or wealth. Furthermore, different ethical issues tend to arise depending on where the texts are located on the continuum. For exam-ple, privacy tends to be more of an issue in relational lives, in which the partners know each other intimately, than in most other forms of collab-orative autobiography. In his memoir of growing up the younger son of deaf parents, Lennard J. Davis tells of suffering physical abuse at the hands of his older brother, Gerald. The publication of such accusations, if true, would qualify as "justified harm"; even so, Davis blunts their force by noting that he and Gerald became closer as a result of Lennard's life writing. When Lennard edited and published their parents' love letters as *Shall I Say a Kiss? Courtship Letters of a Deaf Couple*, Gerald wrote the preface at Lennard's invitation. Further, Lennard notes in *My Sense of Si-lence* that "I have finally shown him this memoir, and he has read it avidly. I think he has come to understand how odious his behavior was to me, and he sincerely regrets it. His is an apology I can fully accept now, and I am grateful to know that he understands me better, even as I think I have come to understand him" (72). Although Gerald evidently was not al-lowed to make or even request changes—and in that sense Lennard re-mains sole author—Gerald's role is not entirely passive. If what Lennard claims is true, the narrative he wrote single-handedly (but in consultation with his brother and others) not only retroactively "re-presents" their relation but also helps to (re)shape its future by precipitating a reconcili-ation through its very production. This claim serves to deflect any accu-sation that Lennard has unnecessarily violated his brother's privacy. The implication is that the project—both as process and as product—has ben-efitted them both by bringing them closer together.

∽

Inequities are possible in two distinct but interrelated aspects of the project: the portrayal and the partnership. The justice of the portrayal has to do with whether the text represents its subject the way the subject would like to be represented, with whether that portrayal is in the subject's best interests, with the control the subject has over it, and with the degree and kind of any harm or wrong done by misrepresentation. Harm can be done to the subjects' privacy, to their reputations, even to their integrity as individuals.[9] Problems in the portrayal may be manifest in the text—or in its relation to other texts—and thus relatively easy for critics to detect. (Of course, critics cannot correct but only correct *for* these problems.) Problems with portrayal are most likely to crop up when the subjects' opportunity to audit and edit the manuscript is limited, that is, mainly in the ethnographic scenario. Despite their apparent advantage of wealth and clout, celebrities are not immune to hostile or negative representations, particularly if they play a passive role in the production of their autobiographies. For example, according to her obituary in the *New York Times,* Hedy Lamarr (unsuccessfully) sued the publisher and ghostwriter of her autobiography, *Ecstasy and Me,* for making it too lurid (Severo para. 35). In cases of misrepresentation, the critic may be impelled to act, in effect, as the advocate of the subject, whose life may have been inaccurately portrayed or unfairly appropriated.

In many, perhaps most, cases of ethnographic collaboration, subjects never confront their published alter egos; their "lives" appear in print elsewhere, among those who do write, and the subjects are less liable to damage by the product (which is not to say that the process may not be exploitative). In some ways, the case of *Black Elk Speaks* by John G. Neihardt confounds the dichotomy between the celebrity and ethnographic scenarios, because within his tribe, at least, Black Elk was no mere "common man." Despite this, he was vulnerable vis-à-vis his collaborator with respect to race, class, and literacy. *Black Elk Speaks* offers an interesting instance in which the subject of the narrative was discomfited by it in ways he could not have anticipated.[10] The production of this story involved not just translation from Black Elk's Lakota to Neihardt's English but a complex cross-cultural collaboration involving members of Black Elk's family and tribe and members of Neihardt's family. Despite Neihardt's good intentions, it is now possible to tell, thanks to the recuperative work of Raymond DeMallie, how Neihardt imposed his own agenda on the resulting text. In particular, he was at pains to suppress the evidence of Black Elk's acculturation. To this end, Neihardt ended the narrative with the massacre at Wounded Knee in 1890, omitting any acknowledgment of Black Elk's conversion to Roman Catholicism early in the twentieth century.

In theory, it would have been possible for Black Elk to have vetted the text; it could have been translated back to him by the same collaborators who produced the transcripts. Such a process would have been laborious, however, and it would not necessarily have enabled him to assess the implications of publishing this account of his life. As it happened, he was not given the opportunity to audit the text. And, as DeMallie reveals, when the book was published, it became a source of some distress to him. The Catholic clergy on the reservation were upset that the book portrayed their model convert as an unreconstructed "longhair." Although we have no way of knowing Black Elk's full response to this depiction, he was apparently impelled to "speak" again, issuing a document that reaffirmed his Christian faith. Indeed, he complained that he had wanted Neihardt to include a chapter narrating his conversion. Although it is tempting to read these complaints as induced by clerical pressure, it appears that Neihardt's representation did not completely conform to Black Elk's self-image and the accepted image of him in his community. The aftermath of publication suggests that he felt that the book did him some injustice (DeMallie 60). I do not want to portray Black Elk as entirely or necessarily a victim in this process, however, for the book may also manifest his shrewd use of an unfamiliar medium—autobiography—to convey his vision to a large off-reservation audience. In any case, although the book did not have much immediate impact, today it is among the most influential representations of Lakota culture, even among the Lakota themselves. That each partner may have manipulated the other in ways of which the other was unaware suggests the intricacy and ethical complexities of such collaborations.

The question of equity in partnership has to do with the conditions and division of labor and the distribution of the proceeds. Since this aspect of the collaboration has more to do with the process than with the textual product, violations may not be manifest in the text and are less easy for critics to detect. (Issues of ownership and distribution of the proceeds are generally least accessible to inspection; assignment of copyright, though public, does not necessarily reflect the division of proceeds.) In the case of Black Elk, the equity of the partnership, as well as of the portrayal, has come into question: DeMallie's research uncovered a letter in which Black Elk complained that he had not been compensated as promised for his contribution to the book (DeMallie 59–63).

A prime concern with any partnership is whether collaboration is truly voluntary (autonomous) or somehow coerced. Most of us would imagine inequities of partnership as occurring exclusively in the case of ethnography, in which writers are advantaged, but they may occur with celebrity autobiographies as well. There the relationship between subject and writer is sometimes effectively that between employer and employee, with all the potential for abuse that lies in such relations. According to Andrew Szanton, a professional writer of autobiographies, writers have more at risk economically in these collaborations than subjects do, since the project often represents the writers' livelihood but rarely that of the subjects, who are generally financially secure.[11] Economic security may, of course, make celebrity subjects generous. In some instances, they give away their life stories (but usually not the most marketable ones). In any case, there is some potential even in the celebrity scenario for economic exploitation.

Such a claim was made by William Novak, who agreed to accept a flat fee for writing his first celebrity autobiography, *Iacocca*, which became a surprise best-seller. When his request for a share of the paperback royalties was turned down, Novak felt he had been cheated out of his fair share of the proceeds. He complained publicly, to no avail (Wyden). Despite the inequity in the distribution of proceeds, Novak had no legal recourse, having signed a contract that afforded him no royalties, and his ethical position was undermined by the fact that Lee Iacocca, chief executive of Chrysler, donated his royalties to charity. In any case, to the extent that Novak's career took off after (and as a result of) *Iacocca*, any inequity was at least partially redressed.

In addition to shedding a good deal of light on the sometimes competitive relationship between authors and celebrity subjects, Quincy Troupe's *Miles and Me* reveals that compensation is not limited to contractual matters such as royalties. After Troupe, a poet and jazz fan, interviewed Miles Davis for *Spin* magazine, Davis invited Troupe to write *Miles: The Autobiography*. (Thus, Troupe, who had thought of himself as interviewing Davis, discovered that Davis had simultaneously been auditioning him.) In addition to his share of the book's proceeds, Troupe benefitted from heightened name recognition—fame by association—which he credits with increasing the sales of his poetry (91). (This would not be the case for an unacknowledged collaborator, of course, so the right to a byline has economic ramifications.)

Troupe also capitalized by producing a spin-off of the as-told-to autobiography, his aforementioned memoir of Miles, which grew out of their collaborative relationship. Although he was freed here from any obligation to Davis, who had died in the interim, Troupe did not produce a significantly different portrayal; indeed, he claims that the autobiography had been forthright and candid, unconstrained by Davis's ego. (Although Davis had asked to see the manuscript before publication, Troupe declined, as was his right under the contract [92].) Yet, Troupe complains that Davis had refused to participate in publicity for the autobiography; fans who showed up at book signings were predictably disappointed to meet "only" the book's author (81–82). Thus, Troupe's memoir casts light on the backstage negotiations between collaborators, illuminating ways in which their interests are linked and ways in which they may be opposed. It also illustrates how separate life writing genres—here as-told-to autobiography and memoir—can be bound up with each other.

An obvious ethical issue in celebrity autobiography is conflict between the writer's obligation to portray the subject as he or she would wish and the obligation to the historical record. It is characteristic of celebrity autobiography for two reasons. First, as suggested earlier, celebrities are in a position—not just as celebrities but as employers—to wield power over their collaborators; second, because they are celebrities, more is known about them, and discrepancies between their autobiographical narratives and other published sources are easy to detect and, in the case of "historic" personages, of public interest. Michael Korda has written instructively on the problems that Ronald Reagan's memory posed for his collaborator Robert Lindsey. For example, Reagan remembered a tête-à-tête with Mikhail Gorbachev in a boathouse on Lake Geneva as a turning point in their negotiations in November 1985; in fact, however, the two had not been alone together but were surrounded by a number of translators and security people (Korda 92). More problematically, although Reagan spent the war years in Hollywood, he recalled having been present with the United States Signal Corps at the liberation of the German concentration camps—a memory appropriated from documentary footage of that operation (93).

Such lapses in—or creations of—memory force collaborators to choose between serving as compliant scribes and acting as reality checks, between loyalty to their subjects and fidelity to historical truth (insofar as that can be determined). Each writer needs to decide how aggressively and extensively to check the accuracy of the record he or she is helping to create. Biographers are differently positioned: for them, there is a clear obligation to check the record and no necessary obligation to their subjects, except in the case of authorized biographers. The professional celebrity autobiographer may, like Andrew Szanton, conceive of his role as analogous to that of the defense attorney, who may know more than he divulges and whose ethical obligation is to put the best possible face on his client's behavior without outright deception. This may be the proper ethical stance for the professional collaborator; the professional critic, however, is justified in putting a higher value on historical truth. In cases, especially ethnographic ones, in which the model or source is taken advantage of by the writer, the ethical duty of the critic may be to defend the disenfranchised subject; in the case of celebrity autobiography, the ethical duty of the critic may be to protect the historical record.

Although autobiographers may be held to an "autobiographical pact" with readers which commits them to tell at least a version of the truth, they are generally not regarded as obliged to research their own lives; the presumed subjectivity of the genre gains them a degree of latitude. Richard Lewontin has suggested that

> the reader of conventional autobiography [i.e., that of a public figure] is, in principle at least, able to test some of the self-indulgences of autobiographers, since much of what is of general interest in a public life has been seen and heard by others who may be consulted. . . . But . . . with not many exceptions, one must be a Napoleon before anyone will bother to check an author's memoirs against the record. For the most part, autobiography is a free ride into history. (231–32)

But, *pace* Lewontin, while autobiographers and their collaborators may not be required to fact-check their stories, others' biographical research may be used to discredit them. And when hitherto unknown individuals generate autobiographies that touch upon sensitive historical and political topics, they may be subjected to withering scrutiny. This tends to occur only in high-profile cases. As manifested in the instances of Rigoberta Menchú and "Binjamin Wilkomirski," these have tended to involve "identity politics" and related ideological investments.

Collaborations with celebrities are always consensual; in any case, they also have built-in checks and balances that may deter or at least minimize exploitation. Each partner may use for leverage the indispensability of his or her contribution. Celebrity subjects would seem to have the upper hand; since presumably their stories are the sine qua non of the project, they can threaten to cease cooperating and choose other partners.[12] But their lives are not copyrightable, and if they cease cooperating, their writers may point out that in order to protect their own investment of time and labor, their only alternative is to turn what were to be autobiographies into heterobiographies. The writers' leverage lies in the fact that, though presumably not as marketable as collaborative autobiographies, biographies do not have to be as flattering. (Biographers' ethical obligations to their subjects are quite different from those of collaborators; indeed, contemporary biography would suggest that biographers feel little or no ethical obligation to their subjects. It is hard to imagine a contemporary biographer concluding, as M. O. W. Oliphant did one hundred years ago, that a biographer who discovers unexpected flaws in his or her subject "might well consider not writing the biography at all" [Bergmann 3].) In the case of collaborative celebrity autobiography, then, the dynamics of the partnership serve to minimize the potential for inequity in both dimensions—that of the portrayal and that of the partnership. Subjects unhappy with their portrayals can demand revisions, and writers unhappy with the terms of the collaboration can try to renegotiate them.

Nevertheless, such checks and balances sometimes fail to prevent dissension; like the marriages to which they are often compared, collaborative partnerships can come apart, often acrimoniously. A pertinent case is the story of the failed collaboration between Fay Vincent, the former commissioner of major league baseball, and David A. Kaplan. Vincent withdrew from the collaboration on his memoir, *Baseball Breaks Your Heart*, as the manuscript was nearing completion in 1994, apparently because he was reluctant to publish a book that would revive the controversies in which he had been involved as commissioner (Sandomir). (Vincent did not challenge the accuracy of the manuscript but rather questioned its tone; the real issue seemed to be hostile references to people he had been dealing with as commissioner, such as George Steinbrenner, the New York Yankees' owner. Implicitly, then, he was suggesting that publication of the book would do him harm: that is, it would cause him pain by rekindling some of the antagonisms of his years in office.) In the summer of 1997, Kaplan took Vincent to court, claiming the right, as co-author and joint copyright owner, to publish the book on his own; his claim was, in effect, that Vincent had deprived him of the fruits of his labor.

Such a conflict between collaborators points up an issue close to the heart of collaborative autobiography: Whose property is a collaboratively produced life story? Vincent's position was that, although he shared copyright with Kaplan, he retained control of the final manuscript; as his lawyer remarked: "How could it be any other way? Otherwise, it's giving your life story to someone else." The answer to the question "Whose life is it, anyway?" may not be as simple as Vincent's lawyer suggests, since the manuscript in question was in part the product of Kaplan's work, including independent research. The nonpartisan legal opinions cited in the *New York Times*, however, came down mostly on Vincent's side, on the principle that, unless he explicitly gave up control over the manuscript, he should be assumed to have retained it. As one copyright lawyer put it, "People working on a collaboration about their own lives tend to control their stories, until they give up control." (This is not as tautological as it sounds.) But Vincent's case rests uneasily on "oral agreements" he claims to have made with Kaplan; in a preliminary ruling, the judge "wrote that he was not persuaded that the co-authors were bound by an oral contract" (Sandomir).

In ethnographic autobiography, where the balance of power favors the writer over the subject, the ethical pitfalls are quite different. Collaboration is supposedly a matter of give-and-take, but in the ethnographic scenario, the most obvious danger is the taking of liberties—the appropriation of a life story for purposes not shared, understood, or consented to by the subject. This is a particular danger of ethnographic writing because—as was evidently the case with Black Elk—differences of culture may impede or prevent the obtaining of truly informed consent. The same may be true, as indicated earlier, of differences in age or somatic condition; indeed, I would put most parental memoirs of children and some disability narratives in the ethnographic category. (*The Broken Cord*, Michael Dorris's narrative of raising an adopted son with fetal alcohol syndrome, is both; I treat this work at length in chapter 4.)

∽

Collaborative autobiography is inherently ventriloquistic. The dynamics of the ventriloquism, however—the direction in which the voice is "thrown"—may vary with the location of the collaboration on the continuum described earlier. In ethnographic autobiography, the danger tends to be that of attributing to the subject a voice and narrative not originating with him or her, and that he or she may not have edited. *Black Elk Speaks* is a classic example; the most frequently quoted paragraphs have turned out to be wholly of Neihardt's authorship. This danger exists, of course, in celebrity autobiography as well; at the time of publication, some celebrities—notably Darryl Strawberry and Ronald Reagan—had notoriously not *read*, much less written, their so-called "autobiographies." But, unlike Black Elk, they *could* have reviewed the prose ascribed to them.

In celebrity autobiography, perhaps the greater danger is the reverse dynamic, in which the subject assumes or is given more credit for the writing than is legitimate. The predicament of the hired writer—whether acknowledged as co-author or effaced as a "ghost"—may involve a kind of *subjection* to its "subject" and putative writer. At least, this is the gist of the testimony of Margot Strickland, co-author of the autobiography of Moura Lympany, the English concert pianist: "In ghosting an autobiographical memoir of a living person the writer is at the mercy of a volatile subject who may or may not capriciously cooperate. The subject has little knowledge or even interest, let alone sympathy, with the writer's craft, method, and difficulties" ("Ghosting" 66). Thus, argues Strickland, writing someone else's "autobiography" can be strenuous and draining work:

> It requires an imaginative plunge into the depths of a human soul, so deep as to threaten the "ghost" with extinction. And the subject, being famous, is likely to be a personality so powerful that he or she can exercise a will that imperils the author's integrity, to exclude material damaging to him, or include trivial episodes which vainglorify him. . . . Since the living subject has the right of veto to the moment of publication, should he disapprove of the finished book, there is no guarantee the work will be published and read. The writer is inevitably fettered, not to the truth as he sees it, but to an economy with the truth, to satisfy the big name and his view of himself. (67)[13]

Although Strickland was listed on the title page as co-author, and was thus not what I would call a "ghost," she complains that the omission of her name from the publisher's brochure and many library catalogues effectively obliterated her contribution: "The experience of 'ghosting' an autobiography had reduced the writer to a specter indeed, for nobody knew she had done the work" (68). An irony of this process is that the greater the success of the writer in creating a plausible simulacrum of the subject's voice—which can be a considerable feat of literary craft—the less credit that collaborator may get, except possibly from an appreciative subject. (Miles Davis was such a subject, according to Troupe: "When I delivered the manuscript to him for his final perusal in October of 1988, he called me after he read it, laughing hysterically and wanting to know how I had managed to nail his speaking voice, his inflections and cadences" [91–92].)

Truly ghostwritten autobiography—that is, a work produced with the assistance of an *unacknowledged* collaborator—is, by academic standards, tantamount to plagiarism on the part of the subject. If the ghostwriter *consents* to being anonymous, as is usually the case, the process is not plagiarism in the sense of appropriating another's intellectual property without permission; the arrangement is that the writer's compensation takes the form of a paycheck and not a byline, so there is no violation of the partnership. And of course the wide acceptance of the practice—like that of presidential speechwriting—suggests that there is not considered to be any dishonesty involved because none but the most naïve might be fooled. In this regard, the ethics of trade publishing and those of academic publishing differ sharply. But ghostwritten autobiography does raise an ethical issue with regard to the truthfulness of the portrayal. Such texts implicitly falsify both the *history* of their subjects—who did not in fact labor single-handedly to produce them—and their *images*, for they may not be *capable* of writing such texts.

From a different angle, the ventriloquism involved in as-told-to autobiography is akin to (legal) forgery on the part of the writer. This occurs mainly with ghostwritten celebrity autobiography, where the name of the source may be worth more than the name of the writer. (As Lejeune points out, with ethnographic collaboration, the "story takes its value, in the eyes of the reader, from the fact that [the subjects] belong [that they *are perceived* as belonging] to a culture other than his own, a culture defined by the exclusion of writing" [196].) A complex but relatively mild form of the forgery of celebrity autobiography seems to have occurred in the literary aftermath of the death of Diana, Princess of Wales. Andrew Morton, the author of a biography called *Diana: Her True Story,* claimed, after her death, that his title had been an understatement: the book was not merely a "true" story but *her* story in the sense that she was its principal source (Hoge). Accordingly, he rushed into print a new version with the amended title: *Diana: Her True Story in Her Own Words.*

In effect, then, Morton claimed that a book presented originally as his biography of her was in fact a covertly collaborative life writing project, a sort of ghostwritten self-biography. His claims raise ethical issues aside from the questionable propriety of his attempt to capitalize on Diana's death by reviving his "life" of her. If his claim is not true, then this case is an instance of one kind of ethical violation, forgery—the false attribution of material to the subject of the book in order to heighten its apparent authenticity (and thus, not incidentally, its already considerable commercial value). If his claim is true, the act may be a violation of a pledge to keep secret her involvement in the production of the original book. Either way, he may be guilty of violating a relationship of trust—which, I would hold, is not necessarily ended by the death of one party.

Forged or ventriloquistic autobiography may take less benign forms than this, if we broaden our scope beyond those practices usually deemed literary or anthropological. As Margreta de Grazia has pointed out, a false confession coerced by torture might euphemistically be described as "collaborative autobiography." Such a text would obviously involve inequity in portrayal as well as of partnership; in such cases, both the process and the product may be extremely harmful to the subject. Indeed, here the faking of a life may quite literally involve the taking of a life. The extortion of a true confession—that is, a confession to a crime the confessor did commit—could also be described only euphemistically as a collaborative autobiography.[14] The confessions of condemned prisoners in England in the eighteenth century illustrate how the ethnographic and the celebrity scenarios may complement each other. In-house confessions "dictated" to prison ordinaries and distributed at the time of execution—as if spontaneous and simultaneous with the execution—were sometimes supplemented by extramural accounts written by journalists for a popular audience. The in-house confessions, which were coerced, manifested the authority of the state in more than one sense: they were scripted according to narrow conventions and reflected the apparent internalization of self-condemning social norms. (They purported to be confessions in the religious and moral as well as the legal sense; as Hal Gladfelder shows, however, even in these accounts there may be an element of resistance or moral ambiguity [*Criminality* 44–57].) At the same time, convicts might arrange to produce, with the collaboration of a journalist such as Daniel Defoe, a quite different sort of testimony, a kind of criminal's celebrity memoir. Prisoners would be treated more favorably in terms of both process and portrayal in the extramural confessions than in the intramural ones. Although the extramural texts might also be formulaic, they were more autonomously produced, and the subject was more in control of his own representation. While these accounts might be preferred on ethical grounds because of their less compulsory quality, they would of course be more at odds with the official ethos.[15]

Further examples of subtly coercive, and thus unethical, collaborative life writing may be found in abuses of psychiatric practice. Most forms of psychotherapy involve—indeed, consist of—what might be seen as collaborative autobiography. What is ideally a beneficent therapeutic process, however, is liable to corruption (like any collaboration with a professional, such as a physician or lawyer). Obvious examples may be found in the "recovery" of false memories of child abuse or other trauma, except that here we have not coerced confession but induced accusation—autobiography as character assassination. (Although this aspect of the "Wilkomirski" scandal remains somewhat murky, his "identity" as a Holocaust survivor emerged in the context of a psychotherapeutic collaboration.)

Testimony generated through "facilitated communication" (FC) is also pertinent here. In facilitated communication, a trained assistant supports the elbow or wrist of someone who cannot or does not speak and who cannot otherwise type. This method and the messages it produces have been highly controversial. Its proponents—such as Douglas Biklen, who introduced facilitated communication to the United States in the early 1990s—believe that it can tap into and express the hitherto and otherwise inaccessible thoughts of individuals with developmental and cognitive disabilities such as cerebral palsy or autism; opponents (and skeptics, including Diane Twachtman-Cullen) believe that it involves the projection (witting or unwitting) onto such subjects of the ideas of overzealous facilitators driven in part by ideological commitment to policies of deinstitutionalization and inclusion. (The official position of the American Speech-Language-Hearing Association is that under controlled conditions, "there is no conclusive evidence that facilitated messages can be reliably attributed to people with disabilities" [qtd. in Twachtman-Cullen 153].)

One of the reasons why such communication has come under suspicion is that in the case of autism, at least, its success would challenge the accepted conception of the disability as involving deficits in cognitive and symbolic functions rather than merely neuromotor problems (Twachtman-Cullen 6–7). Another, more important one is that facilitated communication has often produced accusations of mistreatment. As with the phenomenon of recovered memory, some suspect that the similarity of these accusations derives not from the frequency of abuse—though mistreatment of disabled, especially institutionalized, individuals is common and underreported—but from a script predetermined or overdetermined by idealistic facilitators. In Australia, where the technique was pioneered with people with cerebral palsy in the 1970s by Rosemary Crossley, it was tested in the Victoria Supreme Court when Crossley's student Anne McDonald sought the right to leave an institution for retarded people and move in with Crossley and her husband. (McDonald had to sue because, although she was no longer a minor, her wishes had been ignored on the grounds that she was mentally incompetent.) McDonald won her case and her freedom after a convincing courtroom demonstration of communication facilitated by Crossley (Biklen 5).

When McDonald was offered a contract by Penguin for a book about her life, the public trustee refused permission on the grounds that McDonald could not understand the contract. Crossley notes: "The contract could have been rewritten to list me as sole author, and I could have given Annie her share of the royalties by some unilateral agreement, but I felt strongly that the book was as much hers as mine, and I did not feel able to write it without Annie being recognized as co-author" (236). Another legal hearing declared McDonald to be no longer an infirm person, effectively granting her legal autonomy (even as some continued to suspect that she was only the passive medium of Crossley's ventriloquism). Crossley and McDonald subsequently co-authored *Annie's Coming Out,* which parallels Sienkiewicz-Mercer's book as a narrative of emancipation from stigma, isolation, and institutionalization. In *Annie's Coming Out,* however, the collaborators "speak" in separate voices; each chapter consists of a narrative by Crossley, followed by a short comment by McDonald produced through "facilitation"—a very different medium from the single first person of *I Raise My Eyes.*

I do not wish, nor have I the competence, to adjudicate this controversy (although it seems to me very plausible that FC would work in the case of disabilities such as cerebral palsy), but only want to suggest that such scenarios demonstrate the difficulties of assessing the authenticity, authorship, and authority of collaboratively produced life writing, especially when one party does not write or even speak. That communication produced collaboratively may somehow exceed that produced by the parties single-handedly is not necessarily evidence of its falsity or inauthenticity; as Biklen notes, "all communication is interactional and influenced by context, including the relationship of communicator and receiver" (131). Hence a model of functional independence requiring unassisted communication would be discriminatory and oppressive; autonomy does not mean or require absolute independence. Further, like any testimony from the disempowered, mediated communication with hitherto mute people is subject to backlash from those whose interests it may threaten. As both an instance of, and a metaphor for, as-told-to autobiography in the ethnographic scenario, facilitated communication highlights both the high stakes and the possible pitfalls of the genre. On the one hand, it offers the potential for precious access to otherwise voiceless, and highly vulnerable, subjects; on the other, it holds the danger of the obliteration, by over-writing, of such subjects.

A significant distinction between collaborative life writing scenarios may be found in the degree of professionalization of the authors. Today, ethnography in the narrow sense is produced by professional anthropologists, who are haunted by the complicity of ethnography in imperialism, cultural or otherwise. Indeed, some would say that poststructuralist ethnography and ethnographic life writing have been so thoroughly theorized and analyzed as to have been virtually paralyzed. By a broader definition, of course, ethnography includes amateur efforts, such as Neihardt's collaboration with Black Elk, in which professional ethics are nonexistent or not highly developed. Similarly, those who write celebrity autobiography for a living are not organized professionally; they constitute a relatively small number of freelancers who function according to their own lights rather than any established ethical guidelines (Szanton interview). Finally, those whose work falls in the middle of the continuum between ethnographic and celebrity collaboration—for example, parental biographers of children or those who collaborate with ill or disabled people to write their lives—are generally wholly amateur in their credentials and experience and thus not necessarily conscious of ethical constraints.

∞

Collaborative autobiography is practiced today with great frequency and openness. At least, this is the implication of a Peter Steiner cartoon in the *New Yorker*. The scene is an elementary school classroom, complete with a globe on the teacher's desk and a flag in the corner. Two students, a boy and a girl, stand next to the teacher's desk, facing the rest of their class. The boy smiles smugly, hands clasped behind his back, while the girl reads from a paper: "'What I did last summer,' by Scott Sweningen, as told to Samantha Gerhart.'" The joke is, of course, that collaborative autobiography has trickled down to the level of the clichéd first assignment of the school year. The teacher's expression is impossible to read, but one wonders about the elementary ethics here: what would clearly be cheating, if done surreptitiously—the writing of one student's composition by another—is apparently acceptable when done openly, even brazenly. (While most as-told-to autobiographies involve collaborators of the same sex, one may wonder here, too, about the gender dynamics of this collaboration, in which a girl serves as the recorder of a boy's experience.) If collaborative autobiography becomes more common, as this cartoon humorously suggests, we will need to extend and intensify our consideration of the full range of ethical issues it raises.

Critics of life writing may apply ethical standards in two different scenarios. One is retrospective: we may investigate and assess the ethics of published texts. The other is prospective: we may seek to head off ethical violations by establishing guidelines for future projects. Whichever alternative we choose, our influence and power are indirect and diffuse. We must remember that, as critics of life writing, we occupy a distinct and awkward position with respect to the practice of it; our ethics may be at odds with the ethics of those—professional as well as amateur— who practice collaborative life writing. And we must be attentive to the benefits as well as the liabilities of collaboration. For example, it may be tempting to decry ethnographic autobiography insofar as it may seem inherently to reduce its subjects to types. But such an objection to ethnography may invoke values, such as that of the uniqueness of the individual, that are alien to the cultures it seeks to represent. It may be, too, that the recuperative benefits of ethnography outweigh its costs. For example, it could be argued that, despite Neihardt's taking of some liberties in his collaboration with Black Elk, the text they produced collaboratively has helped to preserve and to disseminate crucial—indeed, sacred—features of Lakota culture. Black Elk and the Lakota may thus have benefited from the collaboration in ways he did not fully anticipate. Similarly, despite my reservations about the language of *I Raise My Eyes to Say Yes*, I am immensely grateful for the existence of the full account of Ruth Sienkiewicz-Mercer's life that it affords. In any case, it would be unwise and unfortunate to formulate ethical principles that would effectively censor or censure whole genres of life writing. Literary critics may have an important role to play in the ongoing development of collaborative life writing, particularly if we extend our consideration beyond the texts traditionally regarded as literary. But we have to be wary of devising, in the isolation of the ivory tower, excessively fastidious or implicitly discriminatory standards.

4

Adoption, Disability, and Surrogacy

The Ethics of Parental Life Writing in *The Broken Cord*

Fatherhood does not confer surrogacy.
— CYNTHIA OZICK, "Who Owns Anne Frank?"

THE BROKEN CORD (1989), Michael Dorris's memoir of raising an adopted son impaired by fetal alcohol syndrome, can be read as several kinds of life writing: parental memoir, Native American auto-biography, and pathography. Despite the urgency of Dorris's concerns and the value of his testimony about the problem of fetal alcohol syndrome, the book's uneasy amalgamation of genres is ultimately at odds with its reformist intentions. Disentangling some of the text's generic and thematic threads exposes these internal tensions. It also illuminates the ethical complexity of parental representation of those most vulnerable subjects, disabled children.[1]

The Broken Cord invites us to read it as a family memoir—more specifically, as a parental narrative of raising a disabled child. Family memoirs are necessarily relational, plural rather than singular in focus; inherently unstable, they oscillate between biography and autobiography.[2] Indeed, such narratives, which involve a relation between author and subject so intimate that the author-narrator also comes under scrutiny, may be termed "auto/biography." The politics and ethics of the parental memoir are inherently problematic. Parental memoirs are akin to authorized biographies insofar as parents have privileged access to their children. Indeed, parents frequently have knowledge of their children's lives that the children themselves lack, for instance, of their origins and infancy. (In the sense that parents provide children with accounts of their earliest years—which often form their first "memories"—parents serve as informal oral biographers, generating their children's "lives" in more senses than one.)[3] Parental memoirs tend, however, to be either unauthorized or *self-authorized*, insofar as parents assume rather than request the right to write their children's lives; this is especially so in the case of an impaired child. They are thus inherently, literally, paternalistic, particularly when they are undertaken before the subject has reached the age of consent. Like other prerogatives of parenthood, of course, this one is open to misuse. What are intended by parents as beneficent acts may be perceived by their children, once grown, as violations of their autonomy, acts of appropriation or even of betrayal. Disabled children are thus doubly vulnerable subjects—triply so if their impairment compromises their competence or diminishes their autonomy.

Parental memoirs often concern adopted or disabled children—for several reasons. One is the general principle of narratability: the uncommon case is more noteworthy than the common one. Another is that such memoirs are considered valuable resources for other parents faced with situations that may be especially demanding. (In the case of disability, a third factor may be the market value of the pathos presumed to characterize such narratives.) Issues of parental rights and prerogatives are especially vexed when a child is adopted, disabled, or both. Parental memoirs are perhaps most problematic when a child is discovered to be disabled after adoption: a narrative that might have served to bind parent and child more closely, in lieu of a blood relation, may become a narrative of disappointment, frustration, or even resentment.

The discovery of congenital problems complicates matters further. Whereas a biological parent may feel implicated in a child's congenital impairments, an adoptive parent may feel betrayed, if not by the child or the adoption agency, then by the child's biological parents. This is very much the case with Dorris, who blames Adam's mother for the boy's plight.[4] (Indeed, so appalled were Dorris and his wife, Louise Erdrich, by the effects of maternal alcoholism on children that they reluctantly endorsed the policy, carried out on some reservations, of incarcerating pregnant women who abuse alcohol [Erdrich, xviii].) As we shall see, one consequence of the discovery of the source of Adam's problems is the tendency to treat him as a type rather than as an individual. Over the course of the narrative, the relationship between father and son moves from initial bonding to gradual estrangement. Unlike most parental narratives of adoption, then, this one sends a very mixed message.

In this instance, the process of adoption was also complicated by issues of race and ethnicity. One dimension of Dorris's parenting of Adam is what I call the narrative of reracination—the rediscovery or reaffirmation of ethnic identity and the rerooting of the self in traditional culture. A Yale-trained anthropologist who taught first at Franconia College, then at Dartmouth, Dorris was a highly assimilated mixed-blood Modoc, whose attenuated relation to his Native American heritage was mediated by his profession. His bold and well-intentioned decision, as a twenty-six-year-old bachelor, to adopt an Indian child afforded him an opportunity to establish a more intimate connection to the Native American community than that provided by his research and teaching (or his upbringing). Significantly, he expressed his initial impulse to adopt a child in terms of the tribal culture he was studying at the time: "In a world of 'we,' I was an 'I,' with no essential responsibilities or links outside myself" (*Cord* 2).

This aspect of the book comes decisively to the foreground in chapter 4, which recounts the visit of father and son to the Standing Rock Reservation in South Dakota at the invitation of Beatrice Medicine, a Lakota anthropologist who had recently taught at Dartmouth. In this episode, father and son bond *as Indians*. In preparation for the trip, both let their hair grow long. En route by car, getting turned away from a midwestern motel that is obviously not full, they experience racial discrimination. On the reservation, however, unlike in Hanover, it is Adam who fits in and his father who stands out; only gradually is the father accepted as a member of his son's tribal community: "Here I felt as though I were his guest. It was he whom elderly women stopped to admire, he who was given the first taste of soup, he who blended" (61). The visit culminates in a ceremony in which both are honored with the bestowal of Lakota names, an episode that serves to incorporate father and son into a larger Native American community. The adoptive father, then, is in turn adopted; Dorris becomes Bea Medicine's son "in the Indian way" (64). The relation between father and son is reinforced and legitimated by a tribal bond.

The incipient narrative of reracination, however, is jeopardized by several elements. For one thing, there is the difference between the father's and son's tribal affiliations: whereas Adam was full-blood Lakota, Dorris was part Modoc on his father's side, a difference elided but not erased by the ceremony at Standing Rock. For another, their reintegration into Native American culture is somewhat depreciated by the fact of Adam's having been initially deracinated by his adoption.[5] But most important, Adam's cognitive impairments interfere with his appreciation of his Lakota heritage and thus impede his development of a Lakota identity.

Had the narrative of reracination not been thwarted by these factors, the story of Dorris's life with Adam might have become a classic example of autoethnography as defined by Françoise Lionnet: "the defining of one's subjective ethnicity as mediated through language, history, and ethnographical analysis; in short, . . . a kind of 'figural anthropology' of the self" (99).[6] But Dorris's unhappy discovery that his son was impaired by fetal alcohol syndrome (FAS) greatly complicates Dorris's relation to his heritage, since it connects him to pathological aspects of contemporary Native American life that he would rather have ignored and requires him to revise some of his intellectual and political assumptions.[7] Insofar as the focus of the narrative shifts away from raising Adam to researching the roots of Adam's impairment in Native American alcohol abuse, *The Broken Cord* is finally more ethnobiography or ethnohistory—indeed, *ethnopathography*—than autoethnography.

The book is provoked and its shape ultimately determined by Dorris's dismay on discovering that his adopted son's most significant kinship group is neither the Lakota nation of his biological parents nor the multitribal extended family of his adoptive parents but rather the multiethnic "family" or "tribe" of victims of fetal alcohol syndrome, with whom Adam shares obvious physical and behavioral characteristics. That is to say, this discovery constructs Adam as essentially, radically, and irredeemably other. As Susan Wendell has pointed out, disabled people are often constructed as alien: "We see them primarily as symbolic of something else—usually, but not always, something we reject and fear and project onto them" (60). They are thus subject to some of the same sorts of patronizing representations as ethnic or racial others. In this instance, the dynamics of the father-son relationship are clearly (de)formed by Adam's reassignment to this group of others.

To put it differently, the book's source is Dorris's reluctant recognition that his son's ethnicity has been overridden—or over-written—by the effects of his mother's alcohol abuse while pregnant. Nature, in the form of congenital disabilities both physical and mental, has foiled nurture, in the form of Dorris's energetic and resourceful parenting; FAS supersedes Native American culture as a factor in Adam's development and impedes his assimilation into the upper-middle-class culture of his adoptive family. Rather than growing up as an embodiment of some optimal blend of indigenous and Western cultures, Adam seems unable to internalize the values of either. Giving up hope that Adam can make up for a "late start," Dorris bitterly concludes that Adam is barred from living "the life of independent choice, of unbounded possibility, that he was entitled to live" (79). (He is also precluded from writing that life, an autobiography on the Franklinian model.) A response to Dorris's new understanding of his son's impairments, *The Broken Cord* is devised to document the existential poverty to which Adam has been condemned and to prevent more such lives from being pre-scripted by alcohol-abusing parents.

In addition to incorporating elements of family memoir and Native American autoethnography, then, *The Broken Cord* draws on the conventions of the personal narrative of illness or disability. The pathographical convention that most decisively shapes *The Broken Cord* is its division into two parts at the point of diagnosis, which provides a kind of classical anagnorisis. In this case, significantly, the anagnorisis occurs in the parent, rather than the child, who is oblivious to the problem and indifferent to its amelioration. The crucial turn occurs exactly midway through the book, when Dorris experiences a shock of recognition upon observing some clients at Project Phoenix, a clinic for teenagers with chemical dependencies in Kyle, South Dakota:

> I stared. . . . They could have been Adam's twin brothers. They resembled him in every facial feature, in every gesture, in body type. . . . [T]here was something uncannily familiar to me about these boys. . . . The correspondences seemed too great for mere coincidence; they were not superficial either. The fact that these boys and Adam shared the same ethnic group was far less central to their similarities than was the unmistakable set of fine tunings that transformed disparate individuals in the same general category. Some common denominator was obvious. (137)[8]

This moment proves a watershed in the narrative; the diagnosis—discovery of the true cause, nature, severity, and intractability—of Adam's impairment decisively changes the father-son relationship. Although the early chapters focus on Adam's problems of development, he is portrayed as a fully individualized character. As is the case in most parental narratives of impaired children, the emphasis is on efforts to maximize his potential, despite his limitations, and on his inherent value as a person and as a son. The emphasis begins to shift to what Adam cannot do

after Dorris and Erdrich adopt other Native American children, who ex-
emplify standards that Adam doesn't measure up to (see, for example,
120, 127–29).[9] (This tendency culminates in the book's peroration, which
offers a litany of things Adam will never understand or appreciate [264].)

After the moment of "diagnosis," Adam tends to become a type and his
story a case history; the emphasis shifts to his generic congenital traits
and to larger cultural problems. (In effect, Dorris acknowledged this in an
essay written after his son died: "When at last I accepted that I could not
affect my by now grown son's life, I elected, instead, to document it. If he
could not contribute to society by his actions, then, I reasoned, let him act
as example, as a flesh and blood object lesson against the dangers of
drinking alcohol during pregnancy ["Power" 114].) An index of this shift
is the inclusion in chapter 9 of *The Broken Cord* of photographs—the only
ones in the book—of a multiracial group of children damaged by FAS, in
effect a "family" album. Adam is quite explicitly represented hereafter as
a synecdoche for a damaged generation. He thus becomes the subject of
a kind of case study in a way that Dorris could not have foreseen when
he was questioned, at the beginning of the adoption process, about the
connection between his profession and his desire for an Indian child (4).
(Adam does not so much act as serve as a human object lesson, then.)

In narratives of illness or impairment, diagnosis is usually a welcome
development. Even if a serious condition is diagnosed, there is often relief at knowing what is wrong and having one's sense of dysfunction officially validated.[10] At first, this is the case here. Hitherto, Dorris had felt
that he and Adam were floundering in uncharted territory: "Child development books were useless in his case. . . . He fell beyond their range
of normal precedence and prediction, a wild card for whom anything was
possible but nothing was promised. . . . Adam and I, as son and father,
were in a land without codified laws" (38). Now the parents, at least,
could take comfort in a definitive explanation for their son's impairments:
"It was heartening for us to discover that Adam was not alone, that his
collection of disabilities had a name, an explanation, a circle of interested
professional researchers. We had a sense of 'Aha!' to the gathering body
of information" (187).

In most illness or impairment narratives, diagnosis provides not only
an explanation of the past but also hope for the future, insofar as it may
determine a plan of treatment. This is Dorris's initial expectation: "I assumed that when Adam's affliction was given a name, it could be treated;
then recovery would commence" (26). Dorris quite explicitly character-

izes Adam's condition as a medical problem for which there will be an appropriate and successful remedy. The narrative he projects is the preferred illness narrative, which Arthur W. Frank terms a "restitution narrative," whose heroes would be medical and rehabilitative professionals (chap. 4). As it turns out, however, Dorris's research is discouraging; indeed, one authority bluntly announces to him that for FAS children, "nothing works" (138). The discovery that Adam's impairments were both intractable and preventable is crucial, for this explains, though it does not necessarily justify, Dorris's shift of energy and emphasis from saving his child to protecting other children from the same impairment. What begins as a project to salvage a damaged and mistreated child becomes a crusade against fetal alcohol syndrome itself. (With this shift, the desired restitution can be achieved only on the collective scale.) It is the diagnosis of a cultural pathology, then, that inspires Dorris's zeal and finally determines his narrative's representation of his son. Unfortunately, Adam's individuality and humanity are sacrificed to Dorris's mission.

Initially, the book was conceived not as life writing of any sort but rather as a scholarly investigation of fetal alcohol syndrome, to which Dorris turned as a way of coming to terms with, but also distancing himself from, an intimate family matter: "My interests on the one hand might be focused on Adam, but his unique history was, in a sense, a microcosm of a much larger picture. I had never expected my son to educate me about Indians, but now I thought that perhaps a vigorous examination of certain aspects of recent American Indian experience could lead me to a new, helpful awareness of him" (76). As an academic, Dorris might have produced a straightforward social science monograph, but he chose instead to drop the pretense of scholarly detachment and objectivity (which he saw as hypocritical) and to acknowledge his personal stake in his topic—a decision that no doubt won the book many more readers than it would otherwise have had and facilitated its adaptation into an HBO movie in 1992.

While the book is cast as a memoir, *The Broken Cord* turns toward ethnography insofar as Dorris treats Adam as a representative other. Indeed, as Dorris's investigation of his son's developmental problems takes him far afield, the book includes scenes of literally ethnographic research, in which Dorris visits his son's native reservation and other pertinent sites as a participant-observer. Although Dorris arrived at his destination by a different route, other contemporary anthropologists, questioning the convention—the fiction—of objectivity in traditional ethnography, have been writing ethnography that admits and foregrounds its own mediation, the way in which it is produced by cross-cultural interaction or negotiation. As James Clifford has noted: "It becomes necessary to conceive of ethnography not as the experience and interpretation of a circumscribed 'other' reality, but rather as a constructive negotiation involving at least two, and usually more, conscious, politically significant subjects. Paradigms of experience and interpretation are yielding to discursive paradigms of dialogue and polyphony" ("Authority" 41). Rather than claiming "ethnographic authority" exclusively for themselves, then, many contemporary ethnographers are now willing to share it, incorporating narratives by their "subjects," giving them a voice as well. That is to say, they are acknowledging, granting, and even fostering the autonomy of their subjects.

In a literal sense, Dorris too has given his subject a voice: *The Broken Cord* is distinguished from most parental memoirs of children with disabilities by the fact that it includes a narrative by the child.[11] This combination of a parental and a filial narrative represents an additional mixing of genres and makes the book as a whole a collaborative venture. (This complicates the book's status as auto/biography; because of the way the two narratives complement each other, with father and son, first and third persons, changing places, it is an interesting, if problematic, example of the phenomenon Susanna Egan refers to as "mirror talk.") The book, then, is even more generically complex and indeterminate than the typical family memoir, which is written from a single point of view.[12]

Insofar as Adam wrote his own story without assistance from his father, his narrative would seem to be an autonomous solo act of self-representation. The father-son collaboration is presented to us—as it was to Adam—as essentially egalitarian: "'Look,' I suggested. 'If I'm going to tell about my life and your life, it would be fair for you to do the same thing. Write down everything you can remember, the good stuff and the bad stuff, and we'll put that in the book too. Then you can tell the story the way you saw it'" (197). While Adam was encouraged to read his father's narrative in progress, Dorris scrupulously avoided reading, much less editing or rewriting, the narrative he elicited from his son. (Dorris did not read Adam's narrative until he had nearly completed his own. Erdrich apparently supervised Adam's project more closely, but, to judge from the published text, which is riddled with surface errors, she did little or no copyediting.)

Nevertheless, Dorris assumes the role of the anthropologist—usually a nonnative—who enlists in a collaborative life writing project a native subject not otherwise inclined to generate an autobiography. In this, and in the fact that Adam's narrative is preceded and introduced by his father's, the book as a whole is akin to what Arnold Krupat calls the "Indian autobiography," which is "jointly produced by some white who translates, transcribes, compiles, edits, interprets, polishes, and ultimately determines the form of the text in writing, and by an Indian who is its subject and whose life becomes the content of the 'autobiography' whose title may bear his name" (30). *The Broken Cord* differs from this paradigm in that the anthropologist is part Native American, and the native informant—the subject of the ethnographic life—is his own son. In addition, this book reverses the conventional proportions of the ethnographic auto/biography; here the father's long biographical narrative overshadows the son's short autobiographical one.

The crucial difference from most ethnography, however, is that here the disparity between the two parties is not a matter of race or culture; rather, that disparity is a function of Adam's congenital FAS-related cognitive impairments, which, though associated with patterns of Indian alcohol abuse, are not intrinsic to his cultural heritage. In practice, then, if for very different reasons from those operating in most earlier texts, this book's production involved the sort of asymmetrical collaboration typical of ethnographic auto/biography, in which the editor inevitably exercises cultural authority over his or her subject. That Dorris is himself part Indian—and the adoptive father of his informant—does not prevent him from reenacting a scenario now seen as implicated in cultural imperialism, in which the Western editor controls the representation of the native subject.

Aware of the potential for exploitation in publishing the story of his son's disability, Dorris went to considerable lengths to secure Adam's authorization for, and cooperation in, the book's production:

> As an anthropologist I was sensitive to the matter of informed consent: I did not want Adam, because of any lack of understanding of what publication meant, to agree that this book reveal material he would rather keep under wraps. But how could I explain to him, who rarely read, that total strangers would thumb through a version of our lives—our weaknesses as well as our strengths—and draw conclusions we might not like to hear? (197)

Thus, in addition to offering Adam the occasion to write his own life, Dorris apparently gave him the opportunity to request that some material be left out of the paternal narrative. (He does not seem to have offered him a veto over the entire project.)

Such gestures, however sincere and well intentioned, could not ensure that Adam's consent would be *truly* informed. Indeed, Dorris admitted as much in an essay written after the death of his son: "[He] was passively agreeable to this idea, just as he would have been if I had proposed we move to Mars, eat only peanut butter, or go live in a cave" ("Power" 114). In any case, the parents' testimony about Adam's intellectual impairments (Erdrich's in her foreword, Dorris's in the main narrative) is at odds with their insistence that he was a fully consenting participant in this project. Just as he seemed incapable of adjusting his appearance in everyday life to the expectations of others, he could evidently not fully imagine, and thus not censor, the way he was being presented to a reading public. In terms of biomedical ethics, it appears that although Adam was granted autonomy as *condition*—that is, he was treated as an independent agent—he lacked autonomy as *capacity*. Indeed, the impetus of the book is parental grief and anger that Adam might never achieve autonomy in this sense. Thus, Dorris's characterization of Adam, here and throughout the book, casts doubt on his competence, and hence on the ethical legitimacy of his participation in the project, if not his father's initiation of it. Similarly, the gesture of using a pseudonym to afford his son, whose real name was Abel, a measure of privacy seems entirely inadequate.[13]

In any case, what is tendered as autonomous self-representation—"The Story of Adam Dorris by Adam Dorris"—is in effect mediated in ways the putative autobiographer could not understand or control. In this case, the subject's vulnerability is a function not so much of his youth or filial status as of his impairment. And although Dorris elicited Adam's testimony, that testimony serves mainly to corroborate Dorris's characterization of Adam in the narrative that precedes, introduces, and frames it. Adam's text is contained and defined by his father's. On the whole, then, in spite of the book's collaborative elements, Dorris seems to have arrogated authority in ways reminiscent of colonial ethnography.

Indeed, his book unwittingly inscribes the theme of the "vanishing primitive" which has characterized much ethnography. It has been a convention of ethnography, according to James Clifford, to claim that the culture being represented is disappearing from the earth even as it appears on the page. The "allegory of salvage," with its motif of the vanishing primitive, has had the effect—presumably unintentional but nonetheless destructive—of diverting attention from actual historical conditions to the static textual residue of "vanishing" peoples ("Allegory," 112–13). The dynamics of this book are ostensibly different because the narrative so strenuously calls for political action to save Native American culture; it is a prophetic autobiography in the sense that it at once predicts a communal catastrophe and attempts to prevent it.[14] Projecting the effect of FAS over generations, Dorris envisions a kind of catastrophe more terrible, because self-inflicted, than those already visited on indigenous Americans (183). According to Dorris, the very nature of FAS makes the future especially problematic. One of Adam's most frustrating deficiencies was that "he could not . . . project himself into the future. . . . He existed in the present tense, with occasional reference to past precedent" (201). Insofar as he is representative of a whole generation of Native American children, the implications are grim. Thus, Dorris's discovery that his son is "a microcosm of a much larger picture" (76) leads him finally to a view of the Native American predicament that is no less apocalyptic than that of *Black Elk Speaks*. Indeed, one of the aspects of *The Broken Cord* that connects it to *Black Elk Speaks* is that both express powerful visions of the disappearance of Native American culture. Dorris's "broken cord" echoes Black Elk's "broken sacred hoop" (as Elizabeth Cook-Lynn has noted [11]); but Dorris's title seems more biological than cultural in reference, with its echo of umbilical cord, the sustaining connection between pregnant woman and fetus. Although Dorris reminds readers periodically that "FAS is an equal opportunity affliction" (152), he focuses mainly on its causes and effects on the reservation.[15] Here, however, the crisis for Native American culture is situated not in the past, where it might be an occasion for pathos in the reader, as in *Black Elk Speaks*, but in the imminent future; hence the need for energetic action to avert it.

The Broken Cord aspires to literal rather than allegorical salvage, then; it seeks to provoke interventions in a scenario that, if not disrupted, will result in the extinction of cultures that are tenuous survivors of previous catastrophes. Dorris does not, however, fully escape the problem of the ethnographic allegory of salvage—its tendency to establish or perpetuate a relationship of dependency between the culture that writes and the culture that is written. Such ethnography implies or assumes that the "primitive" culture is weak and needs to be represented and rescued by another. In the case of *The Broken Cord*, the implication is that Native American culture, at least on reservations, requires the expertise and intervention of outsiders, as well as a reassertion of its own collective will, to survive the current crisis.[16]

Dorris's apocalyptic scenario has been faulted by others on various grounds.[17] My concern, however, is for the relation between Dorris's call for extreme remedies to prevent catastrophe and his representation of, and collaboration with, an impaired son. This concern has two dimensions pertinent to the ethics of the representation of people with disabilities generally. The first has to do with Adam as the subject of representation—the textual other, the embodiment of the condition in question. For in *The Broken Cord*, Adam and others like him are represented as subhuman or barely human. Dorris quotes one authority as saying: "I feel for those children. They'll never be . . . they'll never be *humans*, I guess, as we know humans, because they've never been given that chance" (168). And Dorris himself laments of Adam: "By all evidence, he had been deprived of the miracle of transcendent imagination, a complex grace that was the quintessence of being human" (167). Dorris claims that his presentation, at a scholarly conference on FAS, of his experience trying to raise Adam had the desirable effect of putting a human face on a problem hitherto represented anonymously and statistically (243); but the tendency of the latter half of the narrative is to do the opposite—to obscure Adam's face behind a diagnostic label (indeed, behind the generic facial traits of FAS children). Adam's ultimate function in the text is to serve as a personification of a population whose inherent limitations may doom them. Indeed, he becomes the poster child for a preventable disability, a poster whose implicit caption reads "*Not* Wanted."

One of the saddest aspects of this heartbreaking book is that the language used by the father to describe his son echoes that used by colonizers to describe recalcitrant "primitive" people. That the language is not part of a rationale or rationalization of subjection but rather part of discourse intended to be liberatory makes a significant difference, but the parallels are uncomfortable all the same. The book functions to project Dorris's frustration with his son onto a whole people. With the population of reservation Indians, as with his adopted son, Dorris's patience gives way to angry scolding and vain attempts at discipline. Paternal disappointment with a son turns into backlash against "his kind" for being hopelessly backward, incapable of improvement. A distinction between the human and the nonhuman is mapped onto a distinction between normality and disability, which in turn is in danger of being mapped onto a traditionally racial or ethnic distinction between the "civilized" and the "savage." The implications of Dorris's book are such that parental memoir and Native American autoethnography threaten to merge into what we might call ethnopathography.

This is not to impugn Dorris's motives nor to dismiss his book's importance in bringing overdue attention to a serious problem. Rather, it is to point out the persistence in his book of a kind of discourse that has often worked to the disadvantage of minorities in the past. In his reformist zeal, Dorris risks further stigmatizing disadvantaged members of his own community (as degenerate, a people whose abuse of alcohol is both an identifying ethnic trait [93] and tantamount to collective suicide). More to the point here, it threatens to characterize mentally impaired people as a literally inhuman, unredeemable population.

My second concern with the book's representation of disability has to do with Adam as its consumer, for both parents insist that Adam read the book in manuscript. What would it be like, I wonder, to read a narrative that describes people like you as not quite human and that is devoted explicitly to preventing the future (re)production of people like yourself? If, as I have argued, Adam was unequipped to anticipate the implications of his representation, then perhaps he also would not have been hurt by what he read; the book's tendency to write off his kind may have gone over his head. (Indeed, in a later essay, Dorris recalls his son's apparent inability to remember the book at all ["Fetal Alcohol Syndrome" 98–99].) But to argue this is to use the extremity of his impairment to excuse his (mis)representation—a principle that falls short of the golden rule that Dorris uses to condemn the behavior of pregnant women who consume alcohol (208). The idea that Adam's condition protects him from being hurt by his father's portrayal of him may have some truth to it, but any argument that construes vulnerability as a form of invulnerability seems only to exploit disability.

In any case, there is evidence that Adam was not beyond being hurt by the narrative. Erdrich's foreword contains the following passage: "If one story of FAS could be made accessible and real, it might just stop someone, somewhere, from producing another alcohol-stunted child. Adam does not read with great ease, but he has pressed himself to read this story. He has reacted to it with fascination, and he has agreed to its publication" (xiii). This is intended, obviously, to justify the narrative on consequentialist or utilitarian grounds. But if Adam read this passage, one wonders how he would have responded to its implicit characterization of him. Such concerns are not idle: Erdrich goes on to tell how, after she had exclaimed to him in a moment of frustration, "Don't call me Mom," Adam literally refrained from doing so for months and how full reconciliation took years. Thus, she prefaces what might be read as a parental narrative of disenchantment and disaffection with a story demonstrating Adam's sensitivity to parental rejection (xiv–xvi).

With reference to the issue of the selective abortion of "defective" fetuses, Susan Wendell has expressed an idea relevant here: "Knowing that your society is doing everything possible to prevent people with bodies like yours from being born is bound to make you feel as though you are not valued and do not really belong, especially when there are so many attitudes and conditions in the society that derogate and/or exclude you" (153–54). The matter of preventable birth defects is admittedly difficult. It seems desirable to minimize or eliminate whatever suffering they cause, but it is not easy to do so without at least implicitly devaluing the lives of those who have such impairments. The argument that Dorris's book is intended to stimulate efforts to prevent FAS fails to reckon with the ethical problems of the means to that end. The same goal might have been pursued with different methods.

It is important to recognize how this narrative differs in its political dynamics from other parental narratives of disabled children. In most, political and parental functions are one: the narrator's role as advocate for children with disabilities is an extension of his or her role as parent. But in this case, as narrator, Dorris does not function as an advocate for his impaired child. His politics are a function, but not an extension, of his role as a parent—which is largely confined to his role as a character.[18] The fact that Adam's FAS is preventable adversely affects the portrayal of Adam throughout, since it gives Dorris an interest in presenting his condition in the worst possible light. In any case, after the diagnosis, the emphasis shifts from dealing with Adam's problems to preventing their proliferation in the world, particularly in Indian nations, where it seems to threaten Indian ethnicity by dilution of the racial stock—the sort of claim typically made by eugenicists.

∽

Reviews of *The Broken Cord* generally ignored Adam's own narrative, "The Adam Dorris Story by Adam Dorris," as though it were a mere appendix. Such readings marginalize and silence him. Though brief, his narrative makes a significant contribution to the book—and to autobiographical literature generally—in part because of its defects as narrative, which reflect Adam's limited literacy. Careful reading of it may to some degree recuperate his subjectivity.

It is a tenet of poststructuralist thought that, as Anthony Paul Kerby writes, "a self arises out of signifying practices rather than existing prior to them as autonomous or Cartesian agent" (1). Indeed, in *Narrative and the Self*, Kerby goes so far as to claim that "persons are such only if (among other things) they can be considered to have a history, a history of acts and involvements" (35).[19] Insofar as, according to his father's reports, Adam generally fails to make connections between past, present, and future, he has no history, or at least little sense of his own life as a story he can plot. Similarly, insofar as a person is the product, and implied subject, of an internal autobiographical narrative, Adam seems to have little sense of self; according to Dorris, "he doesn't ask who he is, or why" (264).

In some ways the evidence of his written narrative corroborates his father's image of him as barely a person, lacking a developed identity and a linear history. Although Adam was about twenty years old when he wrote his story, his control over that story was minimal, and the narrative is simplistic, lacking in interpretation or introspection. The events he remembers are those that a child remembers—parties, accidents and injuries, trips, visits to the zoo, and so on—or that are prompted by family photos. There is little that is vividly concrete, and there is even less of a superstructure that binds events in meaningful sequences; transitions are largely associational. Indeed, at one point in his narrative, he repeats a story of getting lost on his way home from school during a sojourn in New Zealand; in effect, he reenacts his disorientation in the world by getting lost in his narrative. His lack of narrative skill suggests his minimal familiarity with autobiographical narrative of any sort—written, oral, or interior. "The Story of Adam Dorris" is disturbing in the extent to which it fails to become meaningfully autobiographical.

At the same time, the narrative offers a perspective that complements his father's in significant ways. It is a relief, though hardly a consolation, to see that Adam does not perceive himself as defective or deprived and thus does not suffer the way his parents do. In fact, it exposes the projection at work in the common construction of people with disabilities as "suffering from" them. (Sometimes they do; sometimes they just suffer from condescension and stigma.) From Adam's point of view, the concerns of his father—with work habits, personal appearance, academic accomplishment, and so on—seem peculiar and irrelevant obsessions. Indeed, in Adam's narrative, Michael Dorris comes across as somewhat authoritarian, lacking in sensitivity and patience, a bit of a nag: Superdad is no hero to his son. This is refreshing insofar as it suggests that Adam, unlike his father, is not tormented by what he might have been, or by his lack of friends or accomplishments. In any case, even as his narrative's defects demonstrate the severity of his limitations, his story also evinces a distinctive, if undeveloped, subjectivity.

Significantly, the single sustained episode involving Dorris as a character has to do with a back injury. As though to answer his father's characterization of him as impaired, here Adam captures his father in a temporary state of dependency and impotence—literally flat on his back. In Adam's portrayal of his father as infirm or invalid there may be an element of schadenfreude, if not unconscious revenge or oedipal conflict. In this way, at least, his narrative does succeed in countering his father's: it answers, even as it echoes, his words. For all of its limitations—which tend to confirm his father's reluctant conclusions about him—it may embody a kind of resistance to paternal and paternalistic discourse. In this sense, the book as a whole does achieve a kind of bi-vocalism rare in parental memoirs, which are typically parental monologues. If, as Kerby argues, "self-narration . . . is what first raises our temporal existence out of the closets of memorial traces and routine and unthematic activity, constituting thereby a self as its implied subject" (109), then it may be that by giving his son the opportunity and motive for this experiment in autobiography, Dorris helped Adam achieve a stronger sense of identity than he had hitherto felt. Giving his adopted son some textual territory of his own may have been in some ways an engendering act; perhaps Dorris should have taken pride and pleasure in it.

As the book's main author, however, Dorris literally has the last word. And his hand is evident in the placement, at the end of Adam's story, of a boxed notice of a foundation to which contributions can be sent to support research on fetal alcohol syndrome; the book then concludes with a brief epilogue, footnotes, and a bibliography. The effect of this framing apparatus is to reduce Adam once again to a case or an exhibit. Ultimately, then, Dorris's voice, with the authority of age and parental and professorial status, threatens to drown out his son's. Adam's story may supply the book's last full chapter, but, surrounded by his father's texts, it functions finally less as complement or counterdiscourse to his father's narrative than as a corroboration of it. The book, though bi-vocal, is not fully dialogical. The two voices speak eloquently to us in their very different registers, but they do not engage in a sustained or meaningful dialogue with each other.

As we have seen, *The Broken Cord* is generically quite complex. It draws on a rather broad range of genres, including family memoir, conversion narrative, autoethnography, ethnography, and pathography. Finally, however, its fusion of these various life writing genres generates a mixed message; in Dorris's desperate attempt to raise consciousness about FAS—and to exorcise his own conflicted feelings about his adopted son— he echoes rather than revises traditional inscriptions of race and disability. Its claim that Adam gave informed consent to the project is not credible, and the book serves finally as a negative model of the representation of vulnerable subjects. Concern for disability should, as Susan Wendell argues, address the ways in which disability is socially constructed. One is quite literal: "social conditions that cause or fail to prevent damage to people's bodies"; others include "cultural representations, failures of representation, and expectations [i.e., inappropriate standards of performance]" (Wendell 45). Dorris's passionate concern with the former evidently blinded him to the latter; his discovery of the way in which alcoholism impairs Native American children caused him to ignore or underestimate the ways in which eugenic discourse dehumanizes people with disabilities. His public advocacy on behalf of Native Americans involved damaging representation of people with disabilities, personified by his impaired adopted son.

∞

A sad postscript to *The Broken Cord* is that Abel Dorris died several years after the book's publication, on September 22, 1992, at the age of twenty-three, after being hit by a car on a freeway ramp. For me, Dorris's most moving writing about his son is found in the essay, "The Power of Love," which recounts his bedside vigil over the unconscious body of his injured son. As Abel lay mute, Dorris continued to address him, in a final series of one-way conversations:

> It was hard not to talk to Abel, even though I didn't know if he could hear me. I had put words in his mouth so often over the years that the process came naturally. I supplied the questions, and I provided the right answers. . . . I kept apologizing for my constant failures of kindness or understanding, and he, as he surely would have done, kept forgiving me. I kept exhorting him to get better, he kept promising to try his best. (115)

Here, in a sense, is the book in microcosm, with the father ventriloquizing his impaired son. Yet in this short posthumous text, the father's pleas for reconciliation and his awareness of having spoken too readily for his son supply a dimension too often missing in the book. Here, as it was before Abel's devastating diagnosis, Dorris's concern is with his son as an individual rather than as a case of a preventable disability. Thus, the posthumous essay is not so much a synecdoche of the book as a confessional coda to it, in which Dorris tries to repair his relationship with his son even as he tries, unsuccessfully, to will him to survive.

5

Beyond the Clinic
Oliver Sacks and the Ethics
of Neuroanthropology

To look in order to know, to show in order to teach, is not this a tacit form of violence . . . upon a sick body that demands to be comforted, not displayed?"

—MICHEL FOUCAULT, *The Birth of the Clinic*

Anthropology no longer speaks with automatic authority for others defined as unable to speak for themselves.

—JAMES CLIFFORD, introduction to *Writing Culture*

Oliver Sacks Presents

OLIVER SACKS HAS made a second career, beyond his primary one as a physician, writing about people with neurological conditions. Sacks's studies are often twice-told tales, published first as articles in magazines such as the *New Yorker* and later collected in books. Reviews of his books are generally very positive; several of his works have, somewhat improbably, been made into feature films (*Awakenings,* with Robert DeNiro and Robin Williams, and *At First Sight,* with Val Kilmer and Mira Sorvino, from "To See or Not See") and a play, *The Man Who,* written and directed by Peter Brook. With the translation of his work into twenty-one languages, he is the preeminent interpreter of neurological disorder in the world today. As such, he has a considerable degree of visibility, celebrity, and power. With the BBC television documentary series *The Mind Traveller: Oliver Sacks* (1998), his visibility became quite literal, and his influence was extended through a popular mass medium.[1] His forte is presenting rare or obscure neurological conditions to a lay audience in non-clinical language. Such work is fraught with potential for the exploitation of subjects whose conditions often marginalize, stigmatize, and silence them. Early on, his subjects came from the obscurity of the back wards of hospitals, and many could literally not speak for themselves. Further, their conditions often rendered them incompetent, incapable of granting informed consent to their representation. His work as a life writer thus warrants careful scrutiny.

Sacks has long aspired to what he calls a "romantic neurology," by which he means a neurology that recovers the "I" or the "who" (the patient's subjectivity) from the "it" or the "what" (the physiological condition). By his own account, this orientation was in part a matter of making a virtue of necessity. In one of his first jobs, he was banished from the lab because of his habitual clumsiness and disorganization: "I was always dropping things and breaking things . . . and eventually they said, 'Get out! Go work with patients. They're less important'" (qtd. in Lesser, para. 5). In mid-career, he identified himself as a "neuroanthropologist . . . in the field" (*Mars* xx) to signal his movement out of the clinic to investigate the role and significance of neurological anomalies in everyday life. His methods have changed accordingly. As a neurologist, he has created a distinctive ethos and even, one might say, a personal medical ethic. As a writer, Sacks is often credited with transforming a clinical genre, the case report (the written version of the case history), into a literary one, and in the process depathologizing his subjects.[2] In most quarters, Sacks has a reputation for treating his subjects scrupulously and sensitively, adopting generous estimates of their capabilities, and presenting them positively and compassionately.

It may come as a surprise to many readers and fans, then, to learn that a couple of reviewers have been quite hostile to Sacks. One of his detractors has charged that his work is, in effect, a highbrow freak show that invites his audience to gawk at human oddities—that Sacks, like a genteel contemporary Barnum, exhibits people with devastating (and generally irremediable) conditions that place them at the border of humanity. This accusation has come from the *Nation* columnist Alexander Cockburn in a piece called "Wonders in Barmy Land": "Don't you hate Oliver Sacks? It suddenly occurred to me yesterday, reading articles by him . . . that Sacks is in the same business as the supermarket tabloids (I meet monster from outer space with two heads) only he is writing for the genteel classes and dresses it up a bit (I meet man who thinks he's a monster with two heads). The bottom of it is a visit round the bin, looking at the freaks" (822). The "bin" is of course the "loony bin," a reference to the phenomenon of public visits to "Bedlam" (the Hospital of St. Mary of Bethlehem, a mental asylum in London), where spectators marveled at the insane inmates. This reference takes issue with Sacks's display of neurological inpatients in books such as *Awakenings* and *The Man Who Mistook His Wife for a Hat.*

Cockburn associates Sacks's work with two discredited institutional venues for the display of the other, the mental hospital and the freak show. Insofar as freak shows often overlay physical differences with cultural exoticism, Cockburn associates Sacks with scenarios that may be viewed as ethically problematic variants of medical and ethnographic practices, respectively: Bedlam, one might say, is to medicine as the freak show is to ethnography. Because Sacks's life writing takes place outside the literal confines of biomedicine and anthropology, it is not, strictly speaking, governed by their professional codes of ethics. His relationships with his subjects, however, are rooted in medical practice and often have a fiduciary dimension; even when his subjects are not his patients, their relationships with him are based on trust akin to that which patients have in their physicians. In the absence of clear ethical standards for nondisciplinary life writing, then, perhaps the ethics of biomedicine and anthropology may be legitimately invoked in assessing Sacks's work. At any rate, we can explore the ethics of life writing, particularly that which concerns vulnerable subjects, by taking up the implications of his self-designation as a neuroanthropologist.

∞

As we have seen, in biomedical ethics a distinction is made between harming and wronging, whereby *harming* involves adversely affecting someone's *interests,* while *wronging* involves violating someone's *rights* (Beauchamp and Childress 116). By today's standards, the exhibition of mental patients would clearly be regarded as *wronging* them. Even if their insanity rendered them insensible to it, and thus in some sense beyond being distressed by it, the practice would be seen as violating their privacy without consent and without therapeutic justification, thus breaching a cardinal principle of biomedical ethics: respect for patient autonomy, or the obligation to respect patients' choices. In contrast, a freak show would be seen as *harming* those exhibited, since freak shows are generally regarded as detrimental to the dignity of those exhibited, whether they participate willingly or not. If, as Rosemarie Garland Thomson claims, the process of "enfreakment emerges from cultural rituals that stylize, silence, differentiate, and distance the persons whose bodies the freak-hunters or showmen colonize and commercialize" (Thomson 10), then freak shows are harmful by definition. Even if they do not violate the rights of the individuals exhibited, the display would be seen as not in their best interests. By analogy, then, Cockburn has accused Sacks of both harming *and* wronging his subjects, violating their dignity and their rights—in effect, violating biomedical ethics in his nonprofessional writing.

Cockburn's analogy, however, oversimplifies a complex phenomenon. Granted, there is a superficial similarity between the scenario of some of Sacks's cases and that of the freak show: like the impresario of the freak show, Sacks selects human oddities, presents them to us, directs our attention (at least at first) to what makes them strange, comments on them, and then returns us to a world of reassuring "normality."[3] And his titles sometimes echo the sorts of epithets given to freak show exhibits, for instance, "The Disembodied Lady." But the similarity with Bedlam is less obvious. Sacks's inpatients are not insane, and they are displayed not as sheer spectacle but rather as instructive illustrations of how the human mind works—or doesn't. Cockburn's analogy ignores other differences between Sacks's work and the exhibition of Bedlamites. To begin with, whenever he uses patients for subjects, he is careful to conceal their identities, referring to them anonymously or pseudonymously. If he successfully conceals their identities, there is no invasion of privacy or betrayal of confidence. Moreover, unlike those who exhibited the mad as public entertainment, Sacks (in *Awakenings,* at least) claims to have the permission and even the encouragement of his patients, who, he says, "have said to me from the first, 'Tell our story—or it will never be known'" (3). If his patients have consented to having their stories told, there is no violation of their autonomy and no appropriation of their stories. And the communication of their stories, which counteracts the silencing effects of their condition, is a benefit to be weighed against any potential harms.

With regard to the question of harm, it is also significant that Sacks is not subjecting people to the sort of staring that can cause distress, shame, and humiliation. In his writing, they are not exposed to direct visual inspection. Even in the documentary films, their exposure, though visual, is not immediate and direct but delayed and mediated. Cockburn's analogy ignores the distinction between an actual, literal stare, which may cause emotional injury, and the metaphorical gaze, which is not directed at a human subject in real time and space.

There is a meaningful distinction, too, between displaying people whose differences are marked on their bodies, and thus instantaneously detectable with the eyes, as is the case with most "freaks," or manifest in outlandish involuntary behavior, as might be the case with Bedlamites, on the one hand, and presenting people whose anomalies are neurological, on the other. The oddness of Sacks's subjects lies not so much in their outward appearance as in their consciousness. By controlling the flow of information and the reader's angle of vision, so to speak, Sacks is able to counteract the sorts of reactions that his subjects might trigger if encountered in the flesh without his mediation. And because he needs to take the reader into his subjects' psyches in order to demonstrate their oddity, his subject matter and method militate against crude forms of distancing and objectification. This is of course what makes Sacks's cases highbrow: they appeal to intellectuals because they represent dysfunctions of the mind and thus of identity. But this does not make them freak shows.

It is difficult to see how Sacks's subjects are harmed or wronged *as individuals* by representation that is anonymous or consensual. With one minor but interesting exception to be noted later, none of his subjects, to my knowledge, has ever claimed harm at his hands. I would say, then, that—*pace* Cockburn—Sacks's written work passes muster, at least on minimal ethical criteria. He seems not to have violated the principle of nonmaleficence. In fact, he seems to have been quite scrupulous about getting consent from his subjects and/or disguising their identities, thus respecting their autonomy and privacy. Even if we regard his relationships with his subjects as fiduciary ones, the principle of beneficence does not necessarily apply beyond his practice as a physician. It is not clear that he is obliged to do them good in his capacity as a life writer.

And yet, there are troubling aspects of Sacks's work. One could argue that Sacks's representation of his subjects is all the more invasive because his commentary establishes difference where the eye cannot easily detect it. Moreover, when he turns from a written to a visual medium, in the television documentaries, the dynamics of display change decisively—and so must the ethical calculus. Presumably, the subjects in the documentaries have consented to being filmed by signing the standard releases, and the sorts of neurological conditions they have do not generally compromise their competence to give such consent. When his subjects are children, presumably their parents have given consent.[4] So here too there seems to be no violation of autonomy. But in a visual medium his subjects are recognizable and thus identifiable even when they are anonymous. And though they are not subjected to a live stare, they are exposed to visual inspection; indeed, unlike the immediate but transitory exposure involved in both Bedlam and freak shows, Sacks's display of his subjects is available on videotape long after its initial broadcast. In a visual medium, too, it is harder for Sacks to counteract viewers' spontaneous reactions to differences in appearance or behavior (such as Tourettisms) that may accompany neurological anomalies.

Most problematic from an ethical perspective is Sacks's practice of asking his subjects—particularly children—to perform certain tasks in order to illustrate their neurological differences. At such moments, the camera metaphorically zooms in on characteristics that distinguish Sacks's subjects from their presumably normal audience; the viewers' gaze is aligned with a diagnostic medical gaze. Similarly, when Sacks presents groups of individuals with the same condition and who share visible physical or behavioral traits, as is the case with Williams syndrome, the medium can stereotype—indeed, enfreak—them in ways that may defeat Sacks's intention to recover the "who" from the "what." Viewing these episodes is more like accompanying Sacks on rounds or house calls, to use his own analogy, than like viewing a freak show or touring an insane asylum; but his work in the visual medium is sometimes troubling because it realizes the voyeuristic potential of all of his work. Although his subjects may not object, and may not feel that they are harmed, the effect can be to reduce them to their neurological differences. It is for this reason that Sacks may be charged with not always fully respecting his subjects' dignity as individuals.

There are, however, compensatory aspects of the visual medium. One is that, much more than in his written work—and in a literal sense—Sacks himself enters the frame; he and his interaction with his subjects are also available for visual inspection. Thus, the visual medium affords his subjects more autonomy and agency than his written work. Documentary film is less free than prose of the process of its production. Granted, film interviews are mediated by editing; still, there is a sense in which the product *is* the process. This gives film a higher degree of transactional accessibility, an ethically desirable quality in any life writing; that is, it gives consumers greater insight into the transactions that allowed it to be produced. By representing Sacks's interaction with his subjects relatively directly, documentary film gives his subjects an opportunity for direct self-expression generally absent from the more clinical studies, in which they are less interacted with than described and assessed. The more open and reciprocal the interaction, the more ethically sound the representation.

An example of this (relative) openness can be found in a sequence of "'Don't Be Shy, Mr. Sacks'" that concerns Heidi Comfort, a six-year-old girl with Williams syndrome, a genetic anomaly that renders individuals unusually verbal and sociable while limiting some of their cognitive abilities. (Heidi is the exception I mentioned earlier, who claims to be harmed by Sacks.) After he talks with her in her bedroom, they go into the kitchen, at her suggestion, to eat some muffins. Heidi is intent on eating the muffins, but Sacks covers a plateful of them with napkins and asks her to estimate their number. She guesses three. Then Sacks uncovers them and asks her to count them; she arrives at the number ten. Sacks then counts them and finds there are actually thirteen. This "test" has no medical justification; it is not necessary for diagnosis, and it will lead to no treatment. (Sacks is not her real doctor, though he plays one on TV.) It is undertaken purely for purposes of confirming her innumeracy and demonstrating it to viewers. Later Sacks accompanies Heidi and her mother to a department store where she shops for a calculator. As Heidi picks one out, Sacks comments to the camera on her "difficulty with numbers." Moments later she looks up at him and tells him in no uncertain terms that she doesn't like what he said, that he has hurt her feelings, and that she hopes he won't do it again.

As Sacks narrates this episode, he deflects her criticism by saying that he had provoked her into revealing *further* aspects of her condition—acute hearing, emotional sensitivity, and "disarming directness." It may be true that Heidi's syndrome, which tends to minimize social inhibition, emboldened her to speak up. But his attribution of her criticism of him to her condition, rather than to treatment on his part that another child might be too timid to criticize, denies her the respect she deserves—indeed, demands—as a person. And, although we cannot be sure that the sequence of the scenes in the documentary corresponds to the order in which they were filmed, Sacks continues to speak of her in the third person in her presence. During another scene, she is given a high-tech cardiac scanning, since Williams syndrome can affect the elasticity of blood vessels. Heidi's cardiologist points out her valves in motion on a large video screen; she submits without complaint as he, Sacks, and we literally look into her heart. Later, however, as Sacks and her mother discuss her capabilities and traits, she objects, saying, "Cut, cut," and drawing her hand across her throat. The segment immediately ends (although this is no guarantee that the cameras stopped rolling).

It would be helpful to know how Heidi knew to signal that filming should cease. Whether she improvised this or had been told ahead of time that this was her prerogative matters because of the question of her autonomy. As Heidi is too young to give legally valid consent, her mother has presumably granted proxy consent. But this does not compel Heidi's cooperation. She retains the right to dissent—that is, to withdraw at any time—and here we see her energetically doing so. So while the inclusion of the scene reveals her displeasure to the audience, it might have been better to describe rather than show the scene to which she objected, or to interview her on screen about what is bothering her. After all, when she says "Cut," she is objecting to something that has already happened. Although the film doesn't silence Heidi, Sacks does try to mute her objection, and one suspects that he fails to see how damaging his display of insensitivity may be to our sense of his relations with his subjects.

Sissela Bok has observed that "the *pursuit of knowledge* can surely justify probing that would ordinarily be indiscreet or even degrading, so long as it is undertaken with the consent of those subjected to the probing, as when individuals agree to examinations by physicians, psychiatrists, and others which they would reject from other quarters" (235). One of the problems with assessing Sacks's life writing is precisely that its status is not altogether clear. The cases in *The Man Who Mistook His Wife for a Hat*, which involve patients, offer no clinical payoff as life writing; that is, these published stories are not elicited as part of a therapeutic relationship. In *An Anthropologist on Mars*, his subjects are no longer patients (for the most part), but neither are they subjects of biomedical research. He is not subjecting them to experiments, therapeutic or otherwise, or seeking generalizable, and empirically supported, results. (If he were, they would be protected by the ethical rules governing research with human subjects.)[5] Rather, he is using them as embodiments of unusual and interesting neurological anomalies. It is precisely because Sacks's life writing occurs outside the confines of academic or medical disciplines that its ethics are uncertain. Thus, while he may not be subject to the professional restrictions placed on writing about patients or research subjects—for example, the need for disclosure, consent, and anonymity—he also no longer has a therapeutic benefit to offer them; indeed, he lacks even the benefit of research results to offer future patients or the public. As a popularizer, the best he can claim is that he may advance public understanding of the mind and its workings. This is not an inconsiderable benefit, of course, but it does not accrue directly to his subjects, nor does it offer much to offset the risk of possible harm to them. Although it is not necessarily exploitative to treat a subject as a literary commodity, doing so lacks the built-in ethical justification of the clinical case history and of biomedical research. The case of Oliver Sacks is, then, far more complex and subtle than Cockburn's attack on him suggests. Any responsible critique of the ethics of Sacks's work needs to attend to the particularities of genre and medium as well as to the characteristics of his subjects.

∽

Detractors of Sacks such as Cockburn are a minority in the sense that they are vastly outnumbered by his admirers. But another of his detractors, Tom Shakespeare, a disabled British academic, represents a minority voice in a different sense. Just as the movement for patients' rights in the 1970s challenged the paternalism of biomedical ethics, introducing and elevating the principle of respect for patient autonomy, so too the movement for disability rights now poses a challenge to the ethics of biomedicine. And as disabled people have claimed their rights, Sacks has come under attack from a new quarter. Too often this criticism is heard only within the disability community. This is unfortunate, because a more subtle and powerful case than Cockburn's can be made against Sacks, on the grounds that his work may injure classes or communities of people that have been historically marginalized.

The new challenge has two distinct but related thrusts, both of which can be seen as corollaries of the principle of respect for autonomy. The first is that full respect for disabled persons involves acknowledging the role of culture in constructing disability and in discriminating against it, rather than seeing them exclusively in terms of the medical paradigm of disability, which locates disability in anomalies, dysfunctions, or defects of individual bodies. According to the minority model of disability, people with particular disabilities are analogous to groups marginalized— indeed, oppressed—on the basis of race, gender, ethnicity, or sexual orientation. One of the major implications of this paradigm is that the autonomy of disabled people may be limited less by their physiological differences than by their social, cultural, and physical environment. That is, even when they may possess autonomy as *capacity*, the competence to make their own choices, they may not be granted autonomy as *condition*, the freedom and power to govern themselves (Feinberg, "Autonomy" 28, 30). The second thrust, expressed in the slogan "Nothing about us without us,"[6] is that respect for their autonomy would entail not merely their consent to but their control over their representation.

In *No Longer Patient: Feminist Ethics and Health Care*, Susan Sherwin has argued that "research should be evaluated not only in terms of its effects on the subjects of the experiment but also in terms of its connection with existing patterns of oppression and domination in society. We need to develop mechanisms to address the hazards that are involved when the repercussions of a research project make the relatively powerless among us yet more vulnerable" (Sherwin 174–75). For obvious reasons, disability ethics is concerned with the danger of systemic harm to a class of vulnerable subjects, as well as harm to particular subjects. Many in the disabled community now see themselves as having been in effect colonized by the various professions that supposedly serve them; in response, they have sought self-determination both as individuals and as a community. Increasingly, they resent and resist being subjected to medical or social-scientific investigation rather than subjects articulating their own values and concerns. Indeed, the disability rights movement implies that the principle of "respect for communities" should be added to the principles already governing biomedical and behavioral research: respect for persons, beneficence, and justice.[7] Thus, the ethical principles of biomedicine may need to be supplemented with those of postcolonial anthropology, with its explicit concern for avoiding harm to communities under study, for establishing a reciprocal relationship with those studied, and for the politics of representation.[8]

Tom Shakespeare's attack on Sacks took the form of a review of *An Anthropologist on Mars* which appeared in *Disability and Society*, a journal little read by the general public. He begins by playing on the title of Sacks's first book of case studies, *The Man Who Mistook His Wife for a Hat*: "Oliver Sacks, the man who mistook his patients for a literary career, violates every principle of disability equality" (137). I take the word "mistook" here to mean not so much "misidentified" as "misappropriated." Thus, I take Shakespeare to be charging Sacks with commodifying his patients as a means of self-aggrandizement and self-enrichment. (Implicitly, he seems to be suggesting a violation of the Kantian ethical imperative "to treat every person as an end and never as a means only" [Beauchamp and Childress 351].)

Shakespeare also faults Sacks for speaking monologically as the disciplinary expert:

> He resembles nothing so much as a Victorian ethnographer, charting the bizarre world of mentally and physically impaired people for the voyeuristic cognoscenti. The majority of description is his, not his subjects: where their views are expressed, it is via reported speech, and it is rare for him to offer their own accounts to us directly. He describes himself as making "house calls at the far border of experience," but he is more like a colonialist than a general practitioner. His interpretation, which bears all the features of his professional medical background, is the dominant voice within this book, and it is his expertise in diagnosis and exegesis . . . at which we are invited to marvel. (137)

Shakespeare lodges another related charge against Sacks: that "he is inclined to individualism, abstracting these people from their social contexts, and giving few clues as to the reactions of others and the consequent societal experience." He ends by expressing the wish that "Sacks would spend less time on the extreme and the bizarre, and pay more attention to the construction of normality, and the taken for granted assumptions which underlie it" (138).

As suggested earlier, one problem with blanket judgments of Sacks's work is that they represent it as monolithic, whereas in fact it has evolved significantly. I have explored important differences between his work in print and that in film or video. There is also great variation within his written work, from his early studies focused on single conditions such as migraine and post-encephalitic Parkinson's (*Awakenings*) to his better-known collections of case studies (*The Man Who Mistook His Wife for a Hat* and *An Anthropologist on Mars*), and from his autobiographical volumes (*A Leg to Stand On* and *Uncle Tungsten*) to his more ethnographic works (*Seeing Voices* and *Island of the Colorblind*). Despite the vehemence of his attack, Shakespeare makes some interesting concessions. One of these is to acknowledge at the outset that he is as concerned with the "reception" of Sacks's work generally as with the volume in question. And in fact, this review more accurately applies to the work on whose title he plays than to the work it purports to review. I suspect that Shakespeare formed a negative opinion of Sacks on the basis of the earlier volume and was unable or unwilling to qualify it in reviewing a subsequent book that is far more ambitious and accomplished. Evidence for this hypothesis is Shakespeare's use of the term "patients," for in the newer volume Sacks's subjects, with one exception, are actually *not* his patients. This does not mean that he is not displaying them in objectionable ways; but Shakespeare's use of the term suggests that he has not fully registered the shift in Sacks's practice from his first book of cases to his second. Although his new role is somewhat ambiguous, Sacks still retains, and presumably trades on, his authority as a physician. Sacks remains in a position of higher status and power than most of his subjects, and he retains complete control over the text. But whereas patients seek out physicians for help, anthropologists generally seek out subjects to study; and even when their subjects seem to choose them, ethnographers are dependent on and obliged to them for their material.[9] This alters the dynamics and the ethics of the transaction and the subsequent representation.

Partly because of its origins in medical practice, Sacks's life writing is a prime domain for the exploration of the ethics of representing vulnerable subjects. Sacks's oeuvre can be divided into categories that correspond roughly to chronological phases of his career. In the first category are those books, *Migraine* (1970) and *Awakenings* (1973), that focus on a single condition or syndrome. These both contain a relatively large number of short and somewhat formulaic case studies subordinated to analysis of a single medical condition. In some ways these are his least satisfying books; they are clinical in context and in language. Nevertheless, in them Sacks devises a personal medical ethic that illuminates all of his work.

The second category includes *The Man Who Mistook His Wife for a Hat* (1985; hereafter *Man*) and *An Anthropologist on Mars* (1995; hereafter *Mars*). Rather than focusing on a single condition, these books collect cases of various conditions. Here Sacks produces a distinctly *literary* case report intended for a lay, rather than a professional, audience, and he moves from pathography toward biography—and even toward memoir insofar as he appears "in the frame." Within this category we can see marked difference and development. *Man* focuses on individual patients' manifestations of neurological conditions, while *Mars* moves out of the clinic to focus on the *person* rather than the patient. In *Man*, the case studies come to the fore—the book consists entirely of them—but they are still quite short, sometimes perfunctory. In *Mars*, the cases expand in length (the book contains only seven) and, significantly, the subjects are generally not patients, which introduces a new ethical scenario. In mid-career, then, Sacks moves out of the clinic into the world, where he visits, interviews, and even travels with his subjects.

A third category contains two autobiographical volumes separated by almost twenty years, *A Leg to Stand On* (1984) and *Uncle Tungsten: Memoirs of a Chemical Boyhood* (2001). *Leg* is the story of a knee injury that had neurological consequences. It is thus a kind of case study of the self. As such, it may seem to stand apart from Sacks's main work, but I will argue that it is crucial to understanding his evolving ethics.

The final category involves a move from the medical and biographical toward the ethnographic; this category comprises *Seeing Voices*, *The Island of the Colorblind*, and at least some of the BBC series *The Mind Traveller*. Here, Sacks investigates neurologically impaired individuals in a cultural context or within their community. So there is a clear, though not entirely linear, trajectory in his work, over the course of thirty years, from a focus on pathology, through a focus on the individual (first as patient, then as person), to a focus on culture or community.

Three threads run through the commentary that follows. One is the relationship between Sacks's medical ethics, which he announces explicitly, and his life writing ethics, which remain implicit. A second is the relationship between his ethics and his literary form. A third concerns relations among Sacks's ethics, his medium of representation, and the various paradigms—metaphorical, medical, and minority—under which disability can be viewed. Although Sacks's work has grown more sophisticated and self-conscious, it has not outgrown ethical critique, nor is there any evidence that it has changed in response to criticism of it; indeed, different problems often arise as old ones are resolved.

All in Your Headache: *Migraine*

Sacks's first book, *Migraine* (1970), is important for my purposes because of its articulation of his personal medical ethic. Here Sacks draws a useful distinction between "looking at" and "listening to" a patient (230). He writes:

> There [is] only one cardinal rule: one must always *listen* to the patient; and, by the same token, the cardinal sin is *not listening*, ignoring. Prior to any and all specific approaches, there must be this general approach, the establishment of a relation, a communication with the patient, so that patient

and physician *understand* each other. A relationship, moreover, in which the patient is not entirely passive and compliant, believing and doing what he is told, and taking what is "ordered." Any such relation, which degrades the patient while exalting the physician, is a travesty of authority, and essentially malign, leading inevitably to a regression and a breakdown of trust. (222)[10]

Here Sacks begins to establish the received image of himself as a maverick physician, the doctor—*pace* Tom Shakespeare—who mistook his patients for *people*. Statements like this develop both an explicit personal "ethic" (an approach to medicine) and an "ethos" (a representation of Sacks's moral character). They are important, then, both as content and as rhetoric.

A synoptic book, *Migraine* looks at the condition from a variety of perspectives: physiological, historical, and therapeutic. But Sacks insists that "the migraine sufferer knows directly what he experiences—*he* is the authority on his own experience" (191). And while he sees migraine as having a definite physiological basis and structure, he is more interested in migraine as a strategy—the creation, usually unconscious, of the patient. Which is to say that he sees at least one type of migraine, "situational migraine," as psychosomatic. He rejects two hypotheses about migraine as psychosomatic: that it is a function of the "migraine personality" and that it reflects unconscious hostility toward loved ones. Listening to his migraine patients convinces Sacks that the conventional understandings of migraine represent reductive oversimplifications—Procrustean hospital beds (179). Instead, he argues that situational migraines represent idiosyncratic responses to difficult circumstances: "Many migraine attacks were drenched in emotional significance, and could not be usefully considered, let alone treated, unless their emotional antecedents and effects were exposed in detail" (xvii). His belief in migraine as a "strategy" and in the autonomy of the patient extends to a recognition or claim that the patient may in the end choose to keep his migraine: "Certain patients— a minority, but an important and often deeply incapacitated group of patients—may be *attached* to their symptoms, in *need* of them; . . . such patients may *prefer* the migraine way of life, with all its torments, to any alternative which is left open to them" (218).

From the start of his writing career, then, Sacks presents himself as opposing a reductively physiological approach to illness and asserting the importance of seeing—or, more properly, *hearing*—the patient as an individual with his or her own idiosyncratic needs and values. Thus, Sacks seems to have particularly embraced the concept of patient autonomy, according to which an individual "acts freely in accordance with a self-chosen plan" (Beauchamp and Childress 58), which requires that the competent patient's choices and actions should be honored so long as they do not harm or infringe the autonomy of others (Beauchamp and Childress 64).

Sacks's emerging ethics can be considered in relation to several paradigms under which medical conditions may be viewed. The birth of the clinic introduced the biomedical paradigm of illness and disability—the view that illnesses and disabilities are defects or abnormalities in the individual body that medicine diagnoses, investigates, and attempts to correct or ameliorate. This paradigm is for the most part an advance over the earlier symbolic or metaphorical paradigm, which ascribes moral or supernatural significance to such conditions—and thus places them virtually beyond human control. Under the symbolic paradigm, people with epilepsy or Tourette's syndrome might be persecuted, even executed, as possessed by demons. The biomedical demystification of neurological conditions such as Tourette's is, no doubt, an improvement over seeing them as indices of the moral or spiritual status of those affected.

One shortcoming of biomedicine, however, with its emphasis on pharmaceutical and surgical remedies, is that it tends to ignore the person to treat the condition; to many, it seems sterile, even dehumanizing, especially in instances in which biomedicine offers no effective treatment or cure. Sacks's ethic and other recent developments, including "alternative" and New Age medicine, attempt to minimize, ameliorate, or even eliminate this objectification. Such approaches, however, run the risk of remystifying illness. A good deal of New Age discourse of illness in effect revives the symbolic paradigm—though ostensibly in an empowering way. A classic articulation of this is the idea that patients may "choose" their illnesses—including such mortal conditions as cancer and HIV/AIDS—and that they may recover from them as soon as they determine why they chose them and decide to "let them go." (See, for example, Louise Hay.) Such a paradigm can add insult—blaming the ill—to the injury of the disease, and may exacerbate that injury by discouraging more efficacious therapies.[11]

Sacks avoids regression to the earlier paradigm. First, there is a significant difference between assigning migraine to a "personality type" (which is essentially immutable) and understanding it as a modus vivendi, which is to some extent elective and thus alterable. Nor does he claim that people with migraines have chosen their illness (i.e., "asked for it"); rather, he claims that for some people, migraine has come to play a functional role in their lives and that, as a result, continuing to have migraines may be preferable to no longer having them. (For example, while painful, migraines may enable workaholics to take "downtime" they would not otherwise allow themselves.) But clearly Sacks has moved away from a physiological model and a pharmaceutical therapy toward psychotherapy and a "talking cure." Sacks's advocacy of attending to the patient (i.e., the person) and to the meaning of the illness in a particular life is the heart of what he refers to as his "romantic neurology."

As a manifestation of his practice as a life writer, rather than as a physician, however, *Migraine* is relatively crude, especially compared to much of his later work. The numbered case studies are short and generally perfunctory. And despite his emphasis on listening to patients, Sacks rarely shows himself doing that; his relation *of* the cases does not demonstrate egalitarian relations *with* his patients. Rather, as in typical clinical case reports, we see the patient through the eyes of an invisible, effaced observer; the physician is outside the frame, not subject to the reader's scrutiny and not shown in dialogue or interaction with patients. Sacks's retention of narratorial authority is consistent with his reservation about patient associations: that "they may encourage 'professionalism' in patients, and make their obesity, their paraplegia, their migraine, or whatever, the chief preoccupation and (narcissistic) center of the patient's life" (228). Whether Sacks's writing displays his self-described medical ethic, then, is open to question. At least, the enactment of his philosophy in this book is only partial.

In sum, *Migraine* is a seminal work insofar as it articulates an ethos distinct from the paternalism prevalent in clinics in the United States and insofar as it hints at Sacks's future approach to neurological abnormalities. In his idea of a neurological condition as a modus vivendi, we can discern the root of his later inclination to revalue deviations from neurological norms. The choice of migraine for his first book is significant, too, since it is—by nature, he claims—not amenable to simple prevention or magic-bullet treatment. As a condition for which biomedicine did not (and still does not) have a quick fix, migraine virtually demands some modification of the reductive biomedical paradigm. As a condition that may emerge from a particular life and take on meaning peculiar to that life, it also is conducive to Sacks's adoption and advocacy of a patient-centered medicine.

The Big Sleep: *Awakenings*

Unlike migraine, post-encephalitic Parkinson's disease would not seem amenable to Sacks's announced medical philosophy; it is therefore all the more notable that his second book is devoted to this illness, which left some survivors of the early-twentieth-century encephalitis pandemic "as passive as zombies" (15), "encysted, cocooned" (22)—so inert that many were consigned to custodial institutions. It was in such an institution, "Mount Carmel" (Beth Abraham Hospital in the Bronx), that, in the late 1960s, Sacks encountered and began to treat a unique population of patients with the new drug L-dopa. The stories of these otherwise anonymous patients on a back ward of an obscure hospital are familiar to many today thanks to Sacks's written account of his treatment of them, and consequently to the film based on the book.[12]

The success of *Awakenings* (1973) with the general public is quite surprising in view of the work's language, which is at times off-puttingly clinical: "Propulsion and retropulsion were readily called forth. In addition to his grimacing and humming, Mr. O. showed a variety of smaller movements of the ears, the eyebrows, the platysma, or chin. He showed a rather unblinking lizard-like stare, except when grimacing, or during his rare paroxysms of blepharoclonus [spasms of the eyelids]" (82). An interesting solution to the conundrum of the book's popularity has been proposed by Anne Hunsaker Hawkins. As she points out, during the two decades between its initial publication and the release of the feature film in 1990, there was significant public disillusionment with modern biomedicine. Two landmarks of the period are the institution of the doctrine of informed consent (in the 1970s) and the passage of the Patient Self-Determination Act (in 1990), "a law requiring all health-care facilities receiving federal money to inform patients of their right to make out an advance directive" (Hawkins, "Myth" 12). As she sees it, *Awakenings* owed its success to the way in which it challenged the "ideology of the medical establishment" (9) at the right historical moment—the moment when the principle of autonomy was gaining parity with other principles of biomedical ethics. In particular, it advanced an effective critique of what she calls "the myth of cure," that is, "the assumption that biomedical science can and will produce some technique or pharmacologic substance capable of restoring health and the collusion of patient and doctor in denying the limitations of modern scientific medicine—its uncertainty, its capricious pharmacopeia, its potential to do harm" (9).

Awakenings exposes the myth of cure by repeating case after case in which a patient, dormant and seemingly without will or even consciousness for years, even decades, is miraculously "awakened"—revivified and returned to a kind of normality and wholeness—only to experience side effects so severe that drug treatment has to be discontinued. Despite their seeming regression, Sacks concludes that these patients have not come full circle but rather have been enabled to make some accommodation to their illness without drugs. Hawkins reads the cases as exemplifying a shift away from paternalism to partnership as the basis of the physician-patient relation. Thus she credits Sacks with using the "failure" of L-dopa to advance a patient-oriented medical ethic—one honoring patient autonomy. One way to articulate the newer ethic is to say that it characterizes the physician as responsible *to* the patient in contrast to a paternalistic ethic holding the physician responsible *for* the patient.

This is a perceptive account of the book's themes and a convincing explanation of the book's surprisingly enthusiastic reception. Yet a number of concerns remain about Sacks's medical and literary ethics. First, one wonders how a physician so skeptical of drug therapy for migraine came to advocate experimental drug treatment for Parkinson's—especially under conditions in which it seems that patients could hardly have given informed consent: by Sacks's own testimony, they were "ontologically dead, or suspended" (15). In a way, the plot of this book seems to be Sacks's *own* awakening to the limits (and dangers) of pharmacological medicine,[13] but such an awakening would not have seemed necessary for the author of *Migraine*. Scrutiny of the ethics of administering the drug is impossible because the book occludes the process by which the experiment was begun.[14] Such an account would give the book greater transactional openness, that is, access to the transactions that typically occur behind the scenes.

One critic, however, has raised a question about Sacks's biomedical ethics that carries over to the ethics of his life writing. Noting the odd coincidence that so many of Sacks's patients seem to be keeping diaries, Ella Kusnetz has suggested that they are doing it at Sacks's instigation; moreover, she argues that any such therapeutic regimen, when coupled with his reading of said journals, amounts to unwarranted intrusion in patients' lives in ways that serve Sacks's needs without compensatory therapeutic benefit. She suggests that if his "sympathetic engagement with his patients" does not "help control their diseases," it is suspect (185). Her claim, then, is that he violates their autonomy by invading their privacy—

as a physician, not as a life writer. Put differently, she is suggesting that by involving them in a nontherapeutic regime that served his interests, not theirs, he violated the Kantian principle of never treating another merely as a means to one's own ends.

Whether this is true is impossible to determine without more information. Still, Kusnetz's critique reminds us of a risk in any patient- or person-centered therapy: that the partnership that supposedly replaces paternalism can shade into manipulation, invasion of privacy, and betrayal of confidentiality.[15] Since Sacks has an increasing investment in his success as a writer, it is possible that his secondary career may motivate him to know more about his patients than is necessary for their therapy.[16] The possibility that physicians who write about their cases may be involved in conflicts of interest should not be overlooked, especially when their patients are also writing about themselves. Kusnetz is right to raise the question of "the ethical considerations involved in writing about brain-damaged people who have no capacity to affirm or deny what is told about their experience" (186).

The issues raised by his medical practice aside, Sacks's practice as a life writer is not always congruent with his announced ethic. Sacks is fond of distinguishing between the medical or neurological condition as an "it" and the patient as an "I," and he prides himself on his ability to see the "I" behind or within the "it." And yet his cases remain highly formulaic; their shared sequence of phases tends to flatten out individual differences. Granted, each begins with a sketch of the patient's life "before L-dopa," and such attention to patients' *life* history—as distinct from their *medical* history—is a departure from the clinical case report. Yet here the biographical run-up to the onset of the illness is very short, so the bulk of this section is devoted to the course of the illness. This is followed by the "course on L-dopa" and sometimes a brief afterword or update. The effect of this is to give much more space to the script of the disease and the drug than to the script of the life. Moreover, there seems to me a significant discrepancy between the individual case studies and the master plot Sacks imposes on them in his conclusion. There he reconstructs his cases in terms of a tripartite plot featuring dramatic reversals from initial "awakening" by L-dopa (and apparent restoration of the self) to "tribulation" (debilitating side effects), followed by accommodation to the impossibility of complete cure or even effective, reliable treatment.

Sacks is at pains to emphasize the reality and value of this accommodation for his patients: "They may still (or again) be deeply Parkinsonian, in some instances, but they are no longer the people they were. They have acquired a depth, a fullness, a richness, an awareness of themselves and of the nature of things, of a sort which is rare, and only to be achieved through experience and suffering" (241). If one rereads the case studies, however, few support this generalization. The discrepancy may result from his having written up more extreme cases while generalizing from a broader base of milder ones. If so, one wonders what, if not sensationalism, justifies such a focus on the extreme cases. Sacks's reiterated urge to inspire "wonder" in his readers is a motive I view with some suspicion, as it tends to "enfreak" the neurologically different. It may be worth noting here that the real source of the book's sensationalism is not pathology but pharmacology. Parkinsonism is not conducive but antithetical to narrative because of the passivity and inertia of the patients. What evokes awe is an entirely iatrogenic phenomenon.

Although Sacks never says as much, this "experiment" with L-dopa must have been traumatic for him; seeing his patients experience such drastic relapses must have been excruciating. I suspect, then, that his emphasis on their successful accommodation has an element of wishful thinking to it. In any case, his final account strains to ennoble them and to represent them as having benefited from their treatment. To the extent that this master plot is imposed on them, rather than implicit in their separate narratives, Sacks may be over-writing their lives.

Perhaps a more telling critique of Sacks's employment of so many individual cases here is that it leads—or permits—Sacks to minimize a significant factor in the patients' distress. As Kathryn Montgomery Hunter points out, most case reports take for granted the clinical context and thus effectively exclude it from scrutiny (63, 98). Notably, admirably, in *Awakenings,* Sacks opens his frame wide enough to admit himself into the picture, acknowledging his emotions for his patients and theirs for him. More important, he acknowledges that changes in hospital administration and philosophy constrained his treatment of patients and had destructive effects on patient welfare. He alludes to this in a section of the introduction called "Life at Mount Carmel," where he indicates that administrative changes in 1969 undid a good deal of the progress accomplished in the preceding years. He refers to this in the final section, "Perspectives" (239), as well. Furthermore, he makes this striking observation in a note: "We have seen that Parkinsonism and neurosis are innately coercive, and share a similar *coercive structure.* Rigorous institutions are also coercive, being, in effect, *external neuroses.* The coercions of institutions call forth and aggravate the coercions of their inmates; thus one may observe, with exemplary clarity, how the coerciveness of Mount Carmel aggravated neurotic and Parkinsonian tendencies in post-encephalitic patients" (288–89n14). Such an acknowledgment, however, exposes the limits of Sacks's ethical concerns because it reveals his acquiescence to forces hostile to his own medical ethic. His responsibility to his patients was trumped by the institution's abdication of responsibility for them. The narrative offers no evidence that Sacks tried to challenge and change those policies. He notes these factors but seems to consider them outside his ethical purview.

In allowing us to see these forces at work, he gestures toward an ethics that would take into account the political, social, and cultural context in which treatment is effected, but he finally stops short of fully reckoning with this. It is typical of Sacks's tendency to dehistoricize his subjects; even when he returns to earlier writings, he rarely contextualizes them in historical and political terms. Rather, he tends to portray his patients within a sort of ethnographic present: he *presents* them in more than one sense. A differently organized book might have made the same point about drug therapy but also constituted a more far-reaching indictment of the asylum as the site of therapy. To require that all accommodation come from the "patient" while minimizing the ways in which institutions might accommodate their patients is to assume an artificially circumscribed ethical viewpoint.

The Cases of Oliver Sacks. I:
The Man Who Mistook His Wife for a Hat

It is in *The Man Who Mistook His Wife for a Hat* (1985) and *An Anthropologist on Mars* (1995) that Sacks really found his form and his fans; his audience and his reputation grew as his cases were no longer subordinated to the study of a single condition and as they moved from pathography toward biography. As Kathryn Montgomery Hunter has established, despite advances in biomedical technology, the narrative of the individual case—in its various conventional genres, including the oral presentation of the case, the serially composed and multiply authored patient's chart, and the written case report—is still at or near the heart of modern medicine. Of these clinical genres, Sacks's case studies come closest to the case report, which Hunter has characterized as follows: "Its purpose is to report a new and newsworthy clinical point for publication in a medical journal. . . . It is the attempt by a scientifically educated, clinically experienced writer to convey a precise and generalizable account of one patient's illness" (93).

In effect, if not in intent, the medical case report registers and enacts the transformation of people into patients and their stories into cases, a process I refer to as *encasement*. In hope of relief from, or at least understanding of, their complaints, individuals "present" to physicians only to be re-presented by those physicians to others as "patients." The process involves a subtle negotiation in which people surrender a degree of privacy in return for diagnosis and therapy; as part of this process, they surrender their stories, which are transformed into narratives that may be unrecognizable to them and are, finally, "incommensurate" (to use Hunter's apt word [122]) with their own. The process is impersonal, perhaps objectifying, but it need not be dehumanizing; the patient's story is appropriated but ideally not expropriated, recounted but ideally not discounted. In the best-case scenario, physicians eventually return to patients stories that will make sense of their illnesses (Hunter 142–44). But as Hunter has argued, some flattening of the story is necessary for it to be useful in diagnosis. Encasement, then, involves a degree of purposeful and presumably benign alienation of patients from their stories.

In *Man* and in *Mars*, Sacks seeks to avoid encasing his subjects. Indeed, he does not so much enrich or deepen the medical case history as turn it inside out. To achieve generalizability, the case history tends to elide the idiosyncratic, matching symptoms against a clinical paradigm so as to verify diagnosis and optimize treatment; in contrast, Sacks's cases highlight idiosyncratic detail. And whereas the case history seeks to isolate the illness in the individual, Sacks seeks to situate the condition in the life. He attempts to convert pathography into biography, patients into people. In doing so, he violates the clinical convention of the effacement of the physician, according to which "a professional self, standardized, with eccentricities erased, presents the case history and is presented by it" (Hunter 162). His case studies are thus doubly personalized. In short, the tendency of Sacks's narratives is what we might call *disencasement*.

Sacks's cases depart in a number of ways from their clinical model. One is in the minimization of clinical language. (The residue helps to maintain Sacks's medical authority.) Another is in the way they are titled. For obvious reasons, the titles of clinical case reports specify, quite narrowly, aspects of the conditions or syndromes in question. In contrast, biographies usually specify their subjects' names, in subtitles if not in titles. Sacks's cases fall in between; rather than using proper names—whether of medical conditions or individuals—they tend to consist of descriptive phrases. In this they come closer to medical than to biographical practice, however, for these phrases tend to refer to conditions or symptoms rather than to identities or individuals. Although titles from *Man,* such as "An Autist Artist," "Witty Ticcy Ray," and "Incontinent Nostalgia," use everyday terms rather than clinical names, they identify their subjects with or as recognizable neurological conditions. The title Sacks chose for the collection, *The Man Who Mistook His Wife for a Hat,* represents this tendency at its most questionable. The formula usually serves to identify an individual with a single famous or infamous act; in this case it identifies a patient with one remarkable, seemingly bizarre symptom of his disorder. (In addition, in *Man,* the chapters are grouped into units according to whether the conditions represent "Losses," "Excesses," "Transports," or "The World of the Simple.")[17] It is one thing for people with disabilities to "identify" as such; it is another for a medical authority to identify them *with* their disabilities, that is, as model cases. When he selects subjects entirely on the basis of the rarity or extremity of their neurological conditions, Sacks sometimes appears to reduce "who" to "what."

Consistent with other shifts in tenor, the titles in *Mars* are less diagnostic: some indicate a condition or loss—"The Colorblind Artist," "To See or Not See"—but others mask impairment completely, such as "The Last Hippie" or "A Surgeon's Life." The title selected for the volume, *An Anthropologist on Mars,* is perhaps the most intriguing one; Temple Grandin, an autistic scientist, uses this phrase to portray her sense of alienation from the everyday life around her, normalizing herself and characterizing "normal" life as Martian. In the second collection of case studies, too, by lengthening the cases and admitting more of the individual's way of living with his or her condition, Sacks explodes the case report. His creation of what is often termed a "literary" case study may thus be seen as an enactment in writing of the ethical principles declared—but not always demonstrated—in his earlier works.

The role of his specialty in this transformation should not be neglected. Neurology is not merely well suited to this trend toward the biographical; in some sense, as Sacks notes, it demands it, for neurological conditions are difficult to isolate from the life and the self. That is, they tend to exist at the fundamental level of personality and consciousness, "for here the patient's personhood is essentially involved, and the study of disease and of identity cannot be disjoined" (viii). Neurology is conducive to such individual attention to cases for two other reasons as well. First, study of many neurological disorders is dependent on patient testimony. In contrast with diseases of most other organ systems, empirical tests—including sophisticated new scanning technologies—go only so far to reveal pathology in the brain. Second, neurology often has little to offer in the way of effective treatment, let alone cure (one of the sad lessons of *Awakenings*). A physician who specializes in neurological abnormality, then, has little to gain from taking a narrowly physiological view of his patients and correspondingly much to gain by departing from narrow medical paradigms.

The limits of Sacks's approach in *Man*, however, are quite evident in the eponymous study of a man who had such difficulty recognizing familiar things that, when he meant to reach for his hat, he reached for his wife's head instead. This is a case that warrants Tom Shakespeare's critique, I think. It is constructed largely as a medical mystery, with Sacks as the intellectual detective in the manner of Poe's Auguste Dupin, whose solutions often depend on his ability to intuit what is going on in someone else's mind. More pathography than biography, the study contains a minimum of biographical context and follow-up, and it ends abruptly with Sacks's determination of the diagnosis of the disorder and its cause. For the author-physician, the payoff is a diagnosis that solves a riddle; since the condition is untreatable, however, the diagnosis is of little benefit or comfort to the patient or his family. While the anonymous subject may be beyond harm, cases like this seem to objectify their subjects unnecessarily, if not cruelly. (Witness Sacks's remark that his patient's attempt to interpret a Bette Davis film with the sound off was "positively Martian" [13].)

A related example would be "The Disembodied Lady," the story of a woman who loses her sense of proprioception. Sacks's title plays on the epithets given sideshow freaks. Indeed, he quotes his subject as comparing herself to such an exhibit: "It's like something's been scooped right out of me, right at the centre. . . . Step up, come and see Chris, the first pithed human being. She's no proprioception, no sense of herself—disembodied Chris, the pithed girl!" (51–52). As her physician, Sacks reassures her, but as author of the case study, he turns to his audience and concludes that "in some sense, she *is* pithed, disembodied, a sort of wraith" (52)—virtually dis-selved. His final judgment seems unduly negative: "She has both succeeded and failed. She has succeeded in operating, but not in being" (53). It is this sort of discourse—speaking as a medical authority over the body of the anonymous "defective" patient to a presumably "normal" audience—that gives Sacks a bad reputation in the disability community and beyond. While no harm may have been done in the physician-patient interview, the same may not be true of the life writing that proceeds from it. Pseudonymity protects against violation of privacy but not against painful self-recognition and a sense of exposure when a former patient reads her physician's work. Sacks may not have failed any of his ethical *obligations* as physician or as life writer, but as life writer, he has fallen short of his goal of producing empathetic biography.[18]

The cases cited thus far are found in the first section of the book, called "Losses," in which Sacks addresses himself to the sorts of problems that neurology has traditionally concentrated on: deficits in function. In the next section, "Excesses," Sacks moves into more congenial territory, citing as precursors his idol, A. R. Luria, and his own work in *Awakenings* (where the excesses were, of course, drug-induced). "Witty Ticcy Ray," his study of a man with Tourette's syndrome, marks a watershed in Sacks's work, for several reasons. Ray is his first Tourettic patient; moreover, meeting Ray puts Sacks in contact with a neurological disorder that defines a hidden community. Finally, unlike the deficits addressed in "Losses," Tourette's is consistent with relatively successful functioning in society.

We would expect a physician to view Tourette's exclusively through a medical lens. But in the course of treating Ray, Sacks moved beyond the medical paradigm. Ray came to Sacks because his Tourettisms were causing increasing problems with his work and home life, but after several years of controlling his tics with the drug Haldol, he decided he would prefer to retain at least some of them, some of the time. In consultation with Sacks, he decided to medicate himself only during the work week; on weekends, he resumed his tics—which were not only functional in certain endeavors, such as playing the drums and playing ping pong, but also, in his view, part of his identity: "I consist of tics—[without them] there's nothing left" (98). Through his work with Ray, Sacks not only came to recognize the syndrome when he saw it but also was put in touch with the society of Touretters and through them came to see Tourette's as a form of identity or even of culture: "Never before have patients led the way to understanding, become the active and enterprising agents of their own comprehension and cure" (95).

Rather than seeing Tourette's, like migraine, as a dispensable psycho-somatic "strategy" for dealing with life stresses, Sacks is forced to see it as entirely organic and completely valid modus vivendi. The physician who, in *Migraine*, warned against the narcissism of patient support groups now praises the Tourette Society of America for providing a basis for community life and affirmation of identity; he has thus moved toward the "minority model" of disability. That is, he has begun to acknowledge that disabilities may bind people together in communities that have distinctive values and customs. The conclusion of his next case, which has to do with an elderly woman enjoying the late effects of syphilis—a constant state of arousal and flirtatiousness—fits "Witty Ticcy Ray" nearly as well: "We are in strange waters here, where all the usual consideration may be reversed—where illness may be wellness, and normality illness, where excitement may be either bondage or release, and where reality may lie in ebriety, not sobriety" (107).

In other cases, however, Sacks's tendency toward melodrama threatens to remystify disability. That Sacks's "romantic neurology" may represent a throwback rather than a step forward is suggested as well by some of the tales in part four, "The World of the Simple." These tales have been warmly received by some for their view of those with cognitive disabilities as being compensated for their deficits with some spiritual depth. But they have been attacked by others for terminology considered offensive—"retardates," "the simple"—and for patronizing their subjects. Over his career Sacks's most consistent theme has been the resiliency of the mind. Again and again he suggests through his studies that when one area of the brain is compromised, others may compensate, and that the "mind," in any case, is not reducible to its "brain functions." Contra Tom Shakespeare, I find the idea of compensation a progressive theme—at least where it can be empirically established, that is, where it is explained as representing the plasticity of the mind and nervous system rather than as some divine consolation prize. But I think that Sacks's claims of compensation at times amount to overcompensation on his part; when he can't demonstrate it, he often claims it anyway.

Compensation sometimes takes the form of "transcendence," which is inherently resistant to empirical demonstration. This theme is evident in some of the cases in *Man*, especially in this section, where Sacks, unable to obtain testimony from his subjects, imagines them, notwithstanding, as experiencing a kind of transcendent peace. Thus, the pictures of Jimmie in the hospital chapel (37), of Rebecca admiring the spring foliage

from a bench in the courtyard (180), and of Martin (188) enrapt in Bach
seem suspect to me, in part because, read serially, his cases manifest too
many similar moments; one senses a formula at work. Rather than listening to his patients, Sacks here seems to be speaking for them without
authority. His occasional assumption of an omniscient viewpoint to "report" what they must be thinking and feeling in some of these passages
(188) is indicative of his overreaching.

The projection onto passive subjects of states of mind they may not be
experiencing is an ethical issue with a number of dimensions. The fact
that the cases are anonymous and lifted out of the clinical context moots
certain ethical concerns—such as direct harm to the individual—but it
also tempts Sacks, I think, to make claims that cannot be disproved. I am
interested not so much in the questions of "truth" (the relation between
the texts and some extratextual reality), which are undecidable, as in the
issue of the relation between the writer and his vulnerable, because inar-
ticulate, subject. Characterizing voiceless patients as transcendent may
serve Sacks's needs more than it serves theirs. It thus comes into conflict
with the principle of autonomy, or respecting the person. It is not a matter of overriding their choices but of over-writing their subjectivities.

Physician as Patient: *A Leg to Stand On*

In the 1980s, Sacks produced books that illustrate both the negative and
positive tendencies in his work. One, *A Leg to Stand On* (1984; hereafter
Leg), moves from pathography toward autobiography, while the other,
Seeing Voices (1989), moves from pathography toward ethnography. *Leg*
is the story of the aftereffects of a knee injury Sacks suffered while hiking.
(He fell while fleeing a charging bull.) What made this incident worthy
of book-length narration was that his physical injury was accompanied
by a complete, though temporary, loss of feeling and function in the injured leg. For Sacks, this was the most interesting—but also most disturbing—thing about the injury. It was interesting because it involved a
condition, loss of proprioception, that he had seen and written about in
his patients but never experienced. It was disturbing because it challenged his very sense of personal integrity: with the psychological "loss"
of the leg, he seemed to have lost an integral part of himself. It was troubling also because his physician did not recognize, and thus refused to
validate, his subjective reality.

Eventually—suddenly and mysteriously—Sacks recovered his feeling and his function, very much in the manner of some of his arrested Parkinson patients: "A true miracle was being enacted before me, within me. Out of nothingness, out of chaos, measure was being made. . . . My soul was transfixed in a rapture of wonder" (140–41). Sacks's language suggests that the "cure" was quite literally miraculous, grace-ful: "The reality of my leg, and the power to stand and walk again, had been given to me, had descended upon me like grace" (147). The reintegration of his injured self, coincident with the repossession of his "lost" leg, owed nothing to medical intervention. The generous estimate of this episode—and the one he himself takes of it—is that Sacks's own fortuitous experience of a condition he sometimes treated gave him access to a point of view unavailable to most physicians; it thus enlightened and empowered him as a healer: "Now I *knew*, for I had experienced myself. And now I could truly begin to understand my patients, the many hundreds of patients with profound disturbances of body-image and body-ego, whom I saw over the years" (202–3). In its conflation of disability narrative and conversion narrative, however, this self-narrative threatens to substitute for the metaphor of the doctor as God the image of *this* doctor as one of the elect. And, as I have argued elsewhere (*Recovering Bodies* 186–89), Sacks's message—that he understands and can empathize with his patients (can mistake them for people)—is to a considerable extent undercut by his language, which expresses deep revulsion for the condition he has just experienced and, by implication, for the condition and status of disability.[19]

At crucial junctures in this narrative, his language draws on two rhetorics—gothic rhetoric and conversion rhetoric—which have historically operated at the expense of disabled people. The language of conversion, with which the account of his miraculous recovery is saturated, cannot be detached from the symbolic paradigm of disability, which has often characterized it as a condition signifying moral corruption. Similarly, this passage from the preface, which may serve here as a synecdoche of the book-length narrative, deploys gothic tropes that also tend to mystify and stigmatize disability:

I had imagined my injury (a severe but uncomplicated wound to the muscles and nerves of one leg) to be straightforward and routine, and I was astonished at the profundity of the effects it had: a sort of paralysis and alienation of the leg, reducing it to an "object" which seemed unrelated to me; an abyss of bizarre, and even terrifying, effects. I had no idea what to make of these effects and entertained fears that I might never recover. I found the abyss a horror, and recovery a wonder; and I have since had a deeper sense of the horror and wonder which lurk behind life and which are concealed, as it were, behind the usual surface of health. (13–14)

The power of physicians over patients is in part the power of the former to define the reality of the latter. Writing here, crucially, from the perspective of complete recovery, Sacks tends to reinscribe, rather than erase, the line between disability and non-disability, and between patient and physician. Such rhetoric is complicit in the marginalization of disabled people, who inhabit what he characterizes as a world of unreality and who, most significantly, lack not physical but spiritual grace.

I have no reason to doubt the veracity of this narrative, but I am suspicious of its convenient anointment of Sacks as the empathetic physician he had already idealized. He grants himself this status after he has been thrust into a humbling position by means of a double injury to his ego: the loss of feeling in his leg suffered in his literal fall on the mountain and the loss of authority in the clinic suffered in his figurative fall into the status of patient. What he reaps from this experience, however, is not only the recovery of a mystical sense of wholeness but also an accession of authority—and thus power—as a neurological pioneer. In terms of the progressive unfolding of Sacks's ethics, then, I would say that this book has more to do with the projection of ethos—that of the "romantic neurologist"—than with the attainment of a new ethical perspective. The danger of such a personal and professional conversion is that it will embolden him to fill in gaps in patients' experience, to presume that their experience can be understood under the cultural rubrics that appeal to him: biblical narrative paradigms, classical music metaphors, gothic conventions, and so on.

This is precisely what Ella Kusnetz has charged him with. In an essay that all students of Sacks should read, Kusnetz claims that Sacks expropriates his patients' stories in a rather literal way. She notes, for example, that Sacks's idea that music played a role in his miraculous recovery is more than merely reminiscent of accounts given by patients in other texts: "Such is the complicated process of projection and expropriation in Sacks—as well as the elaborate fictionalizing, fantasizing, and metaphysicalizing—that in all the books it is virtually impossible to discern whose material is whose" (194).

In effect, she accuses Sacks of being the doctor who mistook his patients for *himself*. If Kusnetz is right that this book involves introjection—that Sacks is to some extent "playing" neurological patient here—then it would be consistent with my suggestions (and hers) that his other work sometimes involves projection, imposing his own narrative schemas on cases that he cannot otherwise resolve.[20] Any such blurring of ego boundaries would be, in my view, a violation of life writing ethics, but one that may stem, paradoxically, from the adoption of a patient-centered medical ethic.

Neurologist as Ethnographer. I: *Seeing Voices*

In a sense, *Seeing Voices* (1989) is not life writing at all—it includes virtually no individual stories—but rather a kind of semiprofessional inquiry into deafness by a neurologist who had little contact with deaf people until well into his career. Yet *Voices* demands treatment here because of what it reveals about the trajectory of Sacks's career and the evolution of his medical ethics. In that regard, it has two crucial aspects. The first is that in this book, Sacks is emphatically no longer operating in the clinic. The inquiry grew not out of his medical practice but out of his reading about the deaf (ix), which led him to visit various schools for the deaf and ultimately to Gallaudet University. The second aspect is related to the first: the book represents his first acknowledgment that disability can be viewed as a cultural phenomenon. Both aspects—of method and content—contribute to the book's status as quasi-ethnography; metaphorically as well as literally, Sacks moves out of the clinic, the site of his earlier neurological work, into a community defined by a condition he does not share and at first does not understand. The book is his attempt to come to terms with, and explain to his readers, the world of the culturally "Deaf"—that is, those deaf people who communicate primarily with sign language.

The book is structured as a sort of field trip for which Sacks obsessively prepares. The bulk of the book involves his working out the answers to questions in an academic way, relying on books and other neurologists (and the occasional examination of a specimen, such as Joseph [38–42]). The major excursion in the first half of the book is to Martha's Vineyard, the site of a community in which, to accommodate an unusually high proportion of congenitally deaf people, sign language was widely used by hearing as well as deaf people in the nineteenth and early twentieth centuries. The trip to Martha's Vineyard marks Sacks's discovery that deafness can be a cultural as well as a neurological phenomenon; but it is not actually an excursion into a deaf community, since that community is extinct. His next, climactic excursion takes him to a vital and functioning—indeed, very nearly autonomous (i.e., self-governing)—Deaf community, Gallaudet University. In fact, what brings him to Gallaudet is precisely the issue of self-government, which was raised by the controversial appointment in 1988 of a new president who was hearing and non-signing; in response, students mounted a protest that brought about the replacement of the hearing appointee with the university's first deaf president, I. King Jordan.

The book becomes ethnography insofar as it involves "fieldwork" done in a community of "others" and represents that culture as much as possible in its own terms, bracketing the ethnocentric assumptions the observer might bring to it. To this end, Sacks passes on what amounts to the creation story of the culture in question—the history of the development of deaf education, Deaf culture, and a Deaf community; the story of the legitimation of sign language in the 1960s, the growth of Deaf Pride and Deaf Power, and so on. The book culminates with his witnessing the "Deaf President Now" movement at Gallaudet University—a successful flexing of political muscle by Deaf students and professors. The book represents his first extensive acknowledgment that a disability can be viewed as a cultural and political phenomenon. Indeed, he goes beyond "neutrality" to partisanship in his affirmation of American Sign Language (ASL) and of the student protest against an insensitive and patronizing administration.

Nevertheless, as ethnography the book reveals occasional traces of a colonial consciousness. In the long preparation for his excursion to Gallaudet, for example, Sacks relies mainly on medical experts—not deaf, much less Deaf, informants. Even at Gallaudet, most of his informants are not "natives"; most are hearing professionals like himself. More important, perhaps, is Sacks's implicit insistence on the role of medical authority in investigating the implications of deafness. From a deaf point of view, the long middle section of the book, in which Sacks explores the neurological implications of early deafness, is unnecessary and potentially insulting in its exploration of whether the deaf are necessarily retarded. Sacks concludes that it is not deafness per se, but the difficulties in language acquisition that may be attendant on it, that threatens intellectual capacity. Still, what for him requires investigation is for the deaf a

long-settled issue. For them the existence of Gallaudet University is itself
an effective answer to any questions as to their educability.[21] While
Sacks's conclusions are in the end favorable toward deaf people and Deaf
culture, he still arrogates the authority to pronounce them healthy. Thus,
the rhetorical scenario is that of a hearing outsider speaking to other hearing outsiders about whether prelingually deaf people are fully human.

Still, the work represents a significant development in Sacks's oeuvre
in that he seems to accept the view that a neurological impairment can be
the basis for an identity, a culture, and a community. His book probably
disseminated this notion of deafness more widely than earlier books by
specialists and advocates such as Harlan Lane. Sacks's acknowledgment
of a disability as a culture, a disabled people as a minority, suggests that
Seeing Voices records yet another awakening of Oliver Sacks to new human possibilities, and it prepares him for a new openness to other neurological irregularities. (Indeed, one might say that awakening is the
master trope of Sacks's oeuvre, considered as *self*–life writing.)

The Cases of Oliver Sacks. II: *An Anthropologist from Mars*

His 1995 collection of case studies, *An Anthropologist from Mars*, is probably the book on which Sacks's contemporary reputation rests. As I indicated earlier, I find Tom Shakespeare's account of it ungenerous—even
unfair—because in *Mars*, Sacks moves beyond the paradigms and practice of his earlier collection in the direction hinted at in *Voices*. As earlier,
he underscores the plasticity of the mind and the resilience of the person,
but now he chooses to play up something treated only glancingly in earlier work, the "creative" potential of "disease": "Defects, disorders, diseases . . . can play a paradoxical role, by bringing out latent powers,
developments, evolutions, forms of life, that might never be seen, or even
be imaginable, in their absence" (xvi). For the most part, then, the new
tales are "tales of metamorphosis, brought about by neurological chance,
but metamorphosis into alternative states of being, other forms of life, *no
less human for being so different*" (xx; emphasis added). Thus, "Jonathan I.,"
a painter who loses his color vision owing to a head injury, not only ad-
justs to what would seem a devastating loss but also moves on to a new
phase in his career, producing black and white art of stunning quality;
"Greg F." develops an appealing new personality despite severe imped-
iments to the memory creation supposedly necessary for self-construc-

tion; "Dr. Carl Bennett," a Tourettic physician, succeeds in an unlikely specialty, surgery; Franco Magnani, an Italian immigrant, produces meticulously detailed and accurate paintings of the small hill town in which he grew up, entirely from memory; Stephen Wiltshire, an autistic teenager, creates vivid architectural drawings and suddenly develops prodigious musical talent; and Temple Grandin, an autistic professor of veterinary science, becomes the premier American designer of humane facilities for slaughtering livestock. (The anomaly is "Virgil," a blind masseur who regains his vision through surgery, struggles to adapt to this "gift," but becomes blind again.)

Juxtaposing pairs of subjects from the two collections of case studies— the autists, José and Stephen Wiltshire; the Touretters, Ray and "Dr. Bennett"; and so on—illustrates the distance Sacks has traveled in his representation of neurological disability. For one thing, his new cases are weighted toward the high-functioning. For the most part, these are not conventional tales of triumph over adversity, however: these individuals are seen not as overcoming—that is, compensating for—impairment but rather as incorporating it into distinctive identities or sensibilities. Disabled people often react very negatively to the common, well-intentioned verbal formula "successful though impaired" because even as it implies that achievement and impairment are incompatible, it holds up "supercrips" as role models for others, with the implicit query: Why can't you all be like, say, Helen Keller? Sacks's portraits demonstrate an antithetical formula, "successful because impaired." In most cases, these subjects owe their distinction to their neurological anomaly. Indeed, some of them are literally capitalizing on impairments. Sacks goes a long way here toward de-pathologizing neurological anomaly, which helps to defend him from the charge that he may be harming a class of people by his representation of them.

In addition to the shift from low to high function, and in large part as a consequence of it, Sacks's new cases are also different in method: "In addition to the objective approach of the scientist, the naturalist, we must employ an intersubjective approach, leaping, as Foucault writes, 'into the interior of morbid consciousness, [trying] to see the pathological world with the eyes of the patient himself'" (xviii–xix). Although his earlier cases were never merely standard clinical reports, his new cases mark a greater departure from the conventions of medical genres. His subjects in this volume are, with a couple of exceptions (Jonathan I., "the colorblind painter," and Greg F., "the last hippie"), not medical patients at all (and only Greg is an inpatient); thus, there is no question of Sacks's being responsible for them (and he can refer to some of them, with permission, by their real names). For the most part, then, rather than their seeking him out for diagnosis or treatment, he identifies them as subjects for his studies. As we have seen, when patients present in the clinic, they implicitly agree to submit to encasement in exchange for medical help. The new cases involve a different scenario: it is Dr. Sacks who presents. Indeed, when his subjects are already well known—for example, Temple Grandin and Stephen Wiltshire—it is not clear whether the life writing project involves the ethnographic or the celebrity scenario (as distinguished in chapter 3).

Since they are not primarily medical patients, Sacks sees them not in the clinic but on their turf, and occasionally in his own home. In addition, the social stature of these subjects puts them in a different relation to Sacks: one is a physician, another has a Ph.D., and two are successful painters. Furthermore, these subjects are generally far more articulate than his earlier ones, which allows for a more fully intersubjective relationship. These new tendencies reflect Sacks's increasing deviation from the medical paradigm, as both an interpretive and a methodological model. Thus, the dynamics, the politics, and the ethics of his cases have changed significantly. Yet even when his subjects' fame equals or exceeds Sacks's, their impairments may still render them vulnerable.

His new approach is less a matter of looking at or listening to patients, more a matter of talking (and walking) with people, entering into a more egalitarian and mutual relationship, for Sacks cannot do justice to these subjects without their cooperation and testimony. Again, however, Sacks seems to have developed an admirable ethic—that of collaboration and reciprocal intersubjectivity—which he cannot always live up to. His reference to the new cases as "house calls at the far borders of human experience" reveals his uncertain stance toward his subjects. For one thing, the metaphor suggests how hard it is for Sacks to surrender his clinical habit and his medical gaze. For another, it marginalizes the very population he seeks to de-pathologize. Thus, even with his new high-functioning subjects, Sacks retains a medical authority that can be exercised unilaterally; although he is not their doctor (with a few exceptions), he is more physician than ethnographer.

Further, the cases vary considerably with regard to intersubjectivity. Some portraits—those of Jonathan I., Greg F., Virgil, and to some extent Stephen Wiltshire—tend toward the monological; at least, they are dominated by Sacks's voice. Indeed, in at least Greg's case, there is no question of informed consent (hence his pseudonym). The portrait of Virgil is perhaps the most medical; in much of it, Sacks gazes appraisingly at him, watching him perform everyday behaviors and classifying them as "blind" or "sighted." Higher-functioning subjects, especially those who are professionals—"Dr. Bennett," Franco Magnani, Temple Grandin—emerge more fully as agents in their own representation, but they seem to have been granted no control over that representation.

At his best, Sacks adopts a multifactorial rather than a pathographical approach to a subject. Thus with Magnani he concludes:

> it would be reductive, absurd, to suppose that temporal lobe epilepsy, seizures of "reminiscence," even if they do constitute the final trigger of Franco's visions, could be the only determinants of his reminiscence and art. The character of the man—his attachment to his mother, his tendency toward idealization and nostalgia; the actual history of his life, including the sudden loss of his childhood paradise and of his father; and, not least, the desire to be known, to achieve, to represent a whole culture—all this, surely, is equally important. (166)

Magnani's risky decision to return to his Italian hometown of Pontito alone after many years of exile seems to arise in part from an empowering relation with Sacks; he consults closely with him before undertaking the trip. Similarly, in Sacks's account of Magnani's trip and its immediate aftermath, which (necessarily) quotes Magnani liberally, it is apparent that Magnani's relation with Sacks may have helped him reflect on and articulate what his inner life means (179–82). Here Sacks seems to be exercising not professional responsibility for a patient but responsibility to a person; and this egalitarian relationship has apparently actually increased Magnani's autonomy. The case ends, however, with a gratuitous and patronizing judgment to the effect that, when it comes to memory art, Magnani is no Proust:

> Instead of achieving a penetration into the inwardness, the "meaning," of Pontito, [Magnani] makes a vast, even infinite enumeration of all its outward aspects—its buildings, its streets, its topography—as if these could in some way compensate for the human void within. He half knows this, yet does not know it, and in any case has no choice. He has no time for, no taste for, no power of introspection and may suspect, indeed, that it would be fatal to his art. (187)

In any case, Sacks's final reference to Magnani's suspicion is at odds with his assertion that he is incapable of introspection.

The case of Stephen Wiltshire is particularly interesting because Wiltshire is a more opaque subject; the nature of autism is at odds with the intersubjectivity that Sacks seeks and sometimes achieves with other subjects. For Sacks, Stephen is, at first, a test case of whether an autist can be a true artist: "Was not art, quintessentially, an expression of a personal vision, a self? Could one be an artist without having a 'self'?" (203). In representing Stephen, Sacks vacillates, sometimes granting that Wiltshire may be moved by what he sees (and may derive pleasure from his own creations), sometimes implying that his art is mere technical performance without "soul," in part because of his ability to produce it without full engagement. (Sacks does not consider whether this would make Stephen the paradigmatic postmodern artist, with a talent for pastiche; that is, he does not consider the extent to which his own aesthetic criteria are relics of an anachronistic paradigm of the artist.)

Some cases achieve an intersubjectivity missing in *Man* because of the circumstances of Sacks's contact with his subjects—its long duration or its extra-clinical context or both. In such circumstances, Sacks has more opportunity to recognize development and depth in his subjects. This is, unexpectedly, the case with Wiltshire, whose sudden eruption of musical talent surprises Sacks and requires him to revise his initial assessment: "Nothing of what I had seen with him before, and nothing in his art, had quite prepared me for this. He seemed to be using his whole self, his whole body, with all its repertoire of movements and expressions, to sing, to enact the song—though it remained unclear to me whether this was basically a brilliant piece of pantomime or a true entering into the words, the feelings, the inner states of the song" (240). Again, however, Sacks ends with a curiously patronizing conclusion of a sort that he might not render so readily with a subject likely to read and react to it: "Stephen's drawings may never develop, may never add up to a major opus, an expression of a deep feeling or theory or view of the world. And *he* may never develop, or enter the full estate, the grandeur and misery, of being human, of man" (243).

Despite their aspiration to the status of biography, Sacks's newer cases betray traces of the conventional case history—especially in their narrative closure. He tends to achieve such resolution by stepping back from his informal interaction with his subjects to assess their capabilities and even to predict their future development, a reversion to the medical habits of diagnosis and prognosis. Such final, summary judgment is less appropriate and necessary in the biography of living subjects—especially, perhaps, young ones—than it is in case reports. Too often, in disengaging himself and his readers from his subjects, then, Sacks seems to "re-encase" and "alien-ate" those subjects, reinscribing a reassuring line between the abnormal and the normal.[22] Part of what limits Sacks's case studies as biography is that he seems to rely less than a nonclinical biographer would on testimony from close relatives, friends, and acquaintances or even on observation of his subjects' interaction with them. Sacks's reliance on his professional methods too often determines his relation to the subject/specimen and may predetermine or overdetermine his conclusions.

Intersubjectivity enters the case of Stephen Wiltshire, however, through a kind of backdoor, in two tantalizing instances of Stephen's staring back at Sacks. When Sacks is traveling in Russia with Stephen and his agent—in search of new buildings for him to draw—Stephen spontaneously draws a portrait of the group, showing himself fanning Sacks: "He portrayed me as cowering under the impact of the fan, and himself as large, powerful, in command—this was a symbolic representation, the first one I had seen him make" (216). In his graphic representation of Sacks, Stephen "shrinks" the neurologist, portraying him in terms of his eccentric behavior: hypersensitive to heat, Sacks always carries a folding fan. Later, at the prompting of his agent, Stephen subjects Sacks to a mock math test. Asked to do his sums, Sacks plays along, faking effort and occasionally producing a deliberately wrong answer. Sacks realizes that, like the earlier incident, this is serious play: "It was a lesson to me, to all of us, never to underestimate him. Stephen delighted in reversing roles, just as in his cartoon of himself fanning me" (221). Sacks understands that Stephen is resisting medical surveillance, and it is refreshing to see this sort of interaction (which Sacks could have chosen to omit). The more open and apparently reciprocal his interaction with his subjects, the more ethically sound the cases appear to be.[23]

Still, Sacks seems sometimes to forget this, reverting to the stance of an authoritative physician assessing a passive subject. One sign of this is his adoption of a near-omniscient mode: "I had the feeling that the whole visible world flowed through Stephen like a river, without making sense, without being appropriated, without becoming part of him in the least. . . . I thought of his perception, his memory, as quasi-mechanical" (218). He doesn't give Stephen full credit for the interiority suggested by his obsession with *Rain Man* or by the perceptiveness of the role reversals; thus, he provides evidence of depth he doesn't seem to acknowledge. Finally, he attributes the failure of his relationship with Stephen to develop solely to Stephen's lack of selfhood.

Similar dynamics are reflected in the case of Temple Grandin. Sacks's direct interaction with her is condensed, taking place over a mere two days. The shortness of his visit means that Sacks has little time to witness the unfolding of different dimensions of her self. Even so, their relationship seems to develop over the course of the weekend, and the case moves from pathography toward biography accordingly. Reporting their first contact, Sacks notes oddities in her gestures and her gait. (With regard to the latter, he even contradicts her attribution of it to a purely vestibular condition [256], trumping her testimony with his professional opinion.) When they visit slaughterhouse sites she has designed, however, her expertise and her great ease with animals impel him to defer to her and acknowledge her visual way of processing information. Finally, her tearful contemplation of her own death surprises him and changes his assessment of her. His biographical portrait of her is one of his most satisfactory case studies, in which he achieves a significant degree of intersubjectivity.

The book's title is drawn from this case; it is Grandin's phrase for describing her sense of living among "normal" others. Significantly, the phrase constructs an alternative center from which customary human behaviors such as dating, romance, and sex seem strange, even unfathomable. Sacks's appropriation of her phrase raises the question whether he can honor her perspective or whether he will helplessly reverse it, treating her behavior as Martian. If the "anthropologist" of the title is taken to refer to Sacks, the question is whether the "Mars" in question is the world of Grandins and Wiltshires or the everyday world in which he lives, in which his idiosyncrasies and eccentricities sometimes make him feel alien. (As a British citizen, Sacks has the legal status in the United States of resident alien.) Although he is capable at times of deploying his eccentricity to blur the border between normal and abnormal, for the most part he conceives of himself as an anthropologist traveling to distant, different neurological states, reporting on them, and returning—illuminated but somewhat relieved—to the familiar world he shares with his readers.

A larger issue arises from Sacks's characterization of himself as a neuroanthropologist (xx). In this regard, anthropology must refer to ethnography, the heart of which is the self-reflexive attempt to enter into and fairly represent a culture different from one's own. (Contemporary ethnographers have made strenuous, self-conscious attempts to negate or minimize any complicity in imperialism.) Meaningful neuroanthropology might study how culture constructs neurological norms or how neurological conditions may produce culture. To some extent, Sacks does the former; at least, he claims, "I am sometimes moved to wonder whether it may not be necessary to redefine the very concepts of 'health' and 'disease,' to see these in terms of the ability of the organism to create a new organization and order, one that fits its special, altered disposition and needs, rather than in the terms of a rigidly defined 'norm'" (xviii). Sacks clearly identifies himself here as a "normativist" (one who believes that attempts to distinguish between the two states of health and disease are ultimately and inevitably value-laden, culture-bound [Caplan 58]; normativists are of course more amenable to the minority model of disability). But he is proposing here not so much an investigation into the cultural construction of norms, and their deconstruction, as a recognition that particular individuals defy simplistic notions of biological norms. (His use of the term "organisms" suggests how little Sacks is concerned with culturally produced norms.) That is, he seems interested only in a reconsideration of norms on a literally case-by-case basis.

Nor does he, in *Mars*, attend much to the notion adduced in *Voices* of disability as an identity or a culture. It might seem that neurological disorders such as autism would, by their nature, be incompatible with culture or community—if, by "community," we mean not just a set of distinctive people but a group that self-consciously nurtures its members. But Wiltshire's art and Grandin's designs are in some sense autistic culture: their very existence and particular qualities are due in large part to the disorder of their creators. Sacks seems reluctant or unable to acknowledge any autistic culture, however. Thus, while his cases in *Mars* represent a significant evolution of his medical and life writing ethics, in some ways they seem not to live up to the promise of *Voices*.

Neurologist as Ethnographer. II: *The Island of the Colorblind and Cycad Island*

Sack's 1997 venture as a neuroanthropologist is the site of conflicting, even contradictory, impulses. In a literal sense the book represents a new direction in his work: it comprises accounts of travels to various islands in Micronesia, to which Sacks is attracted (mainly) by the high incidence of elsewhere rare conditions: color-blindness on Pingelap and Pohnpei and lytico-bodig, "a progressive degenerative condition akin to Parkinson's and amyotrophic lateral sclerosis" (xi), on Guam and Rota. It thus extends, quite self-consciously, the move toward ethnography that we have seen in *Voices* and to a lesser degree in *Mars:* "I went to Micronesia as a neurologist, or neuroanthropologist, intent on seeing how individuals and communities responded to unusual endemic conditions" (xi).

Sacks wonders, for example, about the consciousness and culture of people congenitally without experience of color: "Would they, perhaps lacking any sense of something missing, have a world no less dense and vibrant than our own? . . . Might they indeed see *us* as peculiar, distracted by trivial or irrelevant aspects of the visual world, and insufficiently sensitive to its real visual essence?" (6). And on the tiny island of Pingelap, he identifies some ways in which the island's culture has embraced color-blindness. Although there is discrimination against the color-blind as less able (because of photosensivity) to do the outdoors labor common in the local economy, he notes that their superior night vision is particularly effective in night fishing, which also has economic value. (He speculates that historically the condition might have had some advantages, too, in food gathering on the theory that in an environment so rich in green plants, color alone is of little use in discriminating one plant from another.)

He approaches ethnography, as well, in inquiring from a local *nahmmwarki* (oral historian) as to indigenous beliefs about *maskun* (congenital color-blindness). These beliefs are various and contradictory; color-blindness is alternately seen as a curse upon the sinful, as biological or genetic in origins, and as a product of contamination by Europeans (52–54). On Guam, he is similarly interested in the indigenous view of lytico-bodig—which is fatalistic and averse to aggressive treatment. And he is respectful of the indigenous therapies generated by the natives' folk neurology: "They know well how to unfreeze or unlock patients if they get frozen, by initiating speech or action for them—this may require another person walking with the patient or the rhythmic pulse of music" (158).

But the limits of Sacks's ethnography are also clear here. There's a revealing gap, at times, between what he says and what he shows. He does not explore the genesis of the local "myths" about *maskun*; it might be interesting to know, for example, whether the theory that color-blindness is a curse on the sinful originated with European missionaries.[24] And Sacks does not explore how it is that uneducated natives came to use music and rhythmic activities to mobilize the frozen—a discovery he treats in *Awakenings* as a breakthrough in Western neurological therapy. Indeed, insofar as he inquires into the worldview of the congenitally color-blind, his answers tend to come not from the natives (of color) but from a color-blind Norwegian scientist whom he has invited along on the trip. The scenario is more that of scientists investigating local disease than that of anthropologists investigating local culture.

Traveling for the first time into the zone of classic European imperialism, Sacks is explicitly critical of the devastating effects of the European presence, and he acknowledges that natives sometimes feel used by the medical researchers, who take their blood and tissue samples but return little in the way of information, treatment, or compensation in any other form (135). Sacks is less single-minded than his predecessors, and he is not in Guam to do "medical" research. He makes house calls with dedicated (though not indigenous) doctors who are highly regarded by the natives (and whom he sees as exemplifying personal medicine), and he does his best to register these patients as individuals. But like medical researchers, he does not stay long; he too takes natives' stories and returns nothing to them. Despite their individual characteristics, the patients surveyed remain cases; indeed, the narrative takes the form of a medical mystery in which Western scientists pursue a dreaded killer using clues and testimony supplied by native victims.

This is also true of the BBC documentary "Poison in Paradise: Guam Disease." People with Guam disease—who may be "frozen" or "locked," but who are not insensible—are discussed in their presence as specimens. Their bodies are subjected to a probing medical gaze, with the camera zooming in to expose telltale symptoms such as twitching muscles. The retinas of their eyes are examined for signs of parasites that may be the cause of the disease; at one point, a patient is told on camera that his eyes lack such "tracks." At moments like this, the presence of the camera and crew seems intrusive; at others, I suspect that relatives gave permission for on-camera examination of ailing and incompetent family members out of reflexive deference to Europeans with medical expertise; there seems to be no benefit to them, however. Further, the oral testimony of the patients is at times inaccurately captioned; the film quite literally misrepresents it, as if no one listened very closely to what they said. There is little intersubjectivity in this project in either its verbal or its visual format. Sacks's explicit criticism of medical imperialism does not exempt him from complicity in its legacy of appropriative practices.

Insofar as he functions as an anthropologist, Sacks's manner and his project seem anachronistic, harking back (as Shakespeare has noted) to the Victorian era. There's an element of discrimination in the films' practice of introducing subjects orally, if at all, and rarely by their full names, while the names of clinicians or experts are generally presented in subtitles. And there is a hint of the white man's burden in Sacks's belief that he can bring special insight or help in a short visit to these areas—and some danger, in focusing on disability in exotic climes, of mapping disability onto ethnicity and race. His expedition is one in which white Western "experts" literally descend from the skies onto islands populated by color-blind people of color, yet it never occurs to Sacks to address the notion of color as race or of color-blindness as absence of prejudice. Rather than neuroanthropology, the book verges at times on neuro-tourism, as if Polynesia and Micronesia were the names not of exotic places but of rare memory disorders (like amnesia and hypermnesia, which Sacks documents in *Man*).

In any case, neurological anomaly is not the only lure of the islands for Sacks; another is the presence of cycads, large fernlike palms that have changed little over the millennia and that have fascinated Sacks since childhood. These two major concerns are linked by the possibility that lytico-bodig may be a delayed effect of toxins consumed by natives who eat cycad products. Still, the alternation in Sacks's gaze back and forth between patients and plants will only confirm the suspicion among skeptics that Sacks's books are his means of displaying his collection of exotic specimens for profit. Sacks encourages this suspicion when he cites a biographer's remark about the father of British neurology, W. R. Gowers, to the effect that "to him the neurological sick were like the flora of a tropical jungle" (xiii). His tendency to anthropomorphize the ancient plant species—in terms reminiscent of his remarks on his Parkinson's patients—also blurs the distinction; he regards cycads as "tragic in that they had lost the premodern world they had grown up in . . . [b]ut heroic too, in that they had survived the catastrophe which destroyed the dinosaurs, adapted to different climates and conditions" (183). Whereas in his own clinical practice Sacks exhibits responsibility for his patients, and in his extra-clinical cases he manifests a sense of responsibility to his subjects, when he ranges farthest afield, he sometimes seems neither responsible nor responsive to his subjects.

Visual Representation: *The Mind Traveller*

In the spring of 1999, a year after the original BBC broadcast, PBS television aired the documentary series *The Mind Traveller: Oliver Sacks*, in which Sacks extended his work into a visual medium. Two significant aspects of the shift in medium call for attention here. The first, noted earlier, is that a visual medium, which involves displaying identifiable people, has the potential for reinventing the freak show. Granted, subjects are exposed to the public's gaze only indirectly, through a time delay, rather than in real time before a live audience. For some subjects, such as Jessy Park, who has autism, this sort of representation may be far more acceptable and comfortable than "live" exposure. The fact that the viewing takes place later, rather than simultaneously, as in a freak show, lessens but does not eliminate this potential. The subjects may be shielded from direct and dehumanizing stares, but they are also deprived of the opportunity to respond to staring by engaging with their audience directly; the mediation insulates the audience from the subject as well as vice versa.

Further, there is no temporal or spatial limit to video exposure; there is no quitting this show. Because the subjects are identifiable, there is some danger of harm to individuals by means of false, objectifying, or patronizing representation; there is the possibility, too, that like "poster children" used for charity purposes, they will come to regard as exploitation what had seemed at the time sympathetic, even beneficent representation—with the additional regret that the representation is still available to others forever beyond their reach. Such a result would violate standards that Sissela Bok has called for, to ensure "that those who are unable to consent, being, perhaps, too young or ill, not be exposed to anything that might then or *later* violate their sense of privacy and self-respect" (241; emphasis added).

The problems inherent in visual representation might seem to be offset by the nature of the neurological disabilities, some of which are not visible to the innocent eye. In fact, however, all of the impairments represented in this series—color-blindness, autism, deaf-blindness, Tourette's,

Guam disease, and Williams syndrome—do have telltale visual signs, and Sacks often explicitly directs viewers' attention to them (e.g., the blinking of the achromats on Pingelap). Furthermore, in identifying individuals as having particular disabilities, Sacks necessarily focuses the viewer's attention on characteristics of each disability. Indeed, with the visual medium, his desire to illustrate the effects of impairments sometimes impels him to prompt his subjects to "perform" them—to demonstrate typical behaviors. Sacks thus submits some subjects to public tests—tests they predictably fail.

As we have seen in the discussion of his interaction with Heidi, another aspect of his move to the visual medium may compensate somewhat for the first: that Sacks himself is subjected to the camera's and the viewer's gaze. He has considerable power to direct that gaze, but his control is imperfect.[25] Sacks is on screen more than any other single figure—to a degree that will strike some as excessive. To a certain extent this reflects his tendency to dominate his subjects and to occupy the foreground. But he could be almost as dominant if he confined himself to monopolizing the audio portion of each installment. And in fact, in this aural-visual medium, there is (at times) more dialogue and more intersubjectivity than in the written medium, where the subjects' voices are largely absent (at most mediated through Sacks's writing) and where the subjects are literally invisible, present only insofar as, and in the manner in which, Sacks presents them. Thus, despite the fact that most of the time the sound track carries the sound of Sacks's voice—speaking to his subjects, to experts, to the camera, or as a "voice-over"—his subjects are quite literally "heard" here in a way not possible in writing.

These six episodes or installments are quite various in their approaches and in their success. The segment on color-blindness has all the flaws of Sacks's chapter on that subject. In contrast, "The Ragin' Cajun," which has to do with hereditary deaf-blindness in a group of people of Cajun descent, is more ethnographic than his treatment of deafness in *Voices:* here he deals with a group of people whose disability is linked through genetics to their ethnicity, and thus to a cohesive community. Sacks acknowledges that the documentary focuses on a community, rather than an individual, at the insistence of its main subject, Danny Delcambre; thus, respect for the autonomy of his main subject entailed respect for that subject's community. This sort of intervention by subjects represents for me an ethical ideal. "Ragin' Cajun" is superior to *Seeing Voices* as neuroanthropology in an additional way: as a visual production, it renders the fluency and grace of sign language directly; here the audience really does see voices.

The segment on Williams syndrome illustrates the difficulty of representing disability communities, however. Much of the footage is taken at a summer camp for children and teenagers with Williams, but including large numbers of subjects is not the same as acknowledging community. The people at the camp share a syndrome, but they form only a temporary provisional community. Rather than showing us how each has adapted to his or her home community, or how this summer community might minimize their anomaly, this segment reinforces their similarities to one another—in physical and behavioral features—and their deviation from the norm. The visual medium's potential to allow a greater degree of interactivity and intersubjectivity is here offset by its tendency to type individuals and to submit them to an appraising gaze.

The most engaging segments are "Rage for Order: Autism" and "Shane: Tourette's Syndrome." The former focuses on Jessy Park, a thirty-seven-year-old artist with autism; the latter on Shane Fistell, an artist with Tourette's syndrome. In these episodes, Sacks succeeds in representing the "who" as well as the "what" in part because his concentration on one subject allows him to provide depth to his portrayal. Yet the segments differ significantly in the dynamics of the relationship between Sacks and his single subject, in large part as a function of the syndromes addressed. This variance illuminates the potential and the pitfalls of such representation. A developmental disability, autism involves deficits in social (and possibly self-) awareness; autists tend to be withdrawn and to find spontaneous interaction with others—even familiar people—threatening. In contrast, people with Tourette's tend to initiate interaction with others, even strangers, all too readily; for example, they may violate others' social space and touch them inappropriately. Whereas the scenario of filming—which involves a crew, considerable equipment, and some setting up—may be intimidating to an autist, it may be inviting to a Touretter. Thus, the films demonstrate the need for sensitivity to the relation between the medium and the condition in question. In part because of the nature of his "disorder"—and also his personality, which is inextricably bound up with it—Shane Fistell seems very much an equal partner in his collaboration with his friend "Oliver."[26] In large part because of her condition, Jessy Park cannot function as such.

Jessy was already known as Clara Park's pseudonymous daughter in

The Siege (1967), her mother's account of the first eight years of her life. (The book was reissued in 1982 with an update, and Clara Park has also published a sequel called *Exiting Nirvana*.) Once cloaked in virtual anonymity, however, Jessy Park has become, as an artist, a public figure in her own right—despite herself, in a sense. She is highly protective of her privacy, and being filmed is obviously a strain on her. The complex dynamics of the process are apparent when the director's innocent question, "What is it you are looking for?" evokes an angry retort, "Don't ask me that." This is in some ways analogous to the moment in which Heidi cries "Cut." In this case, though, Jessy does not explicitly ask for the camera to be turned off, but rather wants unwelcome questions to cease. The camera keeps rolling, the director apologizes, Clara Park intercedes soothingly, and Jessy calms down and carries on. A twist occurs when Jessy expresses her sense of shame at her outburst; according to her mother, this is the first time she has expressed embarrassment about "snapping." Sacks interprets this as evidence of her "finally maturing," and it may be. Interestingly, and perhaps ironically, the moment seems precipitated—that is, induced—by the process of filming. Although she clearly feels intruded on, such intrusions may be beneficial in unintentional ways. Such unforeseeable benefits, however, cannot be used to justify intrusion. The filming clearly takes a toll on her, and one wonders whether she has freely agreed to this and, if so, why: what benefit does she expect from it, aside from publicity for her art?

Shane Fistell is her polar opposite. Whereas she is withdrawn, shy, averse to interaction, immersed much of the time in obsessions that seem to provide her with a sort of psychic cocoon, he is aggressively, even transgressively social. Shane's disorder appears seamlessly integrated in a personal style that most people find engaging. There are exceptions, however, and Shane has a history of provoking violence in others. Indeed, one of his complaints about his representation in the documentary is that the presence of the camera protects him from such reactions and thus misrepresents him; that is, the presence of a film crew distorts his public life by legitimating his every move. (He demonstrates this by seizing a camera from a member of a French film crew on another project; the crew observe his antics with tolerance and amusement rather than alarm. Had he done so without the protection of his own trailing film crew, their response would likely have been very different.)

One senses that, far from being controlled by his involuntary impulses, Shane can use them for his own gratification. Thus, as Sacks begins to speak of him in the third person while they are sitting on a park bench, Shane suddenly inserts the donut he has been eating into Sacks's mouth, momentarily silencing him and his objectifying discourse. At another moment, Sacks comments on Shane's habit of pulling Sacks's ear; Shane responds that he does this because "it pisses you off, in lay terms." Such byplay, while genial and good-natured, also seems pointed and subversive. It combines aggression and playfulness in ways that serve Fistell's purposes more than Sacks's (which is not to say that Sacks doesn't enjoy the horseplay). His conduct demonstrates his sense of limits: he often deflects analysis when Sacks becomes intrusive or overbearing.

An interesting aspect of the visual medium is that when Shane is framed tightly, his tics sometimes carry him right out of the picture, whether intentionally or not. Sacks is at pains to demonstrate that Shane—who, like "Witty Ticcy Ray," declines to eradicate his tics with medication—can "mask" or, better, "channel" his impulses in karate. His ticcing while walking is so rhythmic and graceful—almost dancelike—that one suspects it is partly in his control at other times as well. At times, too, he will improvise with the recording apparatus, reaching out of the frame to pull the mike boom into view, even kissing it. Deliberate or not, such behavior establishes that the medium cannot contain him. Further, such exposure of the process of mediation endows this film with a postmodernist dimension. The representation of Shane appears egalitarian in part because he manages, or contrives, to exceed Sacks's analytical and interpretive matrices. In any case, unlike Jessy, Shane seems not to need anyone to protect him; he can set his own limits. (Thus, although he has a serious neurological condition, he is not made especially vulnerable by it; indeed, there are ways in which in Shane, at least, Tourette's is its own protection: the best defense is a good offense.)

One segment of the film follows Fistell through the streets of Paris, where he and Sacks visit sites associated with the initial discovery of Tourette's by the eponymous French physician. Looking at a historical painting in which Tourette watches Charcot exhibit a woman in a hysterical fit, Shane comments on the patient's posture of "surrender" and on the circus-like scene. He then muses aloud on his being exhibited and observed. Clearly, he does not see himself as entirely analogous to the passive, unconscious woman; as we have seen, his is hardly a posture of surrender. And as he says, Sacks is his friend, not his physician or therapist. And yet, he notes, Sacks is a physician and is observing him as a case, a specimen of a syndrome. His shrewd awareness of the dynamics of the process is immensely important. Indeed, one might say that his expression of it is tantamount to his filmed consent. That is, it is evidence, which we so rarely have, of the subject's understanding of what he is involved in. Someone else controls the final cut, but Shane Fistell's personality and character are such that when he is on camera, he is truly *on*.

This combination of ticcing and talking, Fistell's manifest sense of the history of representation of neurological anomaly—going back to Charcot at least, and comprising both the medical theater and the sideshow—reassures us of the fairness and mutuality of the collaboration. Transactional openness remains at best an ideal to be aspired to, but this documentary is notable for the extent to which and the way in which it gives viewers a sense of its ethical integrity and authorization. The spontaneous horseplay and mutual respect between Sacks and Fistell help to allay any concerns about exploitation. Fistell is not cowed, wowed, or overshadowed by the clever Oliver; indeed, *he* functions as a neuro-anthropologist when he points out that hostile reactions to his "improper touching"—of other people, of their automobiles—expose cultural obsessions ripe for deconstruction. He seems fully aware of himself and (mostly) at peace with his condition and its performative dimension. By the sheer force of his Tourettic motion, Shane Fistell tends to dis-encase himself. If anyone can stare back in the canned medium of televised documentary, it is he.

The Prospect of Neuroanthropology

Kathryn Hunter has referred to the "metonymic imperialism" inherent in the process by which persons become patients, their stories, cases; she acknowledges the therapeutic value of the substitution of the case for the person but notes that it can shade into the unnecessary and undesirable substitution of the disease for the person. Perhaps the major thrust in Oliver Sacks's oeuvre has been the undoing of that metonymic imperialism—the "dis-encasing" of the patient. Readers will differ on whether he has achieved that goal. Certainly, he has moved well beyond the tight constraints of his early cases, with their maintenance of the patient-physician hierarchy, to engage his subjects (people rather than patients) in fuller view of his audience (especially in film). It may be, however, that the full undoing of the metonymic imperialism of the encasement of people with neurological conditions can be accomplished only by those subjects themselves—through first-person testimony—or by those who know them more intimately than Sacks's house calls permit. Perhaps, as a physician first and foremost, Sacks cannot be expected to produce genuine biography without a trace of pathography—that is, narrative entirely free of medical perspective.

Although Sacks manages to de-pathologize neurological disorder in individual cases, the very focus on the individual tends to minimize or obscure the relation between the neurological, on the one hand, and the social and the cultural, on the other. He seems reluctant to deconstruct received notions of normality—despite his own provision of cases that cry out for it—and he seems not much interested in the ways in which disabilities (other than deafness) may have cultural value. But Sacks's ethical shortcomings as a life writer are less a matter of commission than of omission, less a matter of violating obligations than of falling short of ideals—often ideals he has developed in deviation from the standards of his own profession. Oliver Sacks should be credited with seeing and showing that the representation of neurological anomaly can take the form of ethnography rather than pathography. He has gone a considerable distance toward demonstrating what neuroanthropology might look like in practice. For example, immersion in a community of people with a neurological condition should erase or at least erode the power differential that obtains between neurologist and patient in the clinic. And neuroanthropology should study both how culture constructs neurological norms and how neurological conditions may produce distinctive cultures. A postcolonial neuroanthropology would also embrace the dialogism and self-awareness of contemporary ethnography. But perhaps Sacks has set himself an unrealizable goal; perhaps the perspectives of medicine and anthropology are so fundamentally different that the two aspects of his self-designation cannot finally be reconciled—at least by someone trained formally only in one discipline. In his best work, Sacks has pointed the way, but postcolonial neuroanthropology still awaits its exemplary theorist and practitioner.

6

Life Writing as Death Writing
Disability and Euthanography

Suicide is the paradigm of our independence from everyone else.
— JAMES HILLMAN, *Suicide and the Soul*

We may not be beyond encouraging *as rational* the self-elimination of those whom we perceive to constitute a burden to themselves and to others, and . . . this is where the risk in manipulated suicide lies.
— MARGARET PABST BATTIN, "Manipulated Suicide"

Life Writing and Euthanasia: Autonomy and Authority

WITH THE PASSAGE of its Death with Dignity statute in 1994, which survived an attempt to repeal it by referendum in 1997 and an effort by U.S. attorney general John Ashcroft to overrule it in 2002, Oregon became the first state to legalize physician-assisted suicide. Subsequently, other states, including Hawaii, have proposed similar legislation. In the United States, the public debate over the ethics of physician-assisted suicide (PAS) has been carried out in a variety of venues—in courts and legislatures as well as the mass media.[1] Of these venues, perhaps the least attended to has been life writing, and the neglect of personal accounts of euthanasia by students of life writing represents an odd omission in a field that has been very attentive to representations of trauma.[2] Narratives of euthanasia warrant close attention today because they may be, as Herbert Hendin has claimed, "the ultimate marketing technique to promote the normalization of assisted suicide and euthanasia" (49).

Most such narratives concern people of advanced years, with illnesses that cause them unremitting and presumably unmitigable pain. Readers not adamantly and unalterably opposed to suicide on religious or moral grounds may find themselves in sympathy with the plight of the ill persons and may accept their suicides as rational and ethical acts. More problematic, and hence perhaps more revealing, are accounts that deal with similar crises in the lives of young persons. Such accounts are useful not just for what they include but also for what they elide as considerations in the choice of death. In particular, they illuminate the role played by disability in the discourse of euthanasia.

What I call euthanography—narratives in which euthanasia (in any form) is considered, but not necessarily enacted—is a distinct subset of the specialized (but expanding) subgenre of narratives by suicide "survivors."[3] Richard K. Sanderson notes that survivors of unassisted suicide "may blame themselves for the death, and they may imagine, often correctly, that they are being blamed by others. Though their grief may be especially intense and prolonged, the shame attached to suicide frequently deprives them of the social support normally available to the bereaved. In short, suicide survivors generally find themselves assuming a new, enduring, and somewhat stigmatized role" (33). Survivor-narrators of assisted suicide are in a significantly different, but equally delicate, position. They are likely to be less hurt and grief-stricken, since the suicides they survive do not surprise them and do not seem directed at them. While some assistants—especially children of suicidal parents—may feel that they were manipulated into giving their assistance, they lack the obvious claim to victimhood of other suicide survivors.

Their situation may be somewhat less difficult emotionally than that of survivors of unassisted suicide, but it is more complicated, both ethically and rhetorically. As Sanderson points out, suicide is almost always a relational act in that it occurs, and acquires meaning, in a social, primarily familial context:

> Suicide, according to most clinicians, is more than a deliberate act of lethal self-destruction: It is also a *communication,* an interpersonal or "dyadic" act, a self-dramatization performed before an audience consisting of the suicide and of *other* persons, usually members of the suicide's family. . . . [T]he most noteworthy feature of narratives by suicide survivors is that they are responses not simply to an experience but to a relational act, to a communication. (35)

Assisted suicide is relational in a very different way: it is co-intentional. Considered as communication—an act of self-definition as well as of self-destruction—assisted suicide is collaboratively composed; the survivor is not so much the recipient of this communication as its co-author and co-performer. The burden of narrating such an act is to re-present it to a larger audience in such a way as to rationalize it in two senses: to make it seem reasonable and to make it seem justified. "Such books tend to be explicit defenses of 'rational suicide' or 'self-termination.' Their authors claim that the deaths they describe should not be regarded as 'suicides' in the usual sense of the term, and they do not regard themselves as 'survivors of suicide'" (Sanderson 45n6). Thus, suicide assistants' role as life writer is effectively determined by their complicity in the death they narrate.

Narratives of assisted suicide, then, tend toward apologia in a different way from narratives of unassisted suicide. Whereas the survivor of an unassisted suicide may simultaneously condemn, struggle to interpret, and seek to deflect blame for precipitating the act, the suicide assistant must defend the act, for to do otherwise is to admit having acquiesced in an unnecessary death, which would negate its status as euthanasia. At the same time, if the act seems to have been initiated or single-handedly authored by the survivor (in which case it would be what Margaret Pabst Battin calls "manipulated suicide"), a narrative of assisted suicide involves the risk that the deceased will be seen as a victim. Like the survivor of unassisted suicide, the suicide assistant must avoid at any cost seeming to have prompted or precipitated the act; but unlike the survivors of solo suicide, suicide assistants are necessarily implicated and complicit in the act. To be rhetorically compelling and ethically satisfying, euthanography must present the suicide as rational, autonomous, and uncoerced, capable of being communicated without obviously self-serving "spin." Thus, issues of autonomy and authority are crucial in euthanography, for even those who approve of "rational suicide" should be concerned that such acts are freely chosen and fairly represented.

Although euthanography does not necessarily advocate legalizing euthanasia, one way for it to make sense of an otherwise isolated and seemingly self-destructive act is to inscribe it within the larger cultural narrative of the "right-to-die movement." When euthanographers do argue for legalization, they shift blame away from those who enact and enable the suicide onto a government that criminalizes mercy killing.[4] In any case, while the survivors of assisted suicide may be spared some of the pain experienced by survivors of unassisted suicide, their narratives are perhaps equally, if differently, fraught. Their charge is less to decipher a shocking act than to de-stigmatize and justify it to an audience of strangers.

Narratives of euthanasia by those who acquiesce or assist in it come as close, perhaps, as any life writing can to realizing the trope of biography as a kind of "taking" of another's life, because they so literally recapitulate and rationalize the process by which death is chosen and brought about. (The locus classicus of this trope is a letter from Henry Adams to Henry James, in which Adams likens biography to literary homicide; the thrust of his letter is to characterize his autobiography as a preemptive taking of his own life as protection against unauthorized biography [512].) Such narratives aspire to present the ending of their subjects' lives as euthanasia in the literal sense, good (i.e., desired or desirable) death; the assistant's understandable and well-intentioned impulse is to close off doubt and second-guessing. Indeed, this is virtually a generic requirement; it is difficult to imagine an assistant suggesting that the death in question was a mistake.

And yet, as Herbert Hendin has noted, "even in cases advocates believe best illustrate the desirability of legalizing assisted suicide, there is ample room to question whether the death expressed the patient's wishes and met his or her needs. To dramatize these model cases, advocates present them in some detail—and this creates the opportunity to see the discrepancy between the theory and the practice of assisted suicide and euthanasia" (49–50). These accounts thus leave themselves open to oppositional reading—reading which suggests that the deaths depicted are not necessarily "good" deaths, despite having been chosen in good faith and after apparently rational consideration.[5] Reading between the lines does not so much tease out emotional ambivalence about the decision to die, which is all too manifest, as uncover aspects of the cases that may have played a significant role in the scripting of the death without having been explicitly considered. That is, close reading can sometimes discover ways in which the outcomes are even more overdetermined—and thus less autonomous—than they initially appear. Indeed, if, as Carolyn Ells has argued, "autonomy is attributable only to socially situated selves" (611), then the idea of self-determined death becomes inherently problematic.

Euthanography may be unpleasant to read in the best of circumstances—that is, when the reader is convinced that the death in question is a good one. Reading against the grain may be particularly uncomfortable, however, because dissenting reading is tantamount to second-guessing an elaborate defense of a painful choice. Since readers operate at a remove from the world in which a real person chose to die, however, readers are not in a position to take issue with the actual decision making; the process by which these life-or-death decisions were reached and carried out is accessible to readers only through the narrative's mediation. As readers, we know only what we are told, and we can respond only to the representation of these events—a second-order phenomenon at best.

Yet that very mediation, which insulates assistants from direct observation, also invites appraisal, since it involves the literal publication of their acts. As readers, then, we may reach different conclusions from those of the individuals represented; indeed, narratives of euthanasia, not surprisingly, may arouse strong—and conflicting—emotions in readers. Critics are justified in articulating those differences; to do so is to respond to the texts' implicit invitation to engage in the debate over euthanasia and PAS. There is, then, a subtle but significant distinction between second-guessing the actual decisions and evaluating their retrospective public representation. If a narrative offers us an account in which some crucial step or consideration is omitted in the procedure of exercising the right to die, then we can say that the text fails rhetorically. (In real life, the step may have been taken; narratives are at best incomplete.) It should be remembered, then, that my discussion concerns textual figures, not their historical counterparts. It may seem presumptuous to take issue with published accounts of such agonized decisions, but it is not invasive, and whatever presumption is entailed may be justified by the importance of the stakes for other lives whose ends are yet to be determined. Painful as it is to read and respond to, euthanography is an extreme instance of contemporary narrative as quality-of-life writing—that is, narrative that rehearses difficult bioethical questions.

Parental Narratives of Euthanasia: Ethical Conflicts and Conflicting Ethics

Two narratives published near the turn of the century present similar scenarios—of suddenly acquired severe disability in young males—with very different outcomes. The first, *Saying Goodbye to Daniel: When Death Is the Best Choice* (1995), is Juliet Cassuto Rothman's account of her son's decision to discontinue life-sustaining medical treatment after a diving accident that paralyzed him at the age of twenty-one. Rothman's book recounts the decision of a young man, with his mother's support, to end his life rather than to live with what he considered unbearable or futile suffering. The second, *Rescuing Jeffrey* (2000), is Richard Galli's account of the ten days following a diving mishap that left his teenaged son with quadriplegia. In the immediate aftermath of this devastating event, his parents determined that Jeffrey, who was not yet eighteen, should die, and they planned to have his physicians "pull the plug" as soon as they were assured that the medical staff would permit them to do so. According to his father's brief account, however, within ten days of the accident (about the time they received permission), his parents changed their minds.

The accounts of Julia Rothman and Richard Galli deviate from the exemplary scenario of assisted suicide in three ways. First, they have to do with young protagonists, men in their late teens or twenties. They are particularly poignant because, as the cliché goes, these young men (should) have their whole life ahead of them. Second, both narratives have to do with severe disability rather than terminal illness (cancer and amyotrophic lateral sclerosis being the paradigmatic illnesses in euthanasia narratives). Third, they are accounts in which parents oversee or make the crucial decision, a significant deviation from the usual generational perspective, which is that of a surviving spouse (Wertenbaker, Humphry), sibling (West), or child (Rollin, Brown). For these reasons, they cast in high relief some of the ethical issues inherent in euthanasia, assisted suicide, and life writing in extremis.

Rothman's and Galli's narratives are especially revealing if read against each other because, while the nature and the circumstances of the young men's injuries are very similar, the outcomes are diametrically opposed. Daniel Rothman and Jeffrey Galli were both injured in diving accidents. In the summer of 1992, Daniel Rothman, a Delaware resident, had completed his junior year at the University of Rochester, where he was a dean's list premedical student; he was working and living with fraternity brothers in Rochester when he incurred his injury. After being treated for a month at a local hospital, he was flown by private jet to Swedish Hospital near Denver to be stabilized in preparation for transfer to adjacent Craig Hospital for rehabilitation. A rising high school junior, Jeffrey Galli was injured, as his father sardonically notes, on Independence Day 1998, during a party at the house of family friends in his Rhode Island hometown. His parents rescued him from the bottom of the swimming pool, and he was rushed to a local hospital. Both men were diagnosed with injuries in the upper cervical area of the spinal column.

Initially, Daniel Rothman's injury was thought to be at the C4 level (he was able to breathe and talk), but he later lost function and was rediagnosed as having a C1 injury—at the very top of his spine. Jeffrey Galli's injury was located at the C1–C2 juncture, also a very high spinal cord injury.

The numerical difference between the levels of their injuries, though seemingly minor, was not trivial. Daniel's injury entailed life-threatening complications, and his condition was considerably harder to stabilize. While both were dependent on ventilators to breathe, Daniel suffered losses of ventilator pressure (a terrifying but apparently quite common occurrence), fevers, blood clots, terrible headaches, adult respiratory distress syndrome (ARDS, a result of a decrease in the elasticity of lung tissue), and a number of cardiac arrests. At the time of his decision to die, the prognosis was that he would improve little if at all and might live only a few years. Hope of returning to college in the near future, much less attending medical school, which had seemed feasible when he was first injured, now seemed unrealistic. Jeffrey Galli's condition also took a long time to stabilize, but he suffered fewer crises, and he was able to resume high school classes six months after his accident.

Whatever the relative degree of their injuries—and the vertebral level is not the only factor—it would be naïve to assume that the radical disparity between their outcomes, literally between life and death, was entirely a function of their physiological condition. Other aspects of their circumstances are also relevant—aspects that are not explicitly discussed in the narratives and that would not be focal points of standard bioethical analysis but still warrant consideration here.[6] Indeed, part of what such narratives teach us is that outcomes may be influenced or even determined by factors that the parties who make the decisions—and here narrate the cases—may not be fully aware of.

Concerning the two accident victims, gender is a constant.[7] That is not to say that it is not an issue: it is worth considering, for example, whether both sets of parents would so readily have entertained the idea of ending their child's life if that child had been female. (Both families include daughters.) Gender bias could work in two opposing ways. It might seem that in a culture that more highly values men than women, female quadriplegics would be more vulnerable to euthanasia in circumstances such as these. Yet it is also the case that in a patriarchal culture, disability may seem more at odds with masculinity, which is associated with physical strength, activity, and aggression, than with femininity, which is associated with physical weakness and passivity; to many people, the sight of a man in a wheelchair is more incongruous than that of a woman in one. Being of the dominant gender may ironically work against young men in these circumstances, in terms of both their own and others' estimates of their anticipated quality of life after becoming disabled; even today, parents may have more invested in the prospective independence and earning capacity of male children.

Class is also a constant. Both the Gallis and the Rothmans are upper-middle-class families of considerable means. (And, significantly, both are intact nuclear families.) Both families seem to have adequate insurance, and economic considerations appear not to have figured into their considerations of their son's fate; thus, there does not seem to have been pressure on either family to decide in favor of death to avoid devastating expenses. Indeed, both families were prepared to assume responsibility for having their son live at home indefinitely, if necessary. Thus, in terms of socioeconomic status, at least, these are "best-case" scenarios: both families appear willing and able to bear the economic and emotional costs of caring for their son. At the same time, the characteristics of both families are consistent with those of advocates of the right to die (or "death with dignity"), as determined by a sociological analysis. In addition to being white, well educated, and upper middle class, such people often have "a need to respond to powerful symbolic changes in their everyday environments that called their previous identity into question" (Fox, Kamakahi, and Čapek 67). Imminent death and/or severe disability may be especially threatening for people used to controlling their own destiny, and suicide may be especially appealing as literally the ultimate act of self-determination.

If we bracket differences between the injuries of the young men, and if gender and class are constants, we may look elsewhere to explain their different fates. This brings us to the parental accounts of the decision in favor of death. One striking thing about euthanography is that it rarely deploys in any sustained way the standard ethical discourse of euthanasia and assisted suicide. Granted, there are moments in both *Daniel* and *Jeffrey* in which ethical issues are addressed explicitly. Galli is a lawyer, and *Jeffrey* includes a chapter in which Galli makes the case to the hospital ethics committee for his right to end his son's life. Juliet Cassuto Rothman is a social worker trained in ethics, and her book shows it. But both books tend to make their case for death more implicitly, by force of narrative, than explicitly, by force of argument. Both authors *assume* the right to die and the rightness of euthanasia when existence becomes unbearable. Both also *assume* that the conditions they describe are self-evidently worse than death. Thus they emphasize a procedural ethic—one concerned with how, and by whom, a decision is made—over a substantive ethic, that is, one concerned with what is decided, from a normative perspective (Campbell 57). At the forefront are the means (how to bring about death in the most expeditious and merciful manner) rather than the ends (whether death really is the best choice).

Readers may agree with the proposition that—in theory, at least—individuals have the right to determine their own fate, yet still believe that they are making a wrong, or at least premature, decision. Thus, although the narratives' conclusions—in two senses, narrative and "logical"—are both predetermined and overdetermined, readers may resist them. This suggests that such narratives, though immensely useful, indeed indispensable, for reflection on this issue—because they are the most detailed and articulate accounts of assisted suicide—may fail rhetorically. In their very attempts to impel readers to a particular conclusion, they may sow doubts about the choices represented. Despite their powerful impulse to justify certain courses of action, then, they may serve as mirrors in which readers discover reflections of their own images and values. Indeed, it may be the narratives' very overdetermination that creates an aporia for the reader. Even as they empathize with the ordeal of parents such as the Rothmans and the Gallis, readers may resist going where the narratives want to take them.

Juliet Rothman's narrative is particularly uncomfortable to resist because she is so single-mindedly devoted to taking care of her son and so scrupulous about his life-or-death decision. The process of reaching that decision begins with Daniel's announcement to his sister, while he is still in the intensive-care unit in Rochester, that he wishes to die; this message is relayed by a nurse to a doctor, who passes it along to Juliet Rothman with his endorsement. At this point, very soon after the accident, she responds primarily as a mother in terms of an ethics of care. According to Thomas A. Mappes and David DeGrazia, such an ethics "pays considerable attention to affective components of the moral life, but with special emphasis on empathy and concern for the needs of others—that is, on caring. . . . [I]t emphasizes the particularities and context of moral judgment and rejects impartiality as an essential feature of morality. The ethics of care also underscores the moral importance of relationships and the responsibilities to which they give rise" (39).

In contrast to the physician, Juliet Rothman considers it her responsibility to keep Daniel alive and well; at this point, she wants above all to save her son. She argues vehemently against the doctor's assessment that her son would be better off dead, and especially his assumption that a decision to die could be made so soon:

> "How can you say that? . . . You have no right. Just because *you* would want to die if you were a quadriplegic doesn't mean Daniel should. Lots of quads leave very fulfilling lives. He says this now, but he hasn't had any rehab. He hasn't tried. He doesn't even know what his function level will be, finally. He doesn't know how he'll feel off the ventilator, and everyone says he'll get off it."
> "I just can't imagine how he could want to live."
> "*You* don't have to imagine. *He* does. And he doesn't have the knowledge out of which to make a decision. He doesn't know what's out there. You could never tell me that, at this point, Daniel could give informed consent. He's not informed. And he's here, in this ICU. He's on medications. He has no idea what his potential is, now." (64)

It is one thing for Daniel, in his circumstances, to express a wish to die; as Herbert Hendin reminds us, "panic and a wish for immediate death are often patients' responses to learning they have a serious or terminal illness" (151)—or, I would add, disability. It is another for his physician to endorse that wish so soon after his accident. Although Daniel's mother is quick to parry the physician's suggestion, she cannot undo the fact that he has communicated a powerful message: in his professional opinion, Daniel's life is not worth saving. As expressed here retroactively, however, her impulse to protect her son and ensure his survival also invokes procedural and substantive ethics. The procedural ethic is evident both in her reference to Daniel's will as decisive and in her assertion that he cannot give valid consent because he is not fully informed and because of his powerful medications.[8] (The invocation of the procedural ethic may also impress on the physician a sense of his liability should Daniel be allowed to make a life-or-death decision when he is arguably incompetent.) She thus introduces, implicitly, the principle of autonomy, according to which Daniel has the right to determine the course of his own treatment. When he can be judged competent, however, she promises to honor his preference regardless of her own.

The rest of her speech concerns the substance, rather than the procedure, of the choice: whether Daniel should live as a quadriplegic or die to avoid that fate. Significantly, however, her initial preference for life over death is qualified by her references to Daniel's potential when he gets "off the ventilator"—which, unfortunately, he never does (until it is disconnected in order to let him die). She tells the doctor and Daniel that if her son reiterates his wish to die after he learns what can be accomplished through rehabilitation at Craig Hospital, she will support him. Daniel accepts this. The narrative thus invokes, though it does not systematically deploy, the cardinal concepts of bioethics. At this point her concern for her son's well-being (beneficence) is in conflict with respect for his autonomy; that is, in order to override his (to her) premature desire to die, she denies his autonomy—or, rather, negotiates a deferral of his exercise of it until it would be meaningful. And she defends against the physician's assessment by invoking, though not by name, the principle of non-maleficence. Her approach at this point is eclectic and opportunistic. She is driven mainly by an ethics of care, but she articulates it in terms of ethical principles Daniel's physician can understand and is obliged to respect. (Thus, the formal discourse of euthanasia may be at once pertinent and ultimately beside the point; her goals seem to determine her ethical arguments, rather than vice versa.)

This episode characterizes Juliet Rothman as an advocate for her son (in terms of the procedural ethic) and as a believer in the possibility of meaningful life with disability (in terms of substantive ethics). Although a decision is postponed, however, the terms are established in such a way that the substantive ethic and the procedural ethic, which early on both favor life, may not always point to the same conclusion. The implication is that if Daniel cannot live without the ventilator, he may—indeed, would—be justified in choosing to die, once judged competent. As it happened, Daniel never got the chance to see what Craig Hospital could do for him or what life might be like off a ventilator.[9] The turning point comes when the Rothmans are informed that Daniel's chances of surviving ARDS are a mere 30 percent. Summoned to Denver, Leonard Rothman, a physician, elicits a dire prognosis articulated as a list of things Daniel will never be able to do: breathe on his own, speak, eat or drink, move anything but his eyes and mouth (120). It is then that they are told that Daniel might live only a few years, and those in poor condition because of complications from his injury. Once his mother acknowledges that he will never recover the function he lost in the first weeks after his accident, her assessment is bleak: "All there was ahead, for Daniel, was pain, and mental torture, and total dependence. He was marking time, until his death somewhere in the next three years, or a little beyond that" (121).

Daniel Rothman's parents had hoped that Swedish Hospital would be able to reduce his level of dependency—a word that recurs regularly in the discussions of Daniel's future. After this pessimistic prognosis, Juliet Rothman's maternal impulse is to let her son go: better death, she thinks, than living "like that," a "death-in-life." Indeed, she now assumes the position of the Gallis, that her son should be not only "allowed to die" but also spared the pain of making the decision himself. She thus reverses position in terms of both substantive and procedural ethics; now she opts *for* death but *against* Daniel's being informed of his condition or permitted—or, as she sees it, forced—to choose his fate. She proposes to his psychologist and to his doctor that he be removed from life support without his consent: "I *know* that he wouldn't want to do this" (122). That is, she nominates herself as his surrogate.

Unlike Jeffrey Galli, however, Daniel is legally an adult, and the doctor correctly insists that any request to discontinue treatment must come from him. There follows a conference involving Daniel's father, mother, and most of his physicians and caregivers—but not Daniel—to decide what to do next. At this conference, Juliet Rothman reports, "I repeated my request to the roomful of people: that Daniel be informed [of his condition and his right to die], and that choices be offered to him. Crying, I begged that he be spared this choice, and that we, his parents, be allowed to make it for him. I could not bear to consider the pain that knowledge of his condition, and the choices ahead, would give to my beloved child, my son, my baby" (126). Thus, like the Gallis, the Rothmans seek the authority to make the life-or-death decision, which they would decide in favor of death. Although she seems to have come around to the position of Daniel's physician in Rochester that Daniel would be better off dead, her language—"my son, my baby"—suggests that she is still responding primarily as a mother. At this point, then, the ethics of care has eclipsed the ethics of justice (of abstract principles, impartially applied); the mother's beneficent impulse—to do the best for her son—has overridden both the principle of doing no harm and the principle of respect for his autonomy.

Despite her plea, the parents are not permitted to act as surrogates: rather, a physician and a psychologist inform Daniel of his present condition and prognosis, and his parents inform him of his options. His mother, who has been the prime caregiver all along, takes the lead, while her husband sits "in a chair in the corner, offering silent comfort" (128).

This passage is at once intensely emotional—because of the delicacy of the subject—and introspective. As she prepares to speak, Juliet Rothman comes to believe that her personal and professional roles are no longer in conflict. As a mother, she desires the best for Daniel (which is now his death); as a social worker, however (but also, she now sees, as a mother), she needs to grant him the autonomy to make the most important—and last—decision of his short life. She must neither resist his impulse to die, as she had done earlier in Rochester, nor reinforce it: "I was afraid of influencing him in any way" (128).

Daniel opens the dialogue by silently mouthing what his doctors had told him: "My level [of injury] is very high and I won't be getting better." His mother then confesses that she had known this for two days but had kept it a secret, breaking a promise to be candid with him. (Her confession that she delayed telling him the truth about his condition implies, of course, an estimation of his prognosis—that she views it as unbearable.) She adds that "there's just another piece that [he] need[s] to know," that he may choose his own fate: he may choose to go through rehab at Craig and then live on his own or at home, or he may choose to refuse further treatment and die. These options are asymmetrical: one choice is indeterminate, the other certain. To choose life is to choose uncertainty and lack of control; to choose death is to choose self-determination and control over one's future.

Daniel seems genuinely surprised to learn that he can simply refuse treatment; assured that this is true, he does not hesitate to choose to have his ventilator turned off. His mother tells him he needs to think the decision through; he replies he has already done that: "That's why all I do is watch TV. I want out." This remark may be taken at face value: I have thought about my future for a long time and am firm in my decision now that I know it is up to me. But as his mother had argued in Rochester and recognized again at Swedish Hospital, medications can compromise competence; Daniel had been continuously medicated until the day before the conference, when his pain medications were discontinued in order to clear his head in preparation for the day of decision. There is some question as to whether one day off medication is enough to endow him with meaningful competence; another question is whether, weaned suddenly from pain medications, he might be unduly influenced by unaccustomed discomfort. Further, although he has been living with his condition for a couple of months, he has only just been given a grim prognosis. What the text presents him as doing, then, is not weighing his options anew but reinforcing an earlier impulse made when he was heavily medicated, exercising his new procedural right without reconsidering the substance of the choice. My point is that, despite her scruples, Daniel's mother cannot present this decision to him, much less re-present it to us, as an entirely symmetrical one. Under these circumstances, to give Daniel liberty is to give him death; his decision is a foregone conclusion. For all the attention to the principle of autonomy, achieving it may be elusive, if not illusory.

There is other textual evidence that casts doubt on whether this decision is completely rational and autonomous. That Daniel's room is by his order barren of cards or other "reminders of his past life" (125) suggests that he is depressed, or at least has willfully isolated himself from sources of emotional support. Similarly, when he is rolled over to Craig Hospital to spend time in the gym—despite the fact that there is nothing he can really do there—he insists on being positioned in front of a fish tank, where he can watch the fish rather than the humans around him. His preference suggests a deep alienation from his fellow patients and from his condition—not denial so much as revulsion. He apparently cannot bear to see others engaged in rehabilitation, either because they are more capable than he or because their incapacity reminds him of his own. Yet no one seems to address these feelings. (We are told he has a psychologist, as does his mother, but we are not told what goes on between them.)

This is not to fault Daniel for his choice, nor his parents for letting him make it, but to point out that as carefully as this narrative is calculated to reinforce what is, after all, its foreordained end, it admits considerable evidence that Daniel may have reached a less than well considered decision under less than optimal conditions; at least, at the narrative moment of truth, it appears that the crucial decision had long since been made. All the attention to procedural ethics, then, may be beside the point. (And this suggests that while such concerns are important, they can carry us only so far toward determination of what is right in given circumstances.) In any case, the rhetorical effect is not always consistent with the author's apparent intentions. Daniel is granted autonomy, but his choice may have been influenced by all sorts of factors that may have tilted his decision toward death. Whether he has had adequate time and opportunity to adjust to his radically new condition and to revise his life expectations accordingly is, to my mind, an open question.

Daniel and his parents may not have reached the point at which they can contemplate his being, disabled, as distinct from his being disabled.

All parties might have benefitted from a moratorium during which to adjust their self-images and self-narratives to radically new circumstances. By suggesting that euthanasia may fall short of full justification even in these apparently best-case circumstances, I do not mean to suggest that it is always wrong—or even wrong in this instance. I mean only to suggest that even narratives like this one, which set out to justify a decision, may leave haunting doubts in the minds of sympathetic readers. To say this is to suggest also that such narratives may implicitly admit what they explicitly deny: that their authors are also haunted by their decision.

∽

The trajectory of *Rescuing Jeffrey* is directly opposed to that of *Saying Goodbye to Daniel:* the initial parental determination is that Jeffrey is so severely injured that he should not be allowed to survive, but in the end he is permitted to do so. Indeed, an odd feature of *Rescuing Jeffrey* is that so much of it makes the case for Jeffrey's death despite the narrative's ultimate turn toward life. To the extent that the book engages the debate over euthanasia—and it does, despite its author's disclaimer that it is entirely apolitical—the book's *overt* discourse is entirely in favor of nonvoluntary passive euthanasia (in the case of a minor); literally at the center of the book, in a section called "The Ethics Committee," Richard Galli makes the case that he and his wife should be allowed to determine their son's fate, without his consent or his knowledge. As narrative, however, the book contradicts the argument it contains and re-presents: without explicitly acknowledging that their original impulse was wrong or fully explaining how their minds were changed, the Gallis ultimately choose to let Jeffrey live.

One of the book's most interesting features is the very ambiguity about what changed the outcome. One factor, significantly, seems to have been a change in Jeffrey's outlook. This is hinted at in a passing, but telling, remark his father makes to the hospital ethics committee: "He may surprise me. He may be turning into a different Jeffrey than the one I knew" (107). That is, his son may be becoming a young man who will want to live with what seems to his father an intolerable disability. And as it happened, whereas early on Jeffrey expressed a desire to die, he began to show signs—not always stated—of interest in living: "This new Jeff wanted to wake up in the morning" (150).

Significantly, too, even as Richard and Toby Galli plot (i.e., plan) to kill their son, they encourage him to live; thus, there is a striking difference, even contradiction, between what his father says to him about his present condition and his future, on the one hand, and what he thinks about them and says about them to the reader, on the other. His father tells Jeffrey that he resides not in his limbs, which are paralyzed, but in his mind, which is intact: "Jeffrey is up here. . .and that means you are still here, all of you" (44). At the same time, noting that paralysis has deprived his modest son of personal privacy, Galli observes to the reader: "Jeffrey's modesty lived inside Jeffrey above the C1–C2 level. Jeffrey's modesty was an incidental casualty of the other losses. Jeffrey was suffering losses of personality. . . . Even in his mind, above the broken neck, Jeffrey was taking losses. The stuff that made Jeffrey our singular, unique, familiar son . . . that stuff was leaking" (94). His father, then, struggles with the paradox that Jeffrey both is still and is no longer the son he had known.

A litigator and former journalist, Richard Galli is alert to issues of procedure, and he takes quite an aggressive stance in his role as Jeffrey's advocate. Since Jeffrey was a few months shy of eighteen at the time of his injury, he had no legal right to self-determination (despite being of sound mind). His lack of competence is entirely a legal artifact, a function of his chronological age rather than of his maturity—he was autonomous in capacity though not in condition—but his parents choose to stand on this distinction. Yet Richard Galli acknowledges being troubled by the irony of his stance as his son's advocate:

> I was being an advocate. . . . As a lawyer, I did that for a living. But out there where I learned my skills, I always asked my clients what they wanted before advocating the position to which they would be bound. In that hospital room, I was advocating a position that my son might never learn about. . . .
> I was being an advocate, all right. But out there in the real world, a defendant's lawyer doesn't argue for the death penalty. (59–60)

The gendering of the narratives may be pertinent here. Whereas in *Daniel* the primary caregiver and narrator is Daniel's mother, in *Jeffrey* the dominant parent and narrator is his father. Jeffrey's mother, Toby, has a more prominent role in the narrative, as partner in decision making, than Leonard Rothman does in *Daniel*, but in tenor *Jeffrey* is a very masculine narrative. Galli's response to Jeffrey's pediatrician, who says that the boy's parents "can't" terminate his life, is a blunt insistence on parental prerogative: "Of course we can . . . Jeffrey is a minor, we are his parents. The hospital's policy—which is posted on the walls—is that any patient can refuse medical treatment. We are the people who make that decision" (22). What drives the Gallis' decision is their desire to spare Jeffrey from having to choose his own death. At first they believe that a decision has to be made before his upcoming eighteenth birthday. As Richard Galli puts it to his wife, "We have to do whatever is best for Jeffrey. . . . I am saying we may have to kill our son" (22). From their point of view, both substantive and procedural ethics militate in favor of an early death for Jeffrey: death is best, they are sure, and it must occur before Jeffrey reaches the age of consent, when the responsibility for the decision will fall on him—which, as with Daniel, his parents consider an unbearable responsibility.

A revealing moment occurs when Jeffrey's pediatrician suggests that the choice should be Jeffrey's. Richard Galli asks if he would say the same thing if he knew that Jeffrey would choose death: "Dr. Bodner had nothing to say in response. Because we both knew that in his mind, and in the minds of many others, the authority to make the decision shifted according to the outcome chosen. The authority shifted to whoever chose life instead of death" (87). That is, from the medical profession's point of view, the procedural issue (who made the choice) is eclipsed by the substantive issue (that it should be for survival). As an advocate for his son, then, Galli uses his legal skills in a struggle for control against the prevailing medical ethic.

In cases of incompetent patients, a surrogate is permitted to make decisions. The preferred surrogate is usually a family member, and the first principle invoked in such cases is that of "substituted judgment," according to which the surrogate tries to decide "as the patient would have decided if he or she were competent" (Brock 338). In the case of minors, parents are generally considered capable of exercising "substituted judgment" on the basis of their familiarity with the patient. As with Daniel Rothman, the rationale for Jeffrey's death invokes his physicality and revulsion for dependence. Thus, Richard Galli says to his wife:

Jeffrey didn't live in his mind. . . . He needs to move. He needs to do things. . . . [F]or the rest of his life, he will be nothing but a head and neck, sitting in a wheelchair. Is that a future Jeffrey would want us to build for him? Would he choose that life?

He will never be able to run or walk. He will never be able to use his hands. He will never be able to move under his own power. He will be dependent on others for practically everything he needs or wants to do for the rest of his life. (33–34)

Richard Galli prides himself on his courtroom skills, and he seems to enjoy making the case for paternalism to those who might stand in his way. At the same time, however, he includes in the narrative soul-searching private dialogues with his wife over what is best for Jeffrey and for the family as a whole; he agonizes, too, over whether personal interest or selfishness might influence their decision. So there are at least four levels of ethical discourse here: the first between parents and son, the second between husband and wife, the third between parents and professionals, and the fourth between author and readers. (The discourse between father and son is ethical in substance, in that it concerns Jeffrey's quality of life; it is perhaps unethical procedurally in its exclusion of him from the decision-making process.) But while there is considerable discussion of principles and motives, of who might benefit and how from either choice, what goes essentially unquestioned is the proposition that quadriplegia is a fate worse than death. Galli declares to his wife: "I try to believe that helping Jeffrey live is the right thing to do, but I can't believe it. If I were in his position, I know what I would want him to do for me. And I know I should do the same thing for him. I'm sure of it" (36–37). At times, Galli seems to operate on the principle of substituted judgment, but here he seems to be projecting his own desires onto his son—that is, substituting his own judgment for his son's.

The decision is rationalized at other times by an intuitive utilitarian calculus of the cost of his disability to Jeffrey: "I still believed that the pain of Jeff's diminishment exceeded the value of living the lesser life of a quadriplegic" (167). Galli's admission elsewhere that he considers an alternative scenario—seeking Jeffrey's consent to kill him (and promising to kill himself, if necessary, in a sort of euthanasia-suicide pact [78])—is further evidence of his desperate casting about for ways to justify what he sees as the inevitable and proper denouement of this episode. And yet, although his parents decide, after an hour's discussion on the second day after his accident, to end Jeffrey's life unless his condition improves, the proliferation of distinct arguments for this decision can be read as suggesting not their moral conviction but their qualms. (And Galli's suicidal impulse may suggest the force of unarticulated yet clearly anticipated guilt—his sense that he would deserve capital punishment for filicide.)

When the Gallis eventually reverse course, the shift is somewhat anti-climactic; indeed, there is no clear moment of anagnorisis and reversal. The crucial shift is less a decision, which suggests conscious choice, than a surrender—not to resistance from physicians or hospital staff, although there is some of that, but to what Galli refers to as "the wave" or "the river," a groundswell of sentiment for Jeffrey's survival among family, friends, acquaintances. Ultimately, although the Gallis continue to maintain their right to end Jeffrey's life, they choose not to exercise that right. They never renounce their procedural ethic, but they defer exercising their prerogative as surrogates until somehow Jeffrey's death no longer seems the right choice. (They defer the decision in part because a physician assures them that should Jeffrey choose to die after he comes of age, there are facilities that would accept him as a patient and honor his request to remove his ventilator [121, 177].) As Jeffrey weathers some crises, and as support from others buoys his parents up, they find themselves swept along by unfolding events. Thus, they opt finally in favor of the uncertainty of Jeffrey's survival over the certainty of his death. Only after he shows signs of wanting to live, however, do they decide that the decision ultimately will be his.

Galli's prose is notably terse and sardonic; his style embodies as well as expresses the tough-mindedness of his lawyerly analysis of the problem and his adversarial take-charge approach. For example, when former colleagues solicit contributions for Jeffrey's care, Richard Galli insists that they keep careful records, not so he can thank contributors later but so he can return their contributions after Jeffrey dies. He imagines sending back the contributions with a note: "Thanks, but we killed our kid" (144). He's good at argument, and seems to take pleasure in vanquishing objections. In sharp contrast to the father's straight-talking, euphemism-eschewing persona (and its implied ethos) are the tone and content of excerpts from sympathy notes distributed throughout the book. (All chapters and many sections within chapters begin with these brief excerpts, apparently quoted verbatim and attributed to their real authors.) The Gallis' friends are educated, thoughtful people, and their notes are sensitive and supportive. Yet, like much writing done in such circumstances, their prose is often banal, and in their optimism and hopefulness they sometimes seem out of touch with the reality that Galli is unflinchingly describing to the reader. For much of the narrative, then, the contrast between their prose and his seems to be at the expense of the note writers; the father's prose seems to expose the vapidity of the outsiders'.

In the end, however, the narrative's resolution in favor of life with disability effects a reevaluation of the book's voices—the constant controlling voice of the father in one register and the intermittent voices of friends and relatives in another. Retrospectively, at least, the background voices function as a wise chorus, encouraging without insisting, supporting without judging, wishing for the best without denying the worst. In the end, their voices do not merely complement but counter Richard Galli's, and Jeffrey lives. The take-charge father, used to arguing cases in court, acknowledges that this decision is not, in the end, his to make alone. The son who is initially rescued by his father from drowning, and whom his father subsequently intends to rescue from a fate worse than death, is in a sense rescued from his father when the parents' initial decision is overridden by a collective will.

One senses—or perhaps wishes, because one cannot be sure—that this is what the father wanted all along, that his express desire for his son's death was merely a function of a parental wish to spare him further pain. In any case, the book as a whole affirms Jeffrey's survival, even as it restates counterarguments to that outcome. The expression of those arguments may function as a public confession and expiation of Galli's lack of faith. At the same time, he readily acknowledges his own emotional vulnerability during this crisis; alternating with moments of apparently steely self-control are moments in which he wails and blubbers in the arms of his wife: "Any stranger passing by would have heard me and would have marveled at how tenderly that striking woman was managing that hysterical old man" (36). The book's most radical implication may be that Richard Galli's seemingly unsentimental approach to this crisis is a front for (or form of) male hysteria.[10]

One could argue that, in the end, Galli's most powerful impulse is fatherly, not lawyerly, and thus reflects, like Juliet Rothman's first and last impulses, an ethics of care. It would be a mistake, then, to associate Richard Galli with a "masculine" ethics of justice and Juliet Rothman with a "feminine" ethics of care. As a lawyer, Richard Galli is attuned to concerns of "justice" and procedure, but as a parent, like Juliet Rothman, he believes at one point that both the ethics of care and the ethics of justice favor death. He sees his decision to kill his son as entirely congruent with his initial impulse to rescue him from drowning; as a father, he rescues him from apparent death and then he seeks to rescue him from an unlivable life. Like Juliet Rothman, he sees his relational ethic as pitted against a biomedical ethic that would reflexively endorse the application of technology to support life, regardless of its quality or the personality of the patient. Once his son is hospitalized, he thinks: "They had to keep him alive; that was their job. I had to be his dad; that was my job. . . . I began to wonder, Can I help them keep him alive and still be his dad? Can I do both of these things?" (11)

Ultimately—and perhaps this is the point—Richard Galli cannot entirely explain how and why his son survives, that is, is allowed to live despite his severe disability. His survival is not attributable to dramatic improvement in his physical condition. Nor does it seem to represent his parents' granting agency to Jeffrey—granting him the competence that he lacks legally. It seems rather to represent a reestimation of what is best for him or what they think he would want; that is, his condition has not so much changed as it has been reevaluated. The quality of his anticipated disabled life has been recalculated by his parents in part in response to the value that Jeffrey and others put on it. The narrative functions, ironically, to discover and affirm quality of life where it had initially been denied.

Parental Narratives of Euthanasia:
Contexts and Outcomes

For all their seeming engagement (by virtue of their topics) with the public debate over euthanasia, neither Rothman's nor Galli's book presents its life-or-death decision primarily in the terms of that debate. Neither one explicitly addresses the larger issues, much less generalizes its lessons; both seek to distance themselves from "causes" (which may be evidence of awareness of their controversiality). Richard Galli makes this disclaimer in his prologue: "Because the story is told primarily from my private thoughts and memories, it is nothing more than a glimpse of one father coping with the ruination of one son. The story is neither universal nor emblematic. It is not political and it may not be instructional. It is just a story" (1–2). He reiterates this claim toward the end: "This tragedy had been delivered to us by chance, not politics. The accident had no agenda. For Toby and me, Jeff was the only agenda. Jeffrey was not a flag bearer for any point of view. He represented no constituency: not handicap rights, not social or medical policy, not religion. I refused to position Jeffrey into someone else's context" (165). One might think that Galli's speech to the ethics committee would address the substance of the decision—whether Jeffrey should live or die—but it does not do so directly. Rather than making the case for his death, it asserts his parents' right and their qualifications to make the decision: only if the board regards the Gallis as responsible and caring parents will it permit them to exercise life-or-death power over Jeffrey. Thus, the presentation is ultimately more about "ethos" and procedural ethics than about substantive ethics.

But despite disclaimers, both books must be regarded as in some sense political. If, as feminists argue, the personal is political, and if, as postmodern theorists insist, the denial of ideology is itself an ideological position, then both books are in some degree both political and ideological, whether overtly or not. And I would argue that while neither book adequately justifies its outcome, they, and narratives like them, are for that very reason a helpful supplement to the ongoing debate about euthanasia. If the authors themselves do not, and perhaps cannot, fully account for their narratives' strikingly different outcomes, we may mine the texts for the "absent but implicit," the factors not factored in, features that may have affected the decisions and that may affect other such choices without being consciously considered. For it is the nature of such narratives to evince issues that elude consideration by their authors. The conventional discourse of "rights"—including the right to die—locates autonomy in an atomistic individual, minimizing or denying the relational, and occluding the context in which life decisions are in fact made. Narratives of euthanasia can be instructive, however, precisely because they afford an opportunity to examine the act in context rather than to contemplate it in the abstract. In this section, then, I propose to tease out some differences that may play an unacknowledged role in the decisions regarding Daniel and Jeffrey (or in similar scenarios).

One such concern may be the matter of parents' expectations for their offspring. In this regard the scenarios exhibit significant differences. At twenty-one, the youngest (and only male) of three children, Daniel had left the parental nest for college; had he survived, his disability would have returned him to his parents' care (that is, if it allowed him to live at home, which was far from certain). In contrast, at seventeen, the elder of two siblings, Jeffrey was still very much in his parents' care; having him at home would be a restoration, not a reversal, of previous living arrangements. Both sets of parents seem to have had high expectations for their sons in terms of achievement, but the four-year difference in age may be significant: the Rothmans may have had more invested in a specific life course for Daniel, a college junior, than the Gallis did for Jeffrey, a high school junior. At the time of his accident, Jeffrey Galli was less far along in shaping his life choices than Daniel Rothman, who was pointed toward his father's profession, medicine.[11] Perhaps more important, Jeffrey had been performing poorly in high school in the years immediately preceding his accident. After a period of withdrawal and dysfunction, he had been diagnosed and treated for depression, and his attitude and performance had begun to improve. Indeed, one of the ironies of his accident, by his father's account, is that his presence at the July Fourth party at which he nearly drowned was a sign of his recovery; at this point, the Gallis were grateful merely for the revival of his interest in other people.

His accident was an ironic reversal but not as severe a disruption of a projected filial trajectory as Daniel Rothman's. Although both young men considered themselves responsible for their own injuries, it may be significant that Jeffrey's first response when seeing his parents was to ask what happened, whereas Daniel's first remark to his father after his accident was "I messed up, Dad. . . . I really messed up" (13). The implication is that he feels responsible not just for screwing up his life but also for disappointing his father. In any case, a full consideration of a son's decision whether to live or die might take into account the implications of his disability with regard to his past and his projected future within the developing family narrative. For all the justified concern with autonomy in the crucial decision, disability is something that happens to families, not just to individuals; its consequences and costs are shared, not borne solely by the disabled person.

One concern about the competence of people who suffer catastrophic injuries like those of Daniel and Jeffrey is that acute depression, which is common in such circumstances, may cloud their judgment. A clinically depressed patient would clearly not be considered competent; a more difficult question is whether "a depressed state of mind that is serious but does not render a patient incompetent" should militate against a decision to die (Beauchamp and Childress 148). Is a quadriplegic's wish to die a function of an irrational state of mind, or is it a rational response to an insupportable condition, a realistic assessment of the likely quality of his or her life? (This is to ignore for the moment the crucial issue of how much that quality of life is determined by physiological deficit and how much by social and cultural conditions.) This is an especially problematic question because those in a position to evaluate such wishes are rarely disabled and may view severe disability as a fate worse than death: witness Daniel Rothman's physician in Rochester. In fact, however, most people who live with severe disability (especially those disabled from birth) rate the quality of their lives higher than the general population. This helps to explain why "no group is more justifiably concerned about legalization [of PAS] than people with disabilities. . . . [I]f assisted suicide and euthanasia are given legal sanction, disabled persons are, in disproportionate numbers, likely to be seen as appropriate candidates" (Hendin 212).

It may seem counterintuitive that Jeffrey, the depressive son, lives while Daniel dies. But perhaps Jeffrey's survival was influenced in part by his parents' familiarity with depression, their understanding of the way in which it can skew judgment of one's circumstances. In any case, one family has recognized and addressed depression as a treatable medical condition; the other has not. Whatever their actual circumstances— and readers are not in a position to diagnose either young man (or his parents, for that matter) as depressed—it is noteworthy that both narratives minimize consideration of the young men's states of mind. Behaviors that seem symptomatic of depression—withdrawal, refusal of visitors, and the like—might raise some questions as to competence, but in neither narrative is this much explored. No one would deny, I think, that the objective circumstances of both young men are grim. But the narratives' failure to consider that depression (on anyone's part) may play a decisive role is worrisome. (In the Gallis' case, of course, Jeffrey's competence is not at issue, since he is not making the decision; but his state of mind is relevant in that parents might be more inclined to end the life of a son who displayed little desire to live.) Although depression does not play an explicit role in either case, the Galli family might be described as having been inoculated, if not immunized, against it in the sense that they had reckoned with it already.

Herbert Hendin warns that "in their depression, their ambivalence about dying, and their need to test the affection of others, medically ill patients who request assisted suicide are not different from patients who become suicidal for other reasons. . . . Most are looking for a response that indicates that their fears will be addressed, that their pain will be relieved, and that they will not be abandoned" (159). It should be obvious, though it is easily overlooked, that it is not only individuals suddenly stricken by disease or disability but also their families who may experience shock, depression, or despair immediately after catastrophic illness or injury. Also relevant is the family's acquisition of the "courtesy stigma" that extends to those closest to individuals whose identities are "spoiled" by disability (Goffman 30–31).[12]

Hendin suggests that the outcome in crises like these is often determined by those closest to the patient, in particular by whether they respond to the undercurrent of ambivalence in the expression of a wish to
die or only to its overt content (185). So the mental state of the immediate
family and prospective caregivers also needs to be considered. All parties
need a period in which to adjust their sense of the future to new realities.
What Hendin says about terminal illness is also applicable to severe disability, which may seem to offer no relief short of death: "Watching someone die can be intolerably painful for those who care for the patient. Their
wish to have it over with can become a form of pressure on the patient
that must be distinguished from the patient's own wants" (57). That wish,
of course, need not be expressed—or even conscious—to be communicated effectively to the diseased or disabled person.

Another factor may have been decisive, though it may seem adventi-
tious and insignificant: Jeffrey Galli was injured and hospitalized close to
home, while Daniel Rothman was injured and hospitalized far from
home. Although friends seem to have rallied around both families initially, support was more intense, immediate (in both senses), and sustained in the Gallis' case. Once Daniel Rothman was hospitalized near
Denver, it was difficult and expensive for friends and family to visit with
any frequency, regularity, or duration. In contrast, Richard Galli speaks of
the constant, at times even claustrophobic, presence of close friends and
family in the ICU waiting room and the logistical and emotional support
of others outside his immediate circle of friends and acquaintances—the
irresistible wave. As Daniel's stay in Swedish Hospital stretched on from
summer into fall, his mother canceled her classes and dropped other professional obligations to stay on with him while her husband maintained
his medical practice. She was thus isolated from the direct support of family and friends in a way that the Gallis were not; she became, in effect,
Daniel's sole companion, interpreter, advocate, and lifeline. (Unable to
speak aloud, he communicated by mouthing words.)

The importance to the injured person of having family present and to
the nearest relative of having other support nearby is evident when Juliet
Rothman returns home to Delaware for a few days to settle affairs. At this
point she is considering commuting from Denver to her job, but when she
returns to Daniel's bedside, she finds that his condition has deteriorated
during her brief absence, and she resolves to be with him for the duration. Although she does not complain, the effect of this arrangement is to
raise the price she pays for his hospitalization: his confinement effectively

sequesters her as well. The more she mothers him, the less time she has for herself; it seems that she can have a son or have a life. (She selflessly gives up her work and home life for the time being.) The Gallis were somewhat insulated from this choice; after nearly living in the ICU waiting room for the first few days, they were able to commute from their home nearby, and were able to resume more normal patterns of life sooner.

Feminist ethics provides a helpful perspective on the ethics of care that impels Rothman much of the time. Some feminists have worried that Carol Gilligan's association of an ethics of care with women may canonize characteristics that are by-products of oppression: exalting an ethics of care risks reinforcing women's roles as the primary nurturers and carers in patriarchal systems. (Consider the relative prestige and remuneration of the "caring" and the uncaring professions.) Such analysis illuminates Juliet Rothman's position; as much as we may admire the sacrifices she makes—of her time, professional gratification, and income—we may see her position as unsustainable and finally unjust. As long as the burden of being Daniel's primary caregiver is exclusively hers, she is called upon to give up too much, and this may redound to his disadvantage. Understandably, none of this is stated in the narrative; the point is that readers are in a position to sense considerations that may escape the notice of narrators.

Another pertinent difference is that while both sets of parents dutifully "do their homework"—that is, they research spinal cord injury and rehabilitation—only Richard Galli seems to have sought out personal accounts of surviving spinal cord injury in response to his son's injury.[13] At one point Galli admits that he would have done more research before buying a toaster than he had done before determining to kill his son (76), and he is perplexed and shocked by this impulse. He then undertakes further research, reading several narratives, including those of the actor Christopher Reeve and the college hockey player Travis Roy. He gives these stories no credit for the positive outcome in his son's case; on the contrary, when he argues for Jeffrey's death in front of the ethics committee, he rejects them as irrelevant on the grounds that both Reeve and Roy, as celebrities, had resources that Jeffrey entirely lacked. This is a fair point: disabled celebrities may be inappropriate models for people like Jeffrey. Nevertheless, one wonders whether reading their accounts may have helped Galli to visualize life after spinal cord injury, to imagine how life as and with a quadriplegic might be manageable and meaningful.

The issue of the imaginability of living with disability is crucial. A rarely discussed but undeniable, perhaps decisive, factor in quality-of-life considerations is the preexisting attitude toward disability on the part of patients and their families. Different individuals may have very different responses to the same level of impairment; indeed, one of the things that reading narratives like these reveals is the wide variation in tolerance of permanent severe disability. Robert Murphy's *Body Silent*, Archie Hanlan's *Autobiography of Dying,* Albert B. Robillard's *Meaning of a Disability,* and Mitch Albom's best-selling *Tuesdays with Morrie* are all narratives in which men—not incidentally all professors of the social sciences—face deterioration and certain death from progressive paralysis (a spinal tumor in Murphy's case, ALS in the cases of Hanlan, Robillard, and Morrie Schwartz). They do so with remarkable equanimity, even curiosity about the way in which their bodily transformation entails stigmatization and ostracism.[14] To my knowledge, none of them committed suicide; at least, none of them reports contemplating, much less planning, suicide. All are saddened and disturbed by their deterioration, but all endure a high degree of paralysis without feeling the need to arrange their death.[15] This has a good deal to do with their age and maturity, of course; they have resources—intellectual and emotional—to fall back on that are not available to men in their teens and twenties. For older men, masculinity and potency are less at stake in disability.

Although there may be, as we have seen, a significant difference in their ages, the relative youth of Daniel and Jeffrey makes them both vulnerable to choosing to die or to having death chosen for them. As we have seen, both sets of parents invoke their sons' physicality to justify their sons' death, as though they might decide differently about less robust young men. Perhaps they might. But to choose death at this point is to assume that such sons could never—would never—outgrow this characteristic, whereas the importance of mobility and athletic skill tends to recede with age for most men. Further, acquaintance with disability—or, lacking firsthand acquaintance, the ability to view it in a certain light—may literally be life-saving; de-stigmatizing disability may make the seemingly unendurable endurable. Richard Galli touches upon the issue of the preexisting attitude toward disability in this passage:

"I have never been in a situation where there was no out," I told [my wife]. . . .
But now this situation had only two possible outcomes: Jeff would die

or he would live trapped in his quadriplegia. I couldn't imagine that, couldn't visualize it. . . .

I suffered from a failure of the imagination. Paralysis was repugnant to my imagination. (171)[16]

Galli's inability to imagine his son as a quadriplegic needing help with toileting (his cognitive impairment, one might say) is not surprising or blameworthy; previous to Jeffrey's accident, he had no need to imagine such a situation. Presumably Jeffrey also struggled to envision living with disability. The narrative affords us little insight into his thought processes—and we need to remember the difficulty of communicating with him during the ten days covered by the book—but it is a good sign when he asks his father whether, once he is able to resume his education, he "will have to go to a school for cripples" (159). In this brief comment, he reveals both a prejudice against disability and an incipient ability to imagine living as a disabled person. (It is important that the answer to his question—no, he could rejoin his classmates in his old school—is a function of public policy and not his degree of impairment.)

Although euthanasia is typically invoked in cases of terminal disease, a difference between disease and disability is pertinent here: whereas "diseases 'follow a *course*' and therefore prove familiar and domesticated by virtue of a belief in their determinate status (i.e., the ability to confidently narrate their future), disability might be characterized as that which exceeds a culture's predictive capacities and effective interventions" (Mitchell and Snyder 3). Thus, part of the challenge of living with disability is precisely that it seems—sometimes, paradoxically, because of its "stability" (stasis)—unpredictable, unnarratable, that is, inassimilable within the usual narrative formulas. This fundamental resistance of disability to domestication—conceptual and literal—may illuminate the phenomenon of the "cure or kill" response to disability, according to which the disabled are tolerated only if and as long as their condition is deemed rectifiable; when cure or improvement proves impossible, sympathy often turns to hostility and aggression. Family members may be capable of supporting disabled people in terrible condition, as long as there is hope of improvement. Once that hope is lost, however, hostility—initially evoked by the damage the disability inflicts on a loved relation—may be deflected onto the person "afflicted" by it. This is manifest in Richard Galli's response to his son's impairment, an implicit but powerful expression of the rationale—or (psycho)logic—of euthanasia: "For myself, I wanted to destroy his paralysis, to get it out of my world, to fix it, to conquer it. I was greedy to loosen its grip on Jeff, on me, and on the whole privileged world in which we lived before paralysis intruded. Jeffrey's death would be a victory over his paralysis" (36). When disability defies correction, the impulse to eradicate it may be deflected onto its "victim." One way to understand this phenomenon is to recognize that "disabling societies" consign the impaired to a state of permanent liminality—a position, according to Victor Turner, "between fixed points and . . . essentially ambiguous, unsettled, and unsettling" (qtd. in Willett and Deegan 139). Liminality is not inherently a disadvantageous position; it is typically occupied, however, in transition from one social status or role to another. But unlike those who are reintegrated through rites of passages into a new status in society, disabled people may remain stuck in a state of permanent liminality, "suspended between the sick role and normality, between wrong bodies and right bodies" (Willett and Deegan 141). Thus, disabled people may be ignored, ostracized, socially and economically marginalized. Worst of all, perhaps, death may be seen as the only way to resolve their ambiguous status: "Symbolic incorporation is often only possible with death, and the accompanying funeral rites. There is a somewhat common perception that suicide is often preferable to disability, suggesting that the disabled occupy a status lower than death" (Willett and Deegan 142).

This cultural phenomenon—not just a "cultural text" but the lack of alternatives to that text—is implicated in narratives of euthanasia in two ways. First, the lack of familiar plausible (i.e., non-celebrity) scripts of surviving, much less thriving, after catastrophic impairment tends to reinforce and perpetuate the inability to imagine it in new cases. Even when such accounts exist, to expect parents to read and assimilate them in the immediate aftermath of accidents such as those suffered by Daniel Rothman and Jeffrey Galli may be unrealistic; parents in such crises have more immediate concerns. But as such accounts proliferate and become better known (without necessarily being read), the easier it is to imagine each new case. If, because such disabled lives have been written, there is known to be life after severe disability, such "lives" may reproduce themselves. Life writing in such cases may less frequently become death writing.

In this regard, of course, *Rescuing Jeffrey* may seem disappointing in its brevity. The narrative covers only the first ten days after the accident; resolution is provided at that point by the shift from the intention to kill Jeffrey to the decision to let him survive. As the narrative proper ends, he is still in the ICU, his condition more or less stable. A one-page postscript summarizes the next twelve months, during which Jeffrey underwent rehabilitation, returned home, and resumed classes at his high school in January 1999. The book jacket updates this sketchy narrative slightly: "Jeffrey Galli will graduate from high school in spring 2000, and he plans to go to college." Additionally, the book's "Contact Information" advises readers that they may visit his Web site and contact him by E-mail. In the fall of 2001, his Web site revealed that he was a student at the University of Rhode Island. So, despite its brevity, the narrative resists definitive closure and invites readers to follow Jeffrey as he adapts to his new life.[17] The open-endedness of the book, whose story is extended beyond the book's covers into cyberspace, is itself an affirmation of the possibility of life after a serious spinal injury and an acknowledgment of its uncertainty.

In the extremity of their scenarios, these two narratives of euthanasia expose the dangers of writing anyone else's life—especially that of an immediate family member—for it is that very immediacy and familiarity that licenses and seems to justify the arrogation of narrative authority. It is inherent in parenthood, I suppose, to imagine and invest (emotionally as well as financially) in scenarios of children's futures and to seek to script those lives to conform to an imagined life course. Such nonverbal prospective "life writing" is unavoidable and usually benign; indeed, most would agree that it is essential to good parenting. Yet there are circumstances in which such efforts may become pathological. The circumstances of Jeffrey and Daniel would not seem to be such; they appear to be "best-case" scenarios of supportive parenting. But when events threaten to rule out the anticipated scenarios and to inscribe futures no parents like to imagine for children, there may be a powerful temptation to prevent them from being written at all.

Although intolerance of disability, not only in the "afflicted" but in relatives and caregivers as well, is hardly ever an explicit consideration in analyses of euthanasia, one cannot read narratives such as these without recognizing that it functions as a powerful conditioner, if not the determiner, of outcomes. No one should judge those who decide that there is no dignity except in arranging death while they are still in control of their bodies; but we should also attend to the examples of those—like Murphy, Hanlan, Robillard, and Morrie Schwartz—who find dignity and gratification in living with severe disability. Not to put too fine a point on it, prejudice against disability can literally be life-threatening.

∞

Justifying another's suicide in narrative restages the problematic ethics of assisting it in the first place. Such narratives, rare though they are, may be particularly useful texts for thinking through some of the ethical dimensions of end-of-life decisions. Even when a life narrative is driven entirely by the desire to justify and legitimize a decision to end that life prematurely, the narrative may deconstruct itself, exposing flaws and gaps in its own implicit argument. The commitment of the decision-making process to writing, while intended to compel assent in the reader, may actually serve to open that procedure to ethical review and revision. Indeed, such narratives may suggest that, contra its advocates, it is euthanasia, not its criminalization, that constitutes a denial of death as a natural part of life by attempting to bring it under human control.

Euthanasia Narrative as Assisted Suicide Note:
But What If She Wants to Die?

But What If She Wants to Die? (1997), George E. DeLury's account of assisting the suicide of his wife, Myrna Lebov, is particularly instructive concerning assisted suicide as a relational act and its narrative as an auto/biographical act. Only fifty-two when she died, Myrna Lebov had multiple sclerosis but was not in pain nor terminally ill, and she had expressed great ambivalence about the idea of killing herself. Nevertheless, with her husband's assistance—and perhaps at his urging—she committed suicide in New York on July 4, 1995. Rather than face a jury trial for what he acknowledged was illegal conduct, DeLury pleaded guilty and served four months in prison. The case did not end there, however. The incident received considerable media attention, and DeLury mounted a narrative self-defense in his book. In response, Myrna's sister Beverly, who believed that DeLury had driven Myrna to suicide, filed a wrongful death suit against him, invoking the "Son of Sam" law, which bars convicted felons from profiting from their crimes (Hendin 58–60).

DeLury's book would be significant if only because it issued from a felon: although assisting suicide is a crime in most jurisdictions, to my knowledge DeLury's is the only narrative of assisted suicide written by someone convicted and imprisoned for the act that it recounts. The controversiality of this suicide is manifest in numerous features of the book aside from its account of the event itself. In addition to acknowledging the usual parties, such as family members, friends, members of his and Myrna's synagogue, and members of the Hemlock Society, DeLury also thanks a corrections officer and notes that he can recognize some supporters only by their first names because "to name some of them might harm their relations with others" (ix). (Notably absent, too, from the list of family members is Beverly, Myrna's closest blood relative.) Unlike most euthanography, which begins with calamity for the deceased subject—a disabling accident or diagnosis with terminal disease—this one starts with calamity for the survivor, spending the night after Myrna's suicide in jail. This narrative thus uniquely registers dissension about the ethics of the euthanasia it narrates within the inner circle of family and friends.

DeLury acknowledges that he is seen by some as guilty and that others will see his narrative as self-serving. His self-defense involves candid—some would say damning—disclosures. He admits that Myrna was not terminally ill or in pain and that she was depressed; that one of her motives may have been to spare him the burden of caregiving; and that she "did not leave behind clear and convincing evidence to a 'moral certainty' that she chose death of her own free will at the time of the act itself" (8). He makes these admissions at the book's opening; he also reiterates them and rebuts them one by one at its conclusion (213–16), putting readers in the position of the jury he chose not to face in court. His argument is that Myrna's suicide was freely and rationally chosen and that she was unable to carry it out unassisted (and no one else would assist her). In life writing, then, he seeks a change of venue, a more receptive and liberal arena than the courtroom in which to make his case for a revision of legal and ethical standards, as well as for his own moral innocence and his wife's heroism.

His book is noteworthy for its handling of the problematic ethics of committing and narrating euthanasia. Suicide assistants typically seek to memorialize the person who committed suicide, but they also need to justify their own participation in the suicide; the two motives, though not necessarily contradictory, may conflict. Indeed, we may think of such narratives generically as extended assisted suicide notes; as such, they often betray mixed motives. With respect to its genre, the subtitle of DeLury's book, *A Husband's Diary*, is somewhat misleading; although the book's latter half is "based on," and often quotes, a diary DeLury kept during his wife's last years, the book as a whole is a fully retrospective account of his life with Myrna, her death, and its aftermath, including his time in jail. As such, it exhibits a crucial difference between suicide notes and assisted suicide notes: the latter have the advantage that they can be written after the act in question. And as we have seen, the aftermath of Myrna's death profoundly shaped the book from cover to cover. As we have also seen, however, the "advantage" of hindsight carries the risk of counterproductive overdetermination and patent self-justification.

In this instance the act of life writing is bound up with the act of euthanasia to a rare extent and in unusual ways. The original life writing text, DeLury's diary, was explicitly organized around the prospect and advent of Lebov's suicide. Its unfortunate but revealing title, "Countdown: A Daily Log of Myrna's Mental State and View toward Death," suggests how life writing may become implicated in suicide; Myrna's suicide served not only as the overt topic but also as the teleological end of her husband's diary. No wonder the diary was among the evidence seized by those investigating Myrna's death. Indeed, at the time of DeLury's indictment, the Manhattan district attorney released the diary to the press, which predictably pounced on incriminating passages. The diary thus helped to indict DeLury, first literally, in the criminal justice system, and then figuratively, in the media. Offered a plea bargain, he accepted immediately; wishing to avoid the trouble, expense, exposure, and uncertainty of facing a jury, he had good reason to believe that his diary and other personal documents would suggest that he actively encouraged or subtly manipulated Myrna to commit suicide. In an important sense, then, DeLury's private sentences convicted him when made public.

Most damning was a passage from a letter he wrote Myrna:

I feel that everyone is perfectly ready to see me die for your sake, but no one is prepared to do anything for my sake. And I am dying. I have only a few years left, ten at most probably, but only two to three if my work load continues as it is. . . . But no one asks about my needs.

I have fallen prey to the tyranny of a victim. You are sucking my life out of me like a vampire and nobody cares. In fact, it would appear that I am about to be cast in the role of villain because I no longer believe in you. (145)

Eric J. Cassell has observed that "suffering is experienced by persons," not merely by bodies (32–33). Even that formulation may be too narrow; much evidence suggests that pain and suffering are strongly affected by context. If so, then they may also be relational—that is, they may be experienced not only by individuals but also by couples or families.

The relationality of suffering functions in two different directions. First, just as physical pain may be felt not (only) in its anatomical source but also "referred" to some other place in the body, as when a person having a heart attack feels pain in his right arm, so suffering is not confined to nominal sufferers but may also be "referred" onto proximate others—partners, family members, caregivers. Second, the degree and kind of pain experienced by nominal sufferers may be in part determined (and thus conferred on them) by those around them. Human pain is distinguished by its social and cultural components; we learn how to experience—and express—pain in social units and according to cultural cues. DeLury's letter is a particularly explicit illustration of the mutual implication of referred and conferred suffering; even as DeLury complains of suffering from Myrna's dependency here, he communicates to her the declining value of her life to him, thus compounding her suffering. One of the attractions of euthanasia is that it promises to relieve the suffering of those around the ill or disabled person. Thus, there is always the danger that those who acquiesce in, abet, or assist suicide are seeking in part to end their own pain, sadness, and disappointment. (Whatever their explicit messages, the narratives that some of them go on to write also are testimony that their suffering does not end with the life of their relative; their suffering may in fact result in part from their role in the euthanasia scenario.)

The letter goes on to inform Myrna that, if she could produce some work that would persuade him she was capable of writing the book she had proposed, he would help her with it on a daily basis. Although this may sound like an ultimatum, he insists that "the issue here was not 'write a book or die.' Myrna's inability to write was merely one sign of the mental deterioration that was destroying her personality" (146). Yet, he confesses, "my offer of help was not made in earnest." Its point was to force Myrna to recognize her own deterioration, the implication being that if she could not "write a book . . . suicide might be the best solution" (146). He feared that her deterioration had begun to cloud her self-awareness; to him, her inability to compose was a sign that it was time to act on her earlier suicidal impulse. He seemed to allow for no retreat from her prior commitment to die rather than lose her mind, and he assumed an active role in precipitating the long-anticipated suicide.

Also among the documents available to the prosecution was Myrna's suicide note; this was incriminating not because of its content but because of its authorship: DeLury "had prepared [it] in case she didn't do one herself" (173). On Myrna's computer, the district attorney discovered another suicide note, which she had apparently written, but never sent, to her sister. In the absence of authenticating handwriting, DeLury argues from its blunt references to her incontinence that she wrote it herself: "I would not have put some of those words in Myrna's mouth" (176). Though not denying his legal responsibility, his book seeks to contextualize and finally to supplant earlier, once private life writing as the public representation of the suicide. In large part, then, his narration is determined by the need to explain (away) these earlier texts: his need to present Myrna's death as a "rational suicide" and the need to rationalize her suicide are inextricable from each other. In short, his book's burden as an assisted suicide note is to convince readers that it is not a ghostwritten note contrived to disguise his authorship of her suicide itself.

Because of his criminal conviction and the notoriety of the case in and around New York City, DeLury's account of assisting suicide is more devoted to self-exoneration than most. It addresses in an ingenious way, however, the related generic motive of memorialization. DeLury's fundamental strategy is to conflate self-exoneration with vindication of Myrna's "decision to die" (6): he claims that to blame him for Myrna's suicide—to argue that he unduly influenced her decision—is to cast her in the role of victim and therefore to dishonor her memory. The book thus cleverly attempts to fuse the genres of memorial and apologia; to the extent that her suicide appears rational—even heroic—his assistance seems blameless, even admirable.

The book also suggests the elusiveness of authorial "ethos." I welcome DeLury's frank admission of doubts and mixed motives, which helps to create the ethos of an honest and self-doubting agent, one who declines to use his vantage as sole witness and grieving survivor to romanticize the act or gloss over its unappealing aspects. DeLury admits that the event was "all rather anticlimactic": "no tearful goodbyes, no jokes, just a let's-get-this-done approach" (175).[18] Indeed, DeLury confesses that Myrna's death was anticlimactic in a more disturbing way. He admits here something he never told the police (who never inquired): when his wife survived longer than expected after ingesting the fatal potion he had mixed for her, he suffocated her with plastic bags to prevent an arriving caregiver from discovering a comatose client and summoning help. He thus acknowledges that commitment to "assisting" "suicide" sometimes entails acts that are tantamount to active killing.

An ethos of candid self-exposure is always vulnerable to the suspicion that it is only gesture—"rhetoric" in the pejorative sense. DeLury's ethos undermines itself in a different way, however: he does not always seem fully aware of how damaging some of his admissions are. His self-defense depends on making Myrna's act appear that of a wise, self-aware, and generous partner. We can distinguish between two tactics that might serve his strategy (or stratagem). One would be to submit and construe particular pieces of evidence, in a lawyerly fashion, to demonstrate that her act was truly autonomous and uncoerced; to this end, he cites letters she wrote to others as well as oral—and hence unverifiable—communication to him. The other would be holistic, to suggest through force of narrative that her death was of a piece with their life together, that it was an act mutually agreed on and not scripted by his needs. That is, if the narrative could convince readers that her suicide grew out of an egalitarian and loving partnership, then they would presumably accept her chosen death and his assistance in it. This passage reflects his awareness of the narrative's burden:

> When I am in the slough of self-doubt and guilt, I ask the question strangers [read: readers] ask, "Did she really want to die?" But when I look back on our years together, on our joys and sorrows, our hopes and disappointments, our years of peace and years of dread, I begin to see that the ending was in the beginning, that it was all a wholeness, complete in each moment of the passing stream, not just in the last one. And then I know a quietness of heart and a new quickness of spirit and say Amen to our life—and death. (15)

The passage candidly acknowledges moments of doubt about a crucial issue, and DeLury's account is exceptional, perhaps unique, in the extent to which it admits such misgivings. (That is, for an apologia, it is highly confessional, in the legal, not the religious, sense.) At the same time, the passage can be read as more canny than candid—acknowledging doubts, but sweeping them aside prematurely. In fairness, the passage represents a claim that the book sets out to support, but the narrative as a whole does not finally compel (my) belief, in part because it ultimately privileges the interests of the caregiver over those of the cared-for partner, in part because DeLury's coupling of self-exoneration with vindication of Myrna is tantamount to emotional blackmail, putting readers in a position such that if they doubt Myrna's motives, they become her victimizers.[19] Here as elsewhere, the narrative reveals in a particularly naked way the close and complicated relation between the ethics of the act of assisted suicide and the ethics of its narrative representation.

A key issue in narratives of assisted suicide is the nature of the collaboration inherent in the act. Ideally, the act is freely initiated by the suicide and acquiesced in reluctantly by the assister, whose role is secondary; the assistant is perforce the "author" of the act's inscription, but has to present himself or herself as not the sole author of the act itself. DeLury has real problems here, but he tries to face them head-on. He acknowledges, for instance, that early in their marriage, he—the older, more worldly, more self-assured and voluble of the two—had a tendency to finish Myrna's thoughts for her: "I, glib and opinionated, would rush in impatiently to finish her thoughts and sentences for her." She resented and resisted this, and "I slowly began to learn to hold my tongue and wait, a wait that always proved worthwhile. . . . The discipline proved very useful years later when Myrna's speech became even more hesitant because the MS affected her memory" (57). One of the burdens of his narrative is to convince readers that he did not merely finish her thoughts but finish her life prematurely; by his account, his acquired patience with her hesitant articulation assumed unexpected importance when she became disabled.[20]

The text is not entirely reassuring on this score, however. DeLury notes that, worried that Myrna's mental deterioration was beginning to compromise her autonomy, he decided to confront her and force her to resolve her ambivalence about suicide before it was too late. Indeed, he very nearly concedes that it already was too late, since she required him to force the issue, to alert her to her own decline:

> I decided that Myrna deserved a chance to make a choice before her mind was too ravaged to do so. So, during one of her normal, rational periods, about mid-January 1995, after dinner, I told Myrna that I had to lay out some unpleasant facts for her. I described our situation, pointing out that she was deteriorating relatively rapidly; her body was close to useless; her mind was showing serious slippage; and her emotions no longer seemed consistently rooted in reality. (131)

Significantly, however, a good deal of his speech is not about her condition but about a deterioration in the quality of her care: "At the same time, I was exhausted, having worked at making a living and taking care of her without a real break for nearly six years. Now, at age sixty-three, I was so tired I could collapse at any time and was not likely to last more than a couple of years in any case. . . . So, the dilemma: If she wanted to be sure of having help to die, she had to consider doing it sometime in the next year." As he continues, his defensiveness is evident: "If this seems unduly harsh, so be it. The circumstances were harsh and it was not my task to sugar-coat them. My job was to cast a clear light on reality, not obscure it. My aim was to give Myrna a choice, not false assurances—a wake-up call, not a sedative" (131–32). The irony of the last word is apparently not intentional.

Granted, DeLury has much of value to say about the problems of the caregiver; as he points out, this perspective is an important and too often neglected one in cases of chronic illness and disability. Sometimes it emerges here in an unfortunate way, however, such that the book—and the act it attempts to vindicate—comes to seem too much concerned with his needs. This is true in the notorious image of Myrna as a vampire in his letter to her. In his defense, he argues that the trope had originated with her. Even if this is so, it may reflect an issue he does not address, that Myrna had come to see herself as a burden, a drain, and a parasite on others, that she had significantly and dangerously devalued herself in proportion to her dependency.[21]

The problem is linked to what I described earlier as DeLury's fundamental rhetorical strategy, to exonerate himself by exalting Myrna as

a heroine of the highest order . . . [who] had waged a valiant and constantly losing struggle against multiple sclerosis for more than twenty years, with little complaint or self-pity. She was always considerate of others, trying to make them feel that she was all right, in good spirits, and ready to fight on. She seldom faltered in her resolve to make the struggle her problem, hers alone, and to present to the world at large and to those close to her an unassuming nobility of spirit. . . . Above all, she maintained her fierce drive for independence, the core of her life project. (6–7)

In his attempt to cast her not as a victim but as a heroine, he inadvertently exposes key dynamics of the caregiving scenario—perhaps especially when the care receiver is a woman. His account implies that disability like

Myrna's requires not only bravery but also dissimulation; she is exalted for disguising her true condition, physical or psychological. What a counterproductive way for Myrna to present herself to others—as not needing their support and assistance. What a burden on her to have to be such a saint. And what a burden on DeLury to have to play a supporting role in this charade. We can see here how isolating and destructive the dynamics of disability and caregiving can be in an individualistic culture. The individual model of disability puts the onus on the disabled person not to inconvenience others, not even to complain. (Such dynamics isolate not only the couple from others but also each partner from the other.) And we can see how the mercy in this mercy killing may serve the caregiver more than it serves the disabled person. ("As one police official put it, George DeLury put Myrna Lebov out of his misery" [Smith, *Forced Exit* 197].) Further, we can see how the preservation of her image as noble and independent might require the self-sacrifice of suicide. A system of values that exalts personal independence may encourage suicide as its ultimate enactment.

Disability, Surrogacy, Autonomy, and Relationality

What is striking about all of these narratives—despite the survival of one protagonist—is that they reveal how quickly life writing can become thanatography in the face of severe disability. When someone becomes terminally ill or disabled, autobiography often gives way to biography; a narrator speaks about or for the vulnerable subject in the third person. (Interestingly, this happens even in *Rescuing Jeffrey*, whose subject survives; the narrative thus reasserts the very parental prerogative that Richard Galli seemed to have surrendered.) Perhaps the extreme version of surrogacy—speaking for another—is choosing death, and thus silence, for another person. Both Juliet Rothman and Richard Galli have this impulse, though neither finally acts on it; George DeLury may not only have had the impulse but also have followed through on it. Indeed, the postmortem narrative can sometimes be seen as an attempt to "channel" the silenced voice of the deceased subject. (In this regard, Juliet Rothman's second epilogue, "Echoes of Immortality," is particularly poignant; in it she makes posthumous contact with Daniel through dreams and numerological signs of his presence [153–57].) In the face of disability, then, life writing may morph from autobiography into euthanography; in such instances, writing of disability may be tantamount to writing off disability.

Richard Galli's book—again, despite its final, crucial turn toward life—illustrates this nicely. Here he projects himself into the situation of his son contemplating his future as he had imagined it before his accident: "He had the memory of that future even now, as he lay limp in his hospital bed. The memory of his future would last forever, but the future itself was gone. . . . Paralysis . . . ruins your future, but it leaves intact the memory of all your expectations" (49). Similarly, he invokes memories of Jeffrey's earlier adventures and concludes that these would always be his best memories; empathizing with his son's (imagined) sense of loss, the father projects regret and nostalgia ahead indefinitely into a literally hope-less future. This exercise of imaginative surrogacy reinforces Galli's primary impulse to kill his son to spare him an anticlimactic life of nostalgia for his potent young body. That is, rather than allow his own sad prophecy to be fulfilled, Galli opts to deny his son any future at all. This seemingly empathetic anticipation of deep regret is a complex and seductive (and potentially fatal) act of surrogacy.

Such narratives also suggest, however, that reckoning with disability might recast the discourse of euthanasia. The argument for euthanasia generally, and PAS in particular, typically pits the "right to die," justified by appeal to the principle of respect for autonomy, against the "duty to live," enforced by the traditionally paternalistic bias of medicine in favor of extending life at any cost. It is worth noting, however, that this picture of medicine may be increasingly anachronistic in an age of managed health care and far from universal health insurance. In Wesley J. Smith's view, with the advent of concepts such as "futile care," the balance has tipped away from the duty to live toward the duty to die, so that the burden may now be on those who wish to be treated; legalization of PAS tips the balance further toward the presumption of a duty to die (*Culture of Death*).

In any case, as Carolyn Ells has argued, the experience of disability exposes the dangers inherent in a narrow definition of autonomy. Traditionally, the notion assumed an isolate atomistic individual: free, equal, and rational. Thus, the "considered moral judgments" of those endowed with autonomy needed only to be respected (Ells 608–9). (This notion is implicit in these narratives insofar as they take at face value their subject's express wish to die, whether it is acted on or not.) As bioethics has evolved—in part, in response to challenges from feminists—it has increasingly acknowledged as well "an obligation to promote autonomy" (Ells 609). In biomedical practice, however, the earlier concept prevails: autonomy is seen as a capacity of the atomistic individual to be respected, rather than as an attribute of the relational self to be nurtured in its existential context.

The experience of disability challenges this narrow conception of autonomy in a number of ways. For one thing, the very oppression entailed by disability may compromise autonomy by eroding self-trust and self-worth (McLeod and Sherwin). And as Ells suggests, the experience of disability exposes the extent to which all individuals are in fact interdependent and interconnected (609).[22] More to the point with the narratives discussed here, the acquisition of disability may be considered an inherent impediment to autonomy insofar as "the dynamic nature of self-identity is frequently noted in times of impairment. . . . Losses can numb and shrink the self" (Ells 610). If autonomy—especially in such circumstances—is not something to be taken for granted as a component of personhood, but rather a state to be relationally achieved, the ethical complexity of our narratives becomes even greater.

I hope that I have established how the narratives discussed here reveal the dangers of a narrow construction of autonomy—how empty a gesture it may be to respect the autonomy of a person (perhaps especially a relatively young person) suddenly beset by a condition that drastically challenges selfhood, rewrites life narrative, and threatens to foreshorten life itself. As Anne Donchin has observed, "the experience of trauma, so common among hospitalized patients, suggests that the self is affected, and perhaps partially constituted, by the changing circumstances to which it is exposed. For . . . it is the loss of connection experienced by trauma survivors that most imperils their autonomous selfhood" (239). When identity is fragile and in flux, when sudden disability or terminal illness demands the generation of new bases for a sense of self-worth, it may be worse than naïve to assume that even an express desire to die reliably represents autonomous will. Under such circumstances, meaningful respect for autonomy may mean allowing and enabling individuals to develop new centers and new equilibria. Accounts that inscribe futures where no future seemed plausible—and Richard Galli's book, extended by Jeffrey's Web site, turns out to be such an account, almost in spite of itself—perform an important service in part because they enact this process.

Further, they help to demonstrate the comprehensive sense of kinship that is crucial to the survival and flourishing of disabled people. Galli's narrative in particular, for reasons that should now be clear, suggests how he, his wife, his daughter, and, most important, Jeffrey benefitted from the support offered by a diverse group of people—some related by blood, most by association. These individuals established themselves as kin in two separate but overlapping ways. First, they offered emotional and logistical support to the family in its crisis; second, but perhaps more significant, they "adopted" Jeffrey and invested in his future. They assumed what his parents privately did not: that he would and should have a life— even if seriously disabled. They thus affirmed "a more expansive sense of kinship across embodied difference that . . . is essential to the public presence of disability in contemporary postindustrial democracies" (Rapp and Ginsburg 534). Those who made up "the wave" assumed, as the Gallis said to Jeffrey, that he was still Jeffrey and that Jeffrey still belonged among them.

Narratives of disability can foster (or stunt) the growth of this sense of kinship—a public, communal rather than private, familial kinship—and can foster an ethics of caring (as distinct from curing). Some narratives, while protesting the contrary, will in effect draw a new line excluding a newly disabled family member from a preexisting kinship; others will retrace and reinforce an old border that includes the disabled family member; still others will draw a new boundary that expands kinship beyond the family. In acquiring a disabled member, a family may acknowledge (or deny) relations with others not hitherto known as "relations"—not only those who may step forward in support, but also those who may have been through a similar experience. Families and narratives that affirm this relation help to create and sustain an inclusive sense of citizenship (Rapp and Ginsburg 537). If the subtext, the subliminal message, of medicine today is all too likely to be "cure, correct, or eliminate," the subtext of robust disability narratives is life without cure, but not without care.

7

Genome and Genre
DNA and Life Writing

Is there anything more redolent of "identity" in the age of the human genome than our biological code?

—SANDER L. GILMAN, "Private Knowledge"

Decoding Genetics

"THE HOLY GRAIL," "the Code of Codes," "the Book of Life," "the Book of Man," "the human instruction book," "the autobiography of a species"[1]—the human genome is often referred to in terms more appropriate for texts, even sacred texts, than for the chemical code of which it actually consists. As these phrases suggest, the genome has become a contemporary icon for the key to a wide variety of human ills. We are periodically informed of the discovery of the "gene for X," and in June 2000, the completion of the sequencing of the human genome was announced, to predictable media fanfare. The Human Genome Project (HGP) promises much benefit; it may eventually lead to effective treatments for dread diseases and even the elimination of certain hereditary conditions. But genetic information has obvious potential for abuse, and its *mis*use necessarily becomes feasible sooner and more certainly than its proper use. If we think of "gene therapy" not narrowly, as the manipulation of genes in particular individuals, but broadly, as the whole range of policies, social as well as biomedical, that may follow from the HGP, then we can see that genetic medicine may have deleterious "side effects"—for example, discrimination against people applying for insurance or health care.[2]

Apart from its specific hoped-for applications, the mapping and decoding of the human genome may encourage popular belief in genetic essentialism insofar as it singles out genes as causes of human characteristics and human behavior. (It may also advance the commodification of the individual; witness the banking and sale of "genius sperm.") One irony of the hype surrounding the HGP is that few if any reputable scientists believe in anything like strict genetic determinism. Genes do not function *in vacuo,* nor are they the sole influence on who we are; rather, they act through complex causal sequences—sometimes characterized as "cascades of events"—especially when it comes to their influence on temperament and behavior, as distinct from the phenotype itself (the physical form of an organism, characteristics such as eye color). In any case, when the project's first stage reached completion in June 2000, what had actually been accomplished was not the decoding of the genome—as was sometimes implied by media coverage—but rather the mapping of it, which is to say the transcription, or enliteration, of the chemical bases making up the genome. This is itself a monumental accomplishment, but a rather mindless one, made possible and accelerated by banks of supercomputers. It is only the prologue to understanding how the genome works.

The next stage of the project will be the annotation, decoding, and interpretation of the genome—distinguishing genes from "junk DNA" and investigating the function of particular genes. If the first stage of the project has produced a "draft," it is an entirely unpunctuated one; indeed, it is harder to read than an unpunctuated text, since so far there is uncertainty about what constitutes a meaningful unit and whether what appears to be meaningless information—which dominates the genome—is in fact "junk." Already the results of the HGP have complicated, if not disproved, some of the assumptions that underwrote it regarding the power of genes or the way in which they act. The discovery that the human genome contains far fewer genes (perhaps thirty or forty thousand) than the one hundred thousand most scientists had estimated has highlighted the crucial role of the proteins produced according to genetic prompts. If we think of DNA as the organism's genetic instructions, it appears that, like most other human instructions, they are not always faithfully followed.

Such nuances often get lost in the popular discourse of genetics, and those advocating the very expensive Human Genome Project have had much to gain by isolating and overestimating the influence of genes—particularly harmful or destructive genes. Part of the problem is that so much media coverage employs misleading shorthand (the code of the

Code). Even the notion of a "gene" is problematic. The term predates modern DNA science, and laymen tend to think of a gene as a discrete molecular unit of human anatomy, but "genes don't . . . exist as discrete physical entities" (Condit 227); rather, the term refers to a functional segment of continuous DNA that codes for a particular protein (Nelkin and Lindee 4). Similarly, the phrase "gene for X," often taken as implying genetic predestination, usually refers to genetic predisposition—a matter of probability rather than certainty.[3] The result of such shorthand is to give a lot of free publicity to the false idea that human beings are merely the sum of our genes. For this and other reasons, we live in an age when genes are given great credence as explanations for human behavior.

I half expect that in the not too distant future, scientists associated with the Human Genome Project will announce that they have located the gene for autobiography. This may sound implausible, since life writing involves such complex behaviors, but phenomena seemingly as complex—alcoholism, criminality, poverty, and homelessness—are commonly referred to as products of genetic influence. Many people consciously or unconsciously subscribe to the proposition that genes are us; thus, humanists (and skeptical scientists such as Richard C. Lewontin) are often reduced to fighting a rear-guard action against popular genetic determinism. Yet the Human Genome Project is too important to ignore; the mapping of the genome represents a major development of what Foucault called "biopower." It represents a significant new stage in biomedicine's progressive development of diagnosis and prognosis independent of the patient's testimony or even cooperation—the achievement, without literal penetration of the body, of the most metaphorically invasive of exposures.[4] It bids to decode the very stuff we are made of, to spell out—to *spill* out—secrets we didn't know we had.[5] Thus, while life writing may not be genetically determined, it certainly will be "genomically" influenced—that is, significantly shaped by the decoding of the human genome. One of the ways in which the HGP's implications will be played out is through a number of life writing genres in a manner that is rarely, if ever, consensual and that renders all human beings vulnerable subjects in a new sense.

Genome and Scriptome

That the HGP raises profound and urgent ethical questions is trite but true. What has not been much noticed is that the mapping of the genome has serious implications for the various practices and genres of life writing, and that, conversely, life writing has much to offer as an arena for reflection on the questions raised by the project. The human genome ("the Book of Life") and the human scriptome (all forms of life writing) are related in a number of senses, separate but overlapping, in which DNA itself functions as a kind of nonverbal "life writing," that is, a predictor or even "scripter" of individual experience.

First is the sense in which genes themselves may influence identity and life course. Consider Huntington's disease (HD), an untreatable and fatal illness caused by a single dominant gene. When the HD gene is activated, usually in mid-life, it threatens to write the script of the remainder of its possessor's life, overriding other factors: for individuals with the HD gene, at some point biography is inseparable from genetics. Cases like this, in which a gene so directly and definitively writes a life script, are rare, but they illustrate the power of genes to shape identity and life history.

Second is the sense in which gene tests may predict or even determine one's identity and life course. Consider the case of a fetus discovered to carry the gene for a condition such as cystic fibrosis (CF). If the fetus is brought to term and develops the condition in question, the CF gene may be said to write his or her life in the sense already discussed—but in a much less definitive way, since cystic fibrosis is variable and can be moderated by various treatments. Thus the genetic script can be edited through medical intervention; the therapeutic regimen becomes a form of self–life writing that attempts to revise the generic script. Not only life course but also identity can be profoundly shaped by the result of such a test. If the fetus is aborted because it carries that gene, however, genetics becomes destiny in a different sense. Here it is not the gene but its detection that is determinative. In the case of fetuses discovered to have "defective" genes, then, "life writing" may take the form of erasure. As the genome is decoded, more and more genetic conditions will become prenatally detectable; some will in effect become fatal.

A third sense in which DNA writes lives is implied by the second: the sense in which it is not the gene but the cultural construction of genetic difference that proves crucial. The most common life-defining bodily attribute is sex itself, which is decisively affected, if not entirely determined, by a chromosomal difference: almost all human beings can be classified as XX or XY. It makes little sense, however, to discuss sexual difference without considering cultural contexts in which anatomical differences are

constructed as gender. It is such constructions that make the possession
of two X chromosomes "the world's most common reason for elective
abortion based on a genetic trait" (Marie Claire King, qtd. in Jolly 271).
(An obvious irony here is that far from being a genetic abnormality, female sex is the default mode for human embryos, all of which begin as
female.)

A fourth sense in which DNA is tantamount to life writing builds on
some of the preceding senses; it is the way in which genetic information
about individuals may be used to represent them officially or publicly—
to inscribe their lives as texts (and thus, in the case of living people, sometimes to affect the course of events). George J. Annas has noted the way
in which DNA stored in gene banks introduces a decisive new element
into medical records: "A medical record can be analogized to a diary, but
a DNA molecule is much more sensitive. It is in a real sense a 'future diary' (although a probabilistic one), and it is written in a code that we have
not yet cracked" (82). When the code is cracked, the public exposure of a
private text, a medical record, may be life-altering. Even without breaches
of privacy, there are dangers in the possession of individuals' DNA by institutions such as hospitals and justice systems, which may draw infer-
ences from, or act upon, the genetic information in ways the individuals
may not be aware of or able to control.

What is new in our time, then, is not the degree to which our genes may
write our lives directly (after all, genes have always done that, and the
novel promise of genomics is to reduce that degree) but the degree to
which "knowledge" of our genes may write our lives—and genomics
promises, or threatens, to increase that degree. Third millennium genomics bids to intervene and prevent illness and impairment at the genetic level, but the new biopower will not manifest itself solely in the (so
far) sci-fi scenario of gene therapy; genetic knowledge will also write our
lives for us in many other subtler ways. If DNA can trace our genealogy,
predict our future, and give us hard news about our actual present condition (as distinct from our subjective sense of that condition), it has man-
ifold implications for life writing.

DNA, Biography, and Historiography

The complex multistage process of DNA fingerprinting (to employ the
inevitable metaphor) involves producing what is known as an autoradi-

ogram. In this process a segment of DNA is washed with a radioactive element that binds to it and is then exposed to x-ray film; the result is a kind of x ray of the individual's DNA (Lander 192) whose most prominent features are dark bands very much like those of a bar code. If we extend the term "autoradiography" from the laboratory technique to the entire process by which an individual's DNA may be gathered, sampled, exposed, decoded, and translated, we can say that autoradiography is a powerful form of life writing (albeit not of self–life writing). The notion of DNA as the ultimate and definitive identifier of the individual is especially interesting because it arises in a postmodern era in which academics have deconstructed the subject and many of its seemingly constitutive physiological characteristics—such as sex and race—almost to the vanishing point. Counterposed against the slippery first-person pronoun that designates my—but also your—individual subjectivity, DNA is a poststructuralist's nightmare, a unique and constant signifier of the self, present in virtually every cell of the body, stable from birth to death (indeed, from before birth to long after death).[6]

The implications for life writing of the conflation of DNA with the unique individual are only beginning to manifest themselves, but some trends are discernible already. If the idea of DNA as unique identifier is a poststructuralist's nightmare, it is a detective's dream—and a biographer's, insofar as biographers sometimes function as investigators. DNA has begun to play a significant role in the writing of biography, and it bids to play an even larger one. As the surest indicator of paternity, DNA has helped to revise the biography of Thomas Jefferson, lending the weight of science (and all but definitive confirmation) to speculation—highly controversial when first aired—that he fathered children with his slave, Sally Hemings. It is not just Jefferson's life story that is altered by confirmation of this speculation; the identities of his descendants are also decisively changed. This is most obvious in the case of African American descendants, whose claim to presidential ancestry is now corroborated, but it is equally true of white descendants, whose denial of kinship with his black descendants is seriously undermined. Other presidents' lives are also under the microscope, so to speak. An interesting example of genetic revisionism can be found in Robert Marion's book *Was George Washington Really the Father of Our Country? A Clinical Geneticist Looks at World History.* Though not working with DNA evidence obtained from his biographical subjects, Marion, a clinical geneticist and amateur historian, uses his knowledge of genetic anomaly to practice a kind of biography that the HGP will make more common. For example, Marion speculates that George Washington's involvement in the American Revolution may have been influenced by XYY syndrome, which would have predisposed him to impulsive and rebellious acts, and that infertility associated with this genetic anomaly, which left him without an heir, may have influenced his disinclination to become king of the United States (41–74). With regard to Abraham Lincoln, Marion concludes that although his body had "Marfanoid" shape, Lincoln probably did not have Marfan's syndrome but rather "another disease that affects connective tissue, . . . mitral valve prolapse syndrome" (110). More interestingly, he speculates that Lincoln's opposition to the enslavement of people who were physically different may have been rooted in his own physical difference, for which he was ridiculed as a child (120–22). These cases represent two quite different uses of genetics: to single out Jefferson from other possible suspects as distinct from characterizing Lincoln. But identifying Jefferson as father of slave children also characterizes him, so the distinction is not as sharp in practice as it might seem in theory.

Biography as posthumous sleuthing, using scientific tools to write the lives of the dead, is not entirely new, but DNA testing represents a significant addition to the biographer's tool kit. Such testing may presage and encourage increasing use of forensic methods in biography. We should expect to see more—and more sophisticated—use of this sort of argument by biographers and historians in the future; DNA obtained from biographical subjects, even those long dead, is an archive yet to be explored. By citing Marion, I do not mean to endorse his hypotheses; his methodology raises obvious questions about the relative roles of different factors—especially how to assess them at such historical distance. In any case, such sleuthing probably does not herald a new biographical paradigm. Although DNA evidence may authoritatively answer some important biographical questions, it is limited in the sorts of questions it can address: it can confirm that Jefferson had a sexual liaison with Sally Hemings, but it cannot tell us much about the nature and dynamics of their relationship. It can tell us "who" but not "how" or "why." As Frank Shuffleton has shown, biographies are "definitive" only for their own times; eventually they are superseded by new "definitive" lives. Definitive biography is an elusive, if not illusory, ideal; DNA evidence will not by itself produce definitive lives.

In any case, Marion's take on history is revisionist only in a very limited sense. Marion's book attempts to demonstrate the effects of genetic abnormality—his medical specialty—on world history by rounding up the usual suspects: European royalty (kings and tsars) and American presidents (especially those canonized on Mount Rushmore).[7] Indeed, Marion seems interested in establishing their genetic abnormalities only if he can link them to events or characteristics that are deemed already historically decisive. To be sure, this is top-down history with a twist— there is a novel element in arguing that history is the *pathography* of great men—but that novelty is limited by Marion's otherwise very traditional historiography.

Although canonical figures may offer more in the way of evidence and relics to analyze, the application of DNA analysis need not reinforce the great man theory of history. Indeed, probably the most prominent and best-known use of DNA testing as identifier has been in criminal investigations. In addition to providing seemingly infallible and definitive evidence of the presence of an individual at a crime scene, autoradiography can be used to generate a list of probable physical characteristics—such as hair color, eye color, and build—of the individual from whom it comes; some believe it may eventually be used to generate a visual image of that person, like an "Identi-kit" portrait (Annas 80).

Merely as a unique trace of the individual, of course, DNA has great potential as a crime detection and criminal conviction tool, especially in cases of rape. DNA evidence also can be used to exonerate suspects; according to Matt Ridley, exonerations outnumber incriminations by a ratio of two to one, and the Innocence Project has already freed a number of falsely convicted people.[8] Interestingly, those exonerated in some cases confessed to the crimes in question; because DNA evidence can trump incriminating as well as self-vindicating personal testimony, it highlights the phenomenon of false or coerced confessions. And the exoneration of death row inmates by DNA evidence—a particularly drastic form of biographical revisionism—has lent considerable weight to the argument that the death sentence should be abolished to protect against the execution of the innocent. The amassing of DNA databases by investigative organizations obviously has the potential to make crime solving a more efficient and precise endeavor. It does so, however, by nominating all those in the data bank as potential criminal suspects; after all, the purpose of such databases is to maximize the pool of suspects. Whether used to ascribe guilt to, or remove suspicion from, a suspect, DNA testing clearly is a contemporary form of technocratic life writing that has the capacity to decisively alter life scripts.[9]

DNA is also implicated in biography when genetic analysis is used to identify the remains of the dead. In the future there will be no more "unknown soldiers," at least in high-tech armies; indeed, there will be fewer in the past, because hitherto anonymous remains can sometimes be identified by new DNA tests long after death. Although soldiers will continue to go missing and be killed in action, they can now be definitively identified when remains are recovered. The use of DNA evidence to identify victims of the terrorist attacks of September 11, 2001, has brought new attention to this aspect of DNA testing. And survivors' testimony to the comfort of the closure provided by the acquisition of actual remains—however incomplete—should establish the significance of DNA for *death* writing. Here DNA quite literally fills in blanks in the historical record and enables the biography of otherwise anonymous figures to be written.

When DNA testing is applied to living people, ethical considerations come to the fore. Consider the case of "Binjamin Wilkomirski," a name I must put in quotation marks. "Binjamin Wilkomirski" (also known as Bruno Grosjean, his birth name, and Bruno Dössekker, his adoptive name) is a Swiss citizen who claims to have been an inmate in Nazi concentration camps before his adoption by Swiss parents in 1945; his Holocaust testimony to that effect, *Fragments: Memories of a Wartime Childhood*, published in translation in the United States in 1996, was honored with various literary prizes here and in Europe. When, in researching his past, he thought he had discovered his long-lost Latvian Jewish father, he took a DNA test that disconfirmed their kinship (Lappin 39). Later, however, when skeptical journalists questioned his testimony, he declined to submit to DNA testing that might have disproved his story by establishing his kinship with the Swiss family named on his birth certificate (Lappin 61).

Assailed by counterevidence, his publisher withdrew the book, and the literary agency that had placed the book commissioned Stefan Mächler, a freelance Swiss historian, to investigate. In 2001, he produced a biography of "Wilkomirski" that exposed his book as a fiction—indeed, a pastiche of various literary, cultural, and historical sources and the memories of actual survivors.[10] (The "truth" of his story seems be at most metaphorical: he was apparently traumatized as a foster child. His "memories" of concentration camps seem to reflect, or refract, a particularly unpleasant foster home in Switzerland.) The volume, which incorporates the text that it debunks, is unprecedented, to my knowledge, in the annals of life writing. A more drastic rewriting of a life can hardly be imagined; Mächler not only contradicts the self-written life, *Fragments*, but also effectively denies "Wilkomirski" his avowed identity as a Jew and a Holocaust survivor (in which he seems to have profound and unshakable belief). Here an autobiographer has been held to the "autobiographical pact" in a very legalistic way. Indeed, he is liable to trial for fraud—not for lying in print but for accepting money (royalties, lecture fees) on false premises (Eskin 236).

In 2002, DNA tests revealed that "Wilkomirski" was in fact the son of the Swiss man named as his father on a birth certificate "Wilkomirski" had claimed was in error. Although the DNA test alone would have disconfirmed his autobiography, it took a good deal of old-fashioned investigative legwork to provide a corrected account of his life. Thus, this example suggests that DNA will serve mainly as a supplement to traditional biographical methodology. But if biographers equipped with DNA tests can "out" Jefferson as a miscegenist, Lincoln as a freak, and "Wilkomirski" as an impostor (or someone with delusions of persecution), modern genomics is already a force to be reckoned with in biography.[11]

DNA and Identity: Autobiography

What are the implications of the genome project for autobiography? To begin with, experiments using genetic engineering to increase memory function in mice suggest the possibility of enhancing memory in human beings as well. Aside from its obvious medical implications, such a development would affect the primary medium of the ongoing construction of personal identity and life narrative; it might thus have interesting implications for autobiographical writing. It might make possible the narration of conditions one of whose symptoms is impairment or loss of memory. More generally, it might make more common the photographic memory of memoirists such as Nabokov (though not his literary skill at recreating what he claimed to remember). Yet it is also possible that a too retentive memory might interfere with the process of culling memories that autobiography requires (Wade, "Hidden Traps"). Mark Twain wrote some comic sketches involving characters who cannot forget enough detail to remember a story, and Oliver Sacks has explored the phenomenon of "incontinent memory" in a very different medium, the case history.[12]

Other ramifications of the Human Genome Project for autobiography depend on whether its implications are seen as deterministic. As Evelyn Fox Keller has pointed out, the HGP gives nature the edge over nurture as the dominant factor in human development. She notes, however, that there is a twist in this outcome, since the HGP involves the novel assumption that nature will prove more susceptible than nurture to human manipulation and thus provide the key to human progress (288–89). The underlying assumption that genes make us who we are may seem deterministic; the idea that we will be able to manipulate our genes is not so, however. The latter promises a kind of freedom to determine who our offspring will be, if not who we are. For those skeptical of genetic therapy as the solution to human suffering, this is a challenging shift in the traditional debate over whether nurture or nature more influences personal development. But until techniques of genetic improvement become more practical, genomics tends to register rather differently in popular culture.

Since one notion of autobiography is bound up with the idea of personal autonomy, it might seem that any form of determinism, especially genetic, might discourage autobiography as beside the point. Historically, however, fatalism has not deterred autobiography. The Puritan view that the true Author of the individual life was God and that the autobiographer could only trace, imperfectly, that Author's mystic script did not inhibit, but may have encouraged, self–life writing. After all, the stakes were high: the status of one's soul and one's ultimate fate. Scientific determinism might seem less conducive to autobiography than theological determinism; conceiving of your life as pre-scripted by an interested God is very different from conceiving of it as being prescribed by your genes. But the awareness that one is predisposed to a medical condition can induce intense, even excruciating self-consciousness and thus be a powerful stimulant to subgenres dedicated to self-monitoring, such as the diary and the journal. Self-examination can become obsessive for people afforded such "self-knowledge."

Similarly, if "bad" genes are the first to be identified, then the HGP may favor apologia, the subgenre dedicated to self-defense. Genetic determinism might cause a decline in confessional narratives and a corresponding upsurge in narratives in which behavior is retroactively explained and excused by reference to genetic influence. Moral transgression, which Benjamin Franklin's autobiography famously reduced to the status of printers' errata, may be treated as a function of errors in one's genetic code: my genes made me do it. In fact, genetic predisposition is already being tried out in an institutional form of apologia, legal defense, and it will find its way into literary and subliterary life writing as well.[13] Indeed, it makes perfect sense to excuse behavior that is genetically "programmed"—for example, involuntary swearing by people with Tourette's syndrome. It is doubtful, however, that the complementary genre, the success story, will begin to credit "good" genes for accomplishment: if success were attributed to genetic makeup, it would hardly seem something to advertise.

Insofar as DNA enables individuals to trace their descent, the HGP may have interesting implications for autoethnography. On the one hand, since human DNA is 99.9 percent identical, modern genetics establishes that humans are all related (and descended ultimately from Africans) and undermines the persistent notion of race as a significant category. On the other hand, population genetics promises to allow individuals to trace their ancestry to a mere eighteen female and ten male members of the original group of approximately two thousand breeding members of our species; it may soon be possible, then, for anyone to establish descent from particular ur-humans (Wade, "Human"). Already a company called Oxford Ancestors will—for a modest fee, and using DNA from a cheek swab—identify descendants of the seven "daughters of Eve" who are the foremothers of most Europeans. Because the founder of Oxford Ancestors, Bryan Sykes, has taken the liberty of naming the seven European "daughters of Eve," their descendants may come to identify themselves not as Irish or English, French or German, but rather as Ursulan or Xenian. Similarly, efforts are under way to use DNA to help African Americans establish links with ancestral homelands and tribes (Goldberg). New notions of lineage or descent could eventually trump race and ethnicity as bases of identity and might therefore manifest themselves in new forms of autoethnography.

DNA and Relational Life Writing

One manifestation of the spread of genetic determinism in contemporary North American culture is the emergence of books claiming that human beings are incontrovertibly shaped by genetic predispositions. An example of this subgenre (which I think of as self-helpless books) is Martin Seligman's *What You Can Change and What You Can't Change* (Nelkin and Lindee 145). Genetic essentialism also shapes a related genre, parenting manuals. As Dorothy Nelkin and M. Susan Lindee note, "Genetic essentialism in this literature constructs the child as a predetermined packet of genes, not a being to be molded into a productive citizen, but one to be passively and fatalistically accepted" (143). This has obvious implications for parental memoirs of children.

Indeed, since it is DNA that relates "blood relatives," the mapping of the genome has obvious relevance to the entire range of relational life writing. Already, the bulk of what is discussed as relational life writing involves people who are genetically related: biological siblings, parents, and children. This is not to say that such narratives are especially or even usually concerned with issues of genetics and heredity; rather, it is to point out that the relations considered and presented as foundational to identity are often genetic relations. Indeed, in an age when surrogate motherhood and donated eggs have made the determination of maternity problematic, one convenient and, to many, natural way of conceptualizing the family has been as the "molecular" family:

> The notion of the molecular family is based on the cultural expectation that a biological entity can determine emotional connections and social bonds. . . . Since it is beyond culture, outside of time, DNA seems to be of durable or permanent significance. Genetic ties seem to ground family relationships in a stable and well-defined unit, providing the individual with indisputable roots more reliable than the ephemeral ties of love, friendship, marital vows, or shared values. (Nelkin and Lindee 60)

Perhaps the clearest and most intense expressions of this concept of the molecular family are found in narratives of the quest for genetic parents by adopted children or, less frequently, of the quest for genetic children by parents who gave them up for adoption, and stories of infertile couples' attempts to produce genetic offspring.

> These are often stories of desperation: the adopted child seeks his parents out of a profound need to connect himself to a biologically related parent; the infertile couple agree to a surrogacy out of a consuming need to have a baby who carries their genes; the aging baby boomer becomes a single mother out of the desperate drive to perpetuate her genes; and individuals track their family genealogies as clues to both social and biological identity. (Nelkin and Lindee 60–61)

In these scenarios, the quest for identity leads not inward through memory and personal history but outward and backward to those whose genes one carries or forward to those who inherit one's genes.

Betty Jean Lifton's book *Twice Born: The Adoption Experience* (1974) was a powerful stimulus to this phenomenon. Her later book, *The Journey of the Adopted Self: A Quest for Wholeness* (1994), further codified the notion of the molecular family, with its assertion that adoptees ignorant of their genetic parents are "people without selves" (qtd. in Nelkin and Lindee 66). The assumption of the adoptive child is that his or her identity will be realized—or at least that his or her life will be completely writable— only when genetic links have been established to a previous generation; the adopted child seeks to inscribe himself or herself into his or her genetic history, to repair broken genetic links with the expectation of some psychic payoff.

This phenomenon also works the other way: with the changing of adoption laws in some states, birth parents can locate children given up for adoption. Beth Broeker notes that even those opposing the retroactive opening of birth records "make the assumption that every child who was given up for adoption burns with an overwhelming desire to meet, and fall in love with, his or her birth parents" (para. 5). This is emphatically not the case with Broeker herself: "At age 6, when I first learned I was adopted, I cried and cried, not because I wanted to know who my birth parents were, or because I felt lost or empty, but because I wanted to have been born to my parents" (para. 12). In "Stalked by My Birth Mother," she recalls the process by which her apparent birth mother traced her and besieged her with letters, documents, phone calls, and gifts in an increasingly intrusive and unwelcome manner. (At one point, not quite sure she had located her birth daughter, the woman asked Broeker to submit to a DNA test to confirm her identity; Broeker refused [paras. 44–45].) The power of this impulse to locate gene kin is a function not of genes themselves but rather of the belief that the unknown genetic connection trumps affectional relationships. The need of some individuals to seek genetic antecedents or offspring is thus not instinctual but a manifestation of the way in which contemporary culture encodes DNA as a mystical covert sign of true identity. Adopting the term for self-replicating units of culture, we might say, then, that such narratives are driven not by genes but by memes.

Not coincidentally, the concept of the molecular family has developed in an era when profound social forces—feminism, gay liberation, high divorce rates, and an increase in "blended families"—have undermined the stability of the "nuclear family." Further illustration of the power of this meme can be found in some memoirs of gay men who have died of AIDS written by their siblings, parents, or children. As I have argued elsewhere, such accounts involve an understandable impulse on the part of the nuclear family to reclaim a member; in the process of representing the dead man's life, however, surviving relatives may minimize his affectional relations and marginalize his life partner. The family plot grounded in DNA trumps the life choices made by the ostensible subject of the memoir. Such life writing does not merely express but depends on genetic essentialism for its very existence.

DNA and Illness Narrative

As a major addition to biomedicine's repertoire, gene therapy should have especially significant implications for personal narratives of illness. At first glance it might seem that, like other radical new forms of therapy such as organ transplants, gene therapy would generate a whole new subgenre of narratives by those who benefit from it. When it is first employed, such treatment may generate narratives precisely and exclusively because of its novelty. But they are not likely to be patients' stories, which are more often generated by arduous, punishing, and uncertain therapies. Though "high-tech," gene therapy should be low-stress, almost magical, in the way it cures—without conventional surgery or drug regimens. Cures that work the way gene therapy is supposed to work—suddenly, dramatically, and without significant suffering or side effects—generate not "quest stories" but "restitution stories," whose hero is the physician (Frank 77–94) and which "bear witness not to the struggles of the self but to the expertise of other" (Frank 92). Consistent with the thrust of contemporary biomedicine, such narratives commodify the body and objectify the patient; they are related by hospitals, treatment centers, and drug companies in advertisements and promotional literature.

This seems to be the case, at any rate, with the first reported success of gene therapy. In April 2000, French doctors announced that they had used gene therapy to treat a rare condition known as severe combined immune deficiency (SCID). Babies with SCID must live in a germ-free bubble, or they quickly succumb to infections that most people resist. The therapy was applied to three babies—aged eleven months, eight months, and one month; success was pronounced when they had remained healthy in normal conditions for nearly a year. This treatment became a narrative as news and a first draft of medical history, not as life writing; all three babies were collected into an anonymous group whose story was a clinical, not a biographical, tale. The real protagonists were the scientists and physicians who devised and applied the treatment; if the therapy continues to be successful, there will be no occasion for further narrative of their cases—except for periodic updates to confirm its success (Kolata A1).[14] Thus, insofar as gene therapy—whether somatic or "germline" (which is performed on an embryo)—is intended to be proactive and preventive, it should reduce or eliminate narratives of certain conditions.

In any case, safe, effective, and routine (as opposed to experimental) gene therapy is probably a phenomenon of the distant future. (Experimental gene therapy has already cost one life, that of eighteen-year-old Jesse Gelsinger, who died in 1999 after undergoing treatment for a liver disease at the University of Pennsylvania.) In the meantime, the decoding of the human genome has profound, though uncertain, implications for the development of first-person illness narratives, for three reasons. The first is that insofar as health is understood in genetic terms (as the absence of genetic error), the notion of it will become narrower, the experience of it rarer, as genetic testing becomes more and more refined: "As clinical diagnostic technologies continue to improve, the definition of health grows more and more narrow and sophisticated" (McGee 113). Clearly, the decoding of the genome and new genetic tests will produce illness where there once was health, not only in individuals but in entire populations.

The second has to do with the prospect of earlier and earlier diagnosis—not only presymptomatic but prenatal and even pre-implantation. It is already possible to test a fertilized embryo for a limited number of medical conditions; it will become possible to test for many more. And "since everyone carries at least several mutations, no embryo will emerge from DNA screening with a perfect score" (Jones 80). When the tests have to do with embryos, new and difficult choices will have to be made. When the tests concern adults, the results will expand the population of the "worried well." And when illness is redefined as the presence of genetic information rather than the presence of discernible symptoms, the nature of personal illness narrative may change decisively. One would expect that such information would promote constant self-scrutiny and self-monitoring and thus favor the journal or diary, but the relation between "life" and "illness" will be redefined; such narratives will tend to be proleptic, and some may aspire to being preemptive illness narratives.

The third reason is that insofar as disease is increasingly understood— correctly or not—as a function of genetic codes, it may increasingly be seen not only as foreordained but as fundamental—indeed, quite literally essential—to the individual's identity. As Barbara Katz Rothman puts it: "You have cancer not because of something you did, or something that happened to you, but because of who you are. This places the disease deep into the body, internally, intrinsically, essentially within" (148). The implications of this, too, are uncertain, but they would seem simultaneously to stimulate and to constrain first-person narratives of illness.

DNA as Master Text: Narratives of Disability

A major factor determining the implications of the HGP for self–life writing is what sorts of genes are first targeted and identified. Although in theory all human characteristics and behaviors are susceptible to genetic investigation, the emphasis early on has tended to be on bad ones. There are good reasons for this, of course; biomedicine aspires to fix what is considered broken, and isolating genetic factors in disease bids to attack health problems at their root—and even perhaps to eliminate them from succeeding generations.[15] But it is also the case that the champions of the genome project have tended to focus on bad genes in part to justify funding a very expensive project that is unlikely to have much immediate therapeutic payoff. In any case, we do not hear much about the discovery of genes for traits such as agreeability or behaviors such as using one's turn signal; rather, we hear about genes for dread diseases and socially undesirable behaviors. Indeed, although the idea that criminality is genetic has been deemphasized—as politically explosive—the language of genetic research often echoes that of criminal investigation. One commonly hears genes referred to as "culprits." Consider this from a *New York Times* story: "One of the genes suspected of contributing to schizophrenia is believed to lie on Chromosome 22 but has not yet been identified" (Wade, "After" para. 11). The Human Genome Project puts genes in a lineup in more senses than one.[16]

This approach exposes a crucial bias built into a master trope of the discourse of genomics, the metaphor of "the human genome" as a kind of master text. As James C. Wilson has noted, the goal of genetic medicine is often expressed as the detection and correction of deviations from, or errors introduced into, a presumably authoritative master text that is *the* human genome: in this metaphor, "disease/disability is cast as textual irregularity, and those in the biomedical community become editors who attempt to amend, delete, and correct the defective texts of disabled bodies" (Wilson 26). But the genome being mapped is in fact no one's genome but rather a composite of samples from many individuals (a number of whom belong to small sub-populations, such as Utah Mormons, who can supplement their DNA samples with genealogical data). Although the trope constructs the composite as a definitive master text against which to match individual genomes, the composite genome is itself a fictive text—and a pastiche, at that. (Giving the composite genome the status of a definitive human text is like passing off a canon of literary works as illuminating the presumably universal "human condition.")[17] In genomics as in textual editing, "there is [actually] no prototypical genetic script by which to measure or evaluate all others" (Wilson 26–27). Rather, "no two human genomes are or can ever be alike: all exhibit mutations, deletions, and other genetic variants. . . . Not only is genetic variation (in the larger sense) the norm; these variations are never fixed, but always in the process of becoming" (Wilson 27). The master trope of "the human genome" as a definitive text suppresses the fact that the "master text" contains genes that were once mutations. It is for these reasons that Matt Ridley has forthrightly stated that "the Human Genome Project is founded upon a fallacy" (145). The ramifications of this master trope for disability are at best ambiguous. One of the declared goals of the project is to identify genes for disabilities so as to correct them; the Human Genome Project is supposed to illuminate and then eliminate the causes of certain diseases and disabilities. In the context of gene research, the reduction or elimination of human misery is often seen as an unobjectionable and unproblematic goal; who would oppose it? The trouble is that historically, too often the means of eliminating misery has been the elimination of people *presumed* to be miserable because they are "afflicted with" or "suffering from" some condition considered intolerable by "normal" people.

The "new eugenics" may be distinguished from the old on three grounds: first, the new originates not with some official determination of tolerable variation but (sometimes) with people who have, or are at risk for, particular medical conditions; second, the new is carried out not through state coercion but through (presumably autonomous) individual choice; and third, the new seeks to eliminate bad genes not by execution and sterilization of the genetically "defective" but by gene therapy or genetic testing and reproductive choice (i.e., selective abortion). Because it is (supposedly) bottom-up, not top-down, in its administration and more humane and elective in its mechanisms, the new eugenics is viewed as kinder and gentler than the old. (Indeed, some argue that it is not "eugenics" at all.)[18] But with increased genetic knowledge, it will become possible to terminate pregnancies for an ever-expanding range of conditions that are considered undesirable. Thus, the crucial question to be answered—for the most part by private citizens—is when a condition warrants preemptive abortion. Of course, such personal (and presumably private) elective choices are not unaffected by the social, economic, political, and cultural environment in which they are made; in particular, they are affected by the perceived future "burden" of having an ill or disabled child.

There are few conditions on which there is a consensus. Agreement varies according to where conditions are located on a continuum of probable life expectancy, the degree and kind of anticipated suffering, and the predictability of their effects. With conditions such as Tay-Sachs disease, which is inevitably fatal in early childhood, there is consensus on the desirability of prevention, and in fact voluntary eugenics has greatly reduced its incidence in the most vulnerable population, Ashkenazi Jews. There is less consensus about conditions whose severity may be variable and unpredictable, such as cystic fibrosis (which may be caused by over one hundred different mutations [Lloyd 110]). Toward the middle of the continuum are conditions that may compromise the quality of life less drastically—in part because they are already controllable—such as bipolar disease, hypertension, heart disease, and diabetes. At the far end are conditions such as dwarfism, obesity, and deafness which are not so much "unhealthy" as socially disvalued; here suffering and life limitation may be socially and culturally generated. (William Wright reports poll results to the effect that many parents would choose to abort a fetus with a fifty-fifty chance of being obese [257–58].)

To read all genetic anomalies as errors to be corrected is to shorten this continuum drastically. The dangers are clearest if we consider conditions at the latter end of the continuum, such as hereditary deafness. Were hereditary deafness to be eliminated by gene therapy, Deaf culture and community would dwindle; deaf life writing—which has only just achieved critical mass (and critical recognition)—would become nostalgic and elegiac and then trail off.[19] In practice, whether parents choose to abort fetuses fated to be deaf depends largely on their own hearing status and their valuation of deafness. Within the deaf community, if not in the general population, there is a consensus against the elimination of hereditary deafness. Thus, under the new eugenics, deafness is not likely to be eliminated as a hereditary condition, precisely because many of the parents in a position to pass on a gene for deafness are themselves deaf and prefer to have deaf children; they consider deafness not a "disability" but an identity.

The case of homosexuality is more complex. Until recently, homosexuality was defined by the *Diagnostic and Statistical Manual* as a mental illness; its de-medicalization was in large part a function of gay liberation and lobbying. The medicalization of homosexuality, though preferable to its stigmatization on moral grounds, was inherently prejudicial, and its *de*-medicalization was a step toward its legitimation as a way of being. If, as some scientists now claim, homosexuality is genetic in origin, then homosexuality could be *re*-medicalized. Parents carrying this genetic trait would generally not be homosexual, and they might not welcome the prospect of raising a homosexual child. Thus, if a predisposition to homosexuality were genetically detectable in fetuses, fewer homosexuals might be born. Gay life, gay culture, gay life writing would all be affected. Thus, under the new eugenics, homosexuality would be far more susceptible than deafness to elimination in what some would call a eugenic holocaust. Such an outcome is even more likely to befall the dwarf community. The gene for achondroplasia was isolated in 1994, and, according to Elsa Davidson, "in the most extreme scenario the emergence of prenatal gene screening could mean the complete extinction of dwarfs" (para. 1).

If the incidence of such hereditary conditions is reduced by the prevention or the termination of pregnancies, some kinds of "lives" will never be written because those lives will never be lived. To be more precise, some lives will never be *self-narrated* because they are not lived. In fact, however, there are popular forms of life writing devoted to individuals who never existed, "Babies Who Left Us Too Soon"—that is, "babies of parents who made the heartbreaking decision to interrupt their wanted pregnancies due to poor prenatal diagnosis." A good deal of such life writing can be found on Web sites like "A Heartbreaking Choice," which offers support to such parents and prospective parents. Part of this site is dedicated to memorials for these babies (www.erichad.com/ahc/garden .htm). Life writing of this sort assumes two distinct forms. One is found in "the memorial garden," a site where parents can memorialize their unborn children. The memorials include the baby's name, death date, cause of death, and a brief message addressed to the baby. (I am employing, without endorsing, the site's terminology.) The listed causes of death are not abortion but genetic anomalies, including trisomy 21 (also known as Down syndrome), trisomy 18, spina bifida, Turner syndrome, Potter's syndrome, skeletal dysplasia, and anencephaly.

The other form consists of more extended messages or letters, usually addressed by parents to the unborn child but occasionally cast as messages from the child to the parents. The subtext—and sometimes the surface text—is a plea for, or granting of, forgiveness for the "interruption" of the pregnancy and the anticipation of meeting in the afterlife. Interestingly, whereas in the memorial garden the unborn children are identified with their genetic anomalies, in the longer messages they are often represented as disembodied and thus non-disabled. In being prevented from being born (the sites generally avoid the word "abortion"), they are saved from disability and restored to perfection or wholeness, as "angels"—an appealing compensation for their having been aborted. We have here, then, virtual life writing about, or even (supposedly) by, virtual children. In using the term "virtual," I do not mean to minimize the pain and loss felt by the parents, but only to draw attention to their use of cyberspace as a repository for the inscription of lives unlived (and presumed unlivable). In this case, the very disabilities that are the cause of death (many of them genetic and thus detectable with DNA analysis) also impel life writing. That life writing can occur in the absence of life suggests the insistent power and flexibility of the impulse to inscribe life in words; here simple messages help to fill the void left by the absent expected child.[20]

The medicalization of disability, then, cuts two ways. On the one hand, it seems preferable to the demonization of disability under the symbolic paradigm, which once condemned the mentally ill or the Tourettic as witches. Medicalization promises to de-stigmatize disability and thus protect disabled people from persecution. But its effects are not always benign; insofar as it conceives of disability as a defect in the individual, it implies that disability ought always to be fixed or better yet prevented. When medicalization takes the form of geneticization, it suggests that the world would be a better place if all genetic anomalies were eliminated.

The Human Genome Project may promise to eliminate or reduce the incidence of disease and disability in the long run, but in the short run it is likely to have a rather different effect. It may prove to be not just a key but a skeleton key to the human genetic code, in two senses—first, in the sense that it will open any DNA lock; second, in the sense that it will expose genetic skeletons in lots of closets. The larger issue that contemporary genomics raises—and that life writing can help to answer—is what the discovery of more and more genetic anomaly will mean. Timothy F. Murphy has framed the issues economically and directly: "To what extent will the genome project generate new classes of human inferiority? To what extent will the genome project generate a theoretical subjugation of genetically atypical people, born and unborn, and thereby establish difference as disease or disability? Will the genome project mark difference as an undesirable trait and justify its eradication?" ("Genome Project" 7).

The establishment of a standard or normal genome tends inevitably to characterize genetic difference as disease; such an identification of anomaly with disease may revive and reinforce the eugenic impulse to clean the gene pool. As Evelyn Fox Keller has said, "There are many problems associated with the geneticization of health and disease, but perhaps one of the most insidious is to be found in its invitation to biologically and socially unrealistic standards of normality . . . a 'eugenics of normalcy'" (97). And Elisabeth Lloyd, a philosopher, argues that since "molecular techniques [offer] an unprecedented amount of social power to label persons as diseased . . . , it is more important than ever to gain insight into the normative components of judgments about health" (101–2). Lloyd makes the point that any determination of what counts as normal, even under a supposedly biomedical model, cannot be detached from cultural—and thus presumably negotiable—standards of "what counts as the proper functioning of a human being" (106).

How the discovery of the full range of human genetic diversity will play out is impossible to predict, but perhaps we can distinguish between two very different scenarios. In one—already rehearsed for us by history and forecast in dystopian science fiction—genetic abnormality will be mapped onto racial, gender, ethnic, and class differences despite the liberal distribution of genetic anomaly in the general population. That is, disvalued differences will be found to be most common among the marginalized and disenfranchised. Genetic testing would be used "to preserve existing social arrangements and to enhance the control of certain groups over others" (Nelkin 180). "We risk, in other words, creating a genetic underclass" (Nelkin 190). A passage from Revelation (20:15) may stand for the paranoid version of this scenario: "And whosoever was not found written in the book of life was cast into the lake of fire" (qtd. in Doyle 52).

Even without this sort of discriminatory construction of abnormality, the effects of genetic medicine are likely to reinforce, rather than to unsettle, racial, class, and ethnic hierarchies: "As with all expensive new medical technology, the fruits of the HGP are likely to go primarily to the wealthy" (Annas and Elias, "Social Policy" 274). Since genetic tests and prenatal care are expensive, it is already the case that genetic counseling is more often sought by those with means; one effect of this is that disabled children are more likely to be born to those with the least means to care for them, and this is turn confirms the belief that the poor are genetically defective and that disabled people are an economic burden on the whole population. If and when gene therapy becomes effective, it will be those with means who will change their genes, further reinforcing, and apparently justifying, their sense of inherent superiority. The unequal distribution of health care will also have the effect of insulating the well-off from concern with such children. Thus, "we risk *increasing* the number of people defined as unemployable, uneducable, or uninsurable" (Nelkin 190).

The implications of the increasing ability to detect disability in utero by means of genetic testing are already evident in a rather disheartening set of what we may consider genetic life narratives. When genetically abnormal fetuses are brought to term and develop serious disabilities, their lives sometimes become the subjects of malpractice suits known as "wrongful birth" or "wrongful life" suits. In a wrongful birth suit, parents sue a physician or other medical authority for not providing tests and counsel that would have enabled them to abort a pregnancy that, brought to term, has resulted in a life of pain or suffering for the child; in a wrongful life suit, the child—or a legal representative of the child—sues on the grounds that he or she should not have been born (Wexler, "Clairvoyance" 226–27). Both kinds of cases are strengthened by DNA evidence that permits the prenatal projection of the fetus's life narrative in time to prevent it from happening. The goal of such suits and their narratives, of course, is to make someone else pay for a disabled life in a society in which severe disability is not just physically compromising but often emotionally stressful and financially ruinous. Such scenarios, then, though adverting to a kind of "genetic determinism" that would settle preemptively the question of the quality of a potential life, also testify powerfully to the social, economic, and cultural contexts in which genes find ultimate expression. That is, they reflect the economic paradigm of disability in which impaired persons are seen as literal liabilities, a burden on the society and particularly the families into which they are born.

A second, more optimistic scenario for the implications of the HGP is that the "outing" of many, if not all, seemingly normal people as latent defectives—carriers of genes for various conditions considered undesirable to perpetuate—will serve to de-stigmatize disability. As Daniel J. Kevles and Leroy Hood argue, "The more that is learned about the human genome, the more it will become obvious that everyone is susceptible to some kind of genetic disease or disability." This could work in favor of systems of universal or community-based health insurance as a way of sharing liability for disability as the human condition ("Reflections" 324–25). The phenomenon of presymptomatic diagnosis will become increasingly common; the worried well will be joined by the asymptomatically ill. Because it assigns a condition to an individual before it manifests itself—or, in some sense, exists—presymptomatic diagnosis gives new meaning to the phrase "preexisting condition," and if one's presumptive illness is preexisting, then it has consequences for insurance and employment. In any case, "inventorying our genomes for defects, mistakes, or abnormalities may make us feel more fragile and vulnerable; it may make us all think of ourselves as sick" (Annas and Elias, "Social Policy" 274). Thus presymptomatic genetic diagnosis will affect both our images of ourselves and others' images of us in potentially damaging ways. Such a proliferation of disabilities could conceivably shift, blur, or erase the border between the sick and the healthy, the "normal" and the "abnormal." If everyone carries some potentially bad genes, and if biomedicine increasingly identifies genetic anomaly with disease or abnormality, who is not disabled, in some sense? As the proportion of defectives approaches 100 percent of the population, the notion of disability will have to be rethought, at the very least. Such a dissemination of disability could significantly change the climate in which genetics and eugenics are understood. In this scenario, we all become both more and less vulnerable—more vulnerable to diagnosis as abnormal, less vulnerable to prejudicial policies and treatment.

In such a context, narratives of those with genetic anomalies will become indispensable data in ethical deliberations, both private and public, about reproductive choices. As deaf life writing and gay life writing may help protect the lives of fetuses apparently genetically predestined to be deaf or gay, narratives by and about people who are otherwise genetically different have the potential to alter the cultural environment in which decisions are made about what is and what is not an acceptable genetic variant. Life writing—preferably self–life writing—can be an important source of testimony as to whether life with a given condition can be worth living. Such narratives would also help to answer the question that Timothy Murphy has identified as the key ethical question underlying the HGP: "Should we . . . be trying to develop methods to identify and eradicate genetically defective individuals through prenatal and neonatal genetic testing (and possibly abortion) rather than undertaking social accommodation of genetically disadvantaged people, finding what ways we can to offer them hope and happiness?" ("Genome Project" 3).

Genetics as Destiny: *Mapping Fate*

Thus far I have been moving mainly from genome to scriptome, tracing or speculating about the effects of genetic research on life writing and using as examples texts or genres that in some way or to some degree accept or exploit the assumptions of genetic essentialism. Such an approach risks reinforcing a kind of literary genetic determinism by implying that contemporary genomics will unilaterally affect life writing. Here I reverse course, then, to suggest ways in which life writing may resist or rebut genomics. Especially pertinent here is an example of life writing directly precipitated by genetic factors. Alice Wexler's *Mapping Fate: A Memoir of Family, Risk, and Genetic Research* (1995) exemplifies a situation that will become more common: the predicament of living in the interval between the discovery of the gene for a dread condition—in this case, Huntington's disease (HD)—and the development of a treatment for that condition. Huntington's disease (or Huntington's chorea) can be psychologically as well as physically devastating, for two reasons. First, it ravages the mind as well as the body, and therefore threatens identity as well as life. Second, most people who get it have already seen it affect a parent; moreover, by the time their own symptoms appear, many will have had children who are vulnerable to it in turn. Thus, the lives of successive generations—past, present, and future—may all seem scripted by the same gene. This scenario, then, involves a quite literal manifestation of the axiom that genes determine destiny.[21] Alice Wexler's initial concern was that her life would follow the genetic script already acted out in her mother's distressing degeneration and death. And while she had no children, her potential childbearing years were overshadowed by her fear of passing on the HD gene. Indeed, the very possibility that she carried the gene gave her serious reservations about motherhood and made her feel less womanly (72).

In response to her complex predicament, Wexler combined quite different sorts of narrative discourse in her book: memoir and family history, introspective personal narrative and journal entries, and a chronicle of research into the genetics of Huntington's, which affected previous generations of her mother's family and for which she and her sister were at risk. Her exploration of the gene's effect on her took the form of autobiography, and her book becomes at times quite confessional: "The disease was often the vehicle for expressing feelings only tangentially related to it" (xx). Tracing the gene's effect on her nuclear family required writing—indeed, rewriting—family history, for her mother had masked the presence of the disease from her husband and completely hidden it from her children: "What my sister and I thought we knew about our family suddenly shifted, and everything had to be rethought, reinterpreted. Who we were had suddenly been called into question and everything had to be reconfigured" (75). The narrative is, among other things, an example of what Barbara Katz Rothman has called a new genetics narrative, a variation on the family saga: the story of the genetic family curse (121).

Alice's mother, Leonore Sabin Wexler, was diagnosed with Huntington's in her mid-fifties, several years after her divorce from Milton Wexler, a prominent psychoanalyst, when Alice and her sister Nancy were in their mid-twenties; she died of the disease several years later. In writing of her mother, Wexler confronted a biographical conundrum: how to distinguish among chorea (disease), character, and culture as determinants of her mother's identity and behavior. She needed to sort out, retrospectively, how much her mother's rather passive behavior was determined by her genetic condition, how much by her personality, and how much by the gender roles of the 1950s—a new twist on a perennial biographer's dilemma. One of Wexler's interesting observations is that her mother's illness may have been veiled at first by depression and anxiety concerning her preordained fate and, more generally, by the role culture assigned to her. Alice and her sister had tended to take their mother for granted: "The idea that our mother was seriously depressed and needed help never occurred to me. If Mom was more passive than most women were, she was merely an extreme version of the ideal American wife" (29). Her mother's hereditary illness, however, resonated with "the fear of many daughters of my 1950s generation—that we would somehow turn into our mothers, that our mothers were mirrors of our future selves" (xvii). Ironically, the illness that inexorably erased her mother's personality and then took her life brings her into focus in Wexler's mind and puts her in the foreground of a complex narrative. While attending to her mother's pathology, Wexler does not reduce her to a syndrome—cultural (oppressed woman), psychiatric (depressed housewife), or biomedical (victim of hereditary disease). Rather, she recuperates her and places her at the center of the family dynamics, effectively displacing her famous husband.

By the time Leonore Wexler began staggering in public and was taken by others to be drunk, the HD gene had decisively manifested itself; her condition was no longer secret. She could no longer pass for normal, though she continued to live in denial. While of course further publicizing what had been private, Wexler's book demystifies her mother's behavior, restoring dignity to her mother and meaning to her life. The inevitable and unwelcome violation of the family's privacy caused by the gene is paradoxically repaired by the publication of the family story. (This revelation is different from Alice Wexler's physician's characterization of her in medical records as "likely" to develop HD. His assignment of a probability to her developing HD without genetic testing is not simply baseless but irresponsible; it is also potentially prejudicial, since her medical records were accessible to her insurer.)

Although her narrative necessarily foregrounds genetics, tracing a particular gene through her family history to its manifestation in her mother and its influence on herself, Wexler's life writing is unlike Robert Marion's reductive single-factor historiography. Wexler explores the myriad and subtle ways in which Huntington's may have "infected" her nuclear family long before it manifested itself as a physiological condition in one rather recessive member of that family. (Indeed, if the depression that was one of her mother's dominant traits—I use the language of genetics advisedly here—was a function of her dread of "getting" Huntington's, then Huntington's cast a shadow over Alice and her sister long in advance of its actual manifestation in her mother.) Considered as family memoir, Wexler's narrative is also a rehabilitation of her mother; understood retrospectively, she is endowed with unexpected depth and complexity. Indeed, in writing this narrative, Wexler comes to realize that an earlier life writing project, *Emma Goldman: An Intimate Life* (1984), was in part a kind of compensatory act; the energetic and rebellious Goldman had served as a kind of surrogate mother, the antithesis of the person she thought her real mother was. (Her writing of both books suggests, among other things, that the HD gene can have generative as well as degenerative effects.) More important, her reflection on her genetic heritage allows her to see that she may have misunderstood and underestimated her biological mother.[22] Her memoir, then, is in part an act of feminist revisionism.

One of the implications of Wexler's book is that the disease had a profound, if covert, impact on her family prior to and independent of its actual manifestation. That is, much of its effect on her mother, her father, herself, and her sister would have been the same had her mother not in fact carried the gene and eventually developed the condition. Wexler does not merely break her mother's silence, giving away a secret borne by her body and borne out in her life; she does not merely perform an act of feminist recuperation; she embeds the gene in a narrative that reckons with its effect in the broadest human terms, not denying its harrowing effects, but teasing out the ways in which it had subtly inflected her own formation and the structure of the intimate world into which she was born.[23] To put it another way, although one could say that this family memoir is driven by and organized around the effect of a single gene, what Wexler explores is not any simple deterministic physiological schema but rather the way in which a gene's effects are mediated by character and culture. She does not reduce her family history to a generic genetic script but rather suggests "the ways in which even this obviously pathological, genetically determined killer may acquire distinct meanings for different individuals, families, and cultures" (xxiv). It is in this way and for this reason an exemplary text.

The only apparent way to revise Huntington's tragic master plot is to identify and turn off the genetic switch. In response to the disclosure of the presence of this gene in their family, the Wexlers put considerable time and energy into the effort to do just that. Unable to change the family plot, the family sought to disable the incapacitating gene—and thus rewrite the genetic script for others. Wexler's father, Milton, organized a foundation to raise awareness and research money. Her younger sister, Nancy, devoted her career largely to research on Huntington's; she wrote her dissertation on the psychology of being at risk for Huntington's and later was deeply involved in genetic research in a community in Venezuela in which the disease was very common. A historian by profession, Alice Wexler eventually assumed the role of family and foundation historian. Her narrative of the genetic research, which successfully located a marker for the gene in 1983 and the gene itself in 1993, provides a demystifying counterweight to the story of her mother's disintegration. The Wexlers, we could say, then, are advocates and exemplars of the new bottom-up eugenics.

The triumphal narrative of the research project very nearly takes over the book. Ultimately, however, Wexler cannot provide a comic resolution—on the personal or the collective level. After much anguished deliberation, she decides not to take the gene test made available by the research her family had called for and helped to underwrite.[24] Indeed, some of the book's most compelling passages are journal excerpts from this period of her life, when she was virtually incapacitated by her fear that she might be psychologically paralyzed by a gene-positive result. (For obvious reasons, "gene-positive" test results for HD can be devastating; they have been known to cause depression and even to precipitate suicide.) Here we can see how the mere prospect of a genetic prophecy can be self-fulfilling: a possible script for the future has a real effect in the present. The uncertainty of these serially composed entries nicely communicates the ambiguity and anxiety of her liminal status as possible possessor of the gene. And it speaks to what will be a more widespread experience in an age when gene testing makes possible presymptomatic diagnosis.

Rather than seeking resolution, she chooses to dwell in, and on, the uncertainty of her fate. Indeed, although she remains committed to the new eugenics insofar as she endorses the quest for a genetic cure for Huntington's disease, she voices troubling questions about who benefits, and how, from genetic research:

The new genetics has already opened a vast arena for contests of power over what it means to be human, who has the power to define what is normal, who has access to what resources and when. Who will control the knowledge of our bodies after the Human Genome Project has mapped and sequenced all human genes? How can we ensure that this will not be another project for enforcing narrow norms of "human nature," . . . for legislating "genetic destiny?" (xxiii–xxiv).

She is at pains to point out that the triumph of science in locating the gene—which brings its own rewards in prestige and publicity—makes a difference at present only for diagnosis; it does not, and may never, produce a treatment, cure, or prophylaxis. The book's combination of narratives with different focuses and registers—personal, family, and scientific—exposes the gap between biomedicine, which successfully cracks the genetic code, and life writing, which secures little comfort from the medical "breakthrough." Whereas the comic resolution of the typical illness narrative insulates its readers from the threat of the condition in question, Wexler's book, in part because of the lack of closure of its personal narrative, effectively underlines the troubling implications of its story.

Although, for all she knows, Wexler's body may not harbor the Huntington's gene, she is vulnerable to the paranoia that awareness of her risk can engender. Indeed, Wexler occupies a liminal zone between sickness and health, disability and normality. Her discursive resourcefulness reminds us how arbitrary and fluid is the border between those zones. It also suggests that the divide between knowing and not knowing one has such a gene may be as crucial as the divide between having and not having the gene. Indeed, her case foregrounds the divide between knowing and not knowing one's genetic status; her knowledge that the gene runs in her family precipitates her complex life writing project, but she resists determining whether it is part of her genetic makeup. Had she taken the test, the book would surely have been very different, depending on the test's outcome.

The book is thus a cautionary tale suggesting the limits of medical discourse, which is of little immediate help to Wexler. At the same time, it makes clear that somatic condition, no matter how "hard-wired," does not entirely determine life script, let alone script the written "life." She suggests, then, that while we are, of course, influenced—sometimes decisively and devastatingly—by our genes, we can resist being reduced to them. And she reminds us that illnesses and disabilities that may seem to set us apart from one another in fact reveal embodiment as our common condition.

Rewriting Genetic Code

The implication of this chapter—and indeed earlier chapters—has been to suggest that life writing, in various media and on different levels, may play a significant role in the creation of a cultural climate in which the nature of illness and disability might be rethought in the genomic age. *Mapping Fate* suggests how life writing may serve as a reality check on the "genohype" that has surrounded the Human Genome Project. Although the involvement of the Wexlers in genetic research is a good example of the "new eugenics," in which the champions of genetic therapy are those at risk for hereditary disorders, Alice Wexler's book does not finally register the progress of genetic research as in any way a benefit for her generation. Rather, it suggests that, in Nancy Wexler's words, just as "prediction outstrips prevention" (223), so knowledge of genetics outstrips understanding of it. It also raises questions about how much and what sort of knowledge we want about our genetic substance. Do we want to scan our genomes if they are read as our destinies? The discovery of the gene for Huntington's clouded rather than clarified Alice Wexler's life. Even as her book illustrates that her mother's life was far from "not worth living," it suggests that her life might have been more satisfying if she had not felt that she carried a stigma as well as a harmful gene. In any case, Wexler's book makes its own contribution to the dilemma of living with disability—which will always be part of the human condition—by demystifying her mother's illness and recuperating her as a subject with some agency, rather than a passive victim of a rogue gene.

∞

A Mike Thompson cartoon on the occasion of the completion of the sequencing of the genome aptly illustrates the dilemma of the prospect of eliminating or reducing disability. A man in a white coat exclaims, "Possible outcome of the Human Genome Project? No more genetically imperfect people!" The woman he is addressing replies, "Like Stephen Hawking?" He responds, "Well, no more depressed people!" She: "Like Vincent Van Gogh?" He: "Well ... No more physically challenged people!" She: "Like FDR?" And so on with blind (Stevie Wonder) and multiply handicapped people (Helen Keller). To some, the use of such venerated—and exceptional—figures will seem rhetorically unfair; but the essential division in this dialogue is between those who think of disability in terms of generic conditions "suffered" by nameless, faceless people, on the one hand, and those who think of it in terms of actual individuals living with those conditions, on the other. Contemporary life writing can articulate the latter side of the debate by representing living with disability as manageable and meaningful. A good deal of recent life writing about disability may thus serve to dampen the enthusiasm in some quarters for altering our genes.

A model book in this regard is Michael Bérubé's *Life as We Know It: A Father, a Family, and an Exceptional Child*, an account of having and raising a son with Down syndrome. The book challenges the conventional understanding of Down syndrome in two distinct registers. As family memoir, it recounts the integration of a "defective" child into a loving and appreciative family. As explicit critique of geneticism (especially its first chapter, "Genetic Destiny"), it reminds us that a good deal of "genetic" determinism is actually cultural and that social practices can ameliorate what chromosomes would seem to determine. It points out that the notion of people with Down syndrome as ineducable was a self-fulfilling prophecy: so they proved as long as no one really tried to educate them. A related example of counterdeterministic life writing is a memoir written by two young men with Down syndrome, in which one of them explicitly rebukes his mother's physician for doubting that lives like his would be worth living (Kingsley and Levitz).

Glenn McGee has noted that as genetic testing becomes more comprehensive and more common, "parents want to know what it is like to have a baby with the genetic coding for a disease. They want to know whether they can handle the responsibilities, and whether a child is likely to have a life filled with pain. . . . [T]he parents need to know things that genetic testing alone cannot reveal" (92). This suggests the powerful counterdiscursive potential of narratives, for personal stories can put conditions such as Down syndrome in meaningful contexts, not of I.Q. figures but of human potential and relationality. As the genome is decoded, there will be an increasing need for richly detailed and thoughtful real-life narratives of all sorts of medical conditions to help parents and potential parents find their way to decisions and strategies for dealing with disability.

Much contemporary life writing implicitly or explicitly contests one of the assumptions of modern biomedicine: "that disease and suffering are evils to be resisted, threats to our happiness, events without meaning that we would do better to extinguish and avoid because there is nothing to learn from then [sic], no purpose, no achievement in their endurance" (Murphy, "Genome Project" 11). To raise questions about the Human Genome Project—as Murphy does here—is to risk being regarded, and dismissed, as someone with such an investment in illness and disability that one wants to preserve and cherish them. Admittedly, it is difficult to strike a balance between the laudable desire to reduce human suffering and the desire to affirm the value and dignity of people with medical conditions and disabilities. It is well to remember that even if the new eugenics did greatly reduce or even eliminate hereditary disability, people would continue to be disabled by illness and accident. And if disability were attributable only to birth trauma, accident, and illness, disabled people might be further marginalized and stigmatized as representing even more than now that which is to be feared because it is out of or beyond our control. "This, in turn, may result in the deviating individuals being regarded and treated as 'mistakes' or 'social impurities'" (Kavka 172). In a post-HGP world, then, the sort of autobiography that claims somatic aberration as a source of pride and identity might become rarer but all the more important.

∽

Richard Dawkins has argued that evolution, even human evolution, is merely or mainly a matter of selfish genes perpetuating themselves. If we can say anything definitive about being human, however, it may be that to be human is to be self-reflexive. To revise Dawkins's phrase, then, we are self-conscious genes; in the blind process of selection, human genes have evolved a species cursed and blessed with self-awareness. And life writing is one of the powerful means we have of expressing and deepening our self-consciousness, as individuals and as a species. Part of that project will increasingly be reckoning with what is, and what is not, our genetic destiny. Life writing may not be able to put the genome back in the bottle, but it may help to provide the genome with a human face.

Epilogue

Writing Wrongs: In Defense of Ethical Criticism

DELIBERATION ON THE ETHICS of life writing entails weighing competing values: the desire to tell one's story and the need to protect others, the obligation to truth and the obligations of trust. In the United States, at least, where freedom of expression has strong legal and cultural protection, the interests of life writers have historically been favored over those of their subjects. Because those who do not write may be particularly and peculiarly subject to harm, however, the thrust of this book has been to shift attention to those who are customarily on the receiving end of life writing, those who get represented by others, often without their permission, especially when they may be particularly vulnerable to misrepresentation or their stories to appropriation.

Although I feel that this emphasis is warranted—indeed, overdue—I am aware that it can provoke resistance from different quarters and on various grounds. One such response is the charge that I, or those who may follow my lead, want to "police" life writing—to patrol and control those who expose their lives and others' in print. Some academics find it inappropriate—intrusive and presumptuous—to criticize the subjectivity of any life writer; others express concern that scrutiny of familial life writing may disadvantage women, who, historically by necessity and recently by choice, have tended to write relational narratives.

With regard to the first issue, while tact and fairness are especially desirable in assessing life writing that addresses painful personal issues—

for fear of gratuitously causing further anguish to the writers—criticism of published works does not, indeed cannot, invade the privacy of their authors. Such writing should not be beyond criticism, especially when it concerns issues of public moment, such as disability, disease, genetics, and euthanasia. Publishing one's life renders it public property, and those who do so cannot (or should not) expect that their representation of themselves, and especially of others, will meet with universal approval.

With regard to the second issue, women in a patriarchal society may justly claim consideration as a vulnerable class; in addition, the predicament of caregivers, most of whom are women, needs to be weighed against the interests and rights of those they care for. The paramount concern of my recent work, however, has been with subjects who are rendered vulnerable because of impairments or illnesses, some of which limit or preclude self-representation in ways not characteristic of gender. In any case, no group has an exclusive or unique claim to vulnerability. Rather than calibrate protection according to some theoretical hierarchy of vulnerable classes, it seems preferable to determine vulnerability on a case-by-case basis. Granting blanket exemption from ethical scrutiny to life writing on the basis of genre or to familial life writing on the basis of gender would not be advisable.

In any case, when used in such circumstances, the term "policing" itself warrants scrutiny. The sense invoked here seems to be peculiar to academics, who use it to refer to criticism that covertly asserts power over the disadvantaged in a manner that exploits professional or class privilege. It evokes a scenario involving domination and subjection. My first objection to the term lies in the fact that it makes a prejudgment, thus begging the question. Like the term "political correctness," with which it is bound up, it is typically used to preclude or cut off, rather than to initiate, debate; "policing" is implicitly repressive and therefore wrong: end of argument. My second objection is that it often falsely imputes power to those identified as the police—or at least overestimates their power for rhetorical effect. Granted, academic critics derive some power from their professional standing, but vis-à-vis many life writers, whose books are far more widely reviewed and whose audiences are far larger, their actual influence is often not very substantial. For better or worse, such critics are hardly in a position to suppress writers who reach audiences quite independently of academic sanction. My third objection is that the term suggests a degree of coercion and a motive not usually inherent in the discourse to which it is applied.

There are several related and overlapping questions here: first, whether life writing is, or can be, controlled at all; second, whether I think life writing should be regulated and in what way; third, whether I myself want to regulate or control life writing. Underlying these questions is a fourth: whether *criticism* constitutes regulation, control, or "policing." To answer the first, life writing has always been and will always be, in some degree, controlled by the powerful. After all, not all life writing gets published; life writing is always already monitored by mostly anonymous cultural forces that operate through the literary marketplace.[1] The winnowing process of publishing literally silences many life writers by denying them access to print; marketing—or the lack thereof—may minimize the readership of others (often for arbitrary, ill-considered, or self-fulfilling reasons). Further, this process is largely inaccessible and the parties un-accountable. It is carried out by agents, editors, and marketers behind the scenes, and the invisibility of the process protects it from scrutiny by the general public and by critics like myself, who are trained to read texts, not to investigate how they negotiate their way past cultural gatekeepers. Because it is preemptive, the control of publishers over life writing is far greater than that of critics and potentially far more insidious than any retroactive commentary. By nature, the former may qualify as policing; the latter may not.

The gatekeeping process cries out for thorough ethnographic analysis. It would be highly illuminating to know more about what sorts of life writing do *not* get published and why—that is, what sorts of life writing get written but never published. To cite one pertinent subculture, the disability community is rife with anecdotal evidence of editors and agents who demand or favor a particular angle, emplotment, or tone in disability memoir. In this regard, buzzwords found in blurbs, like "uplifting" and "life-affirming," are revealing indices of what gets published and what does not. Poster lives may be welcomed; narratives by angry former poster children may not be. My sense is that there is much vital and valuable life writing that does not reach print—that, as with other genres, publishers usually favor familiar stories but also, as is less likely with other genres, paradoxically and maddeningly rule out narratives on the grounds that "that has been done already." (Certain kinds of lives seem to be subject to quotas.) I am suggesting, then, that life writing is, and has always been, regulated, but not by academic critics, directly or indirectly, and not necessarily for good reason. In this regard, I would like to see life writing "deregulated," liberated from excessive control; the process of cultural gatekeeping would ideally be more liberal and more transparent.

I would like to see greater diversity in life writing, in two distinct respects: more kinds of *lives* represented and more kinds of *representation*.

With regard to the second question—do I want life writing to be regulated in any other way?—my answer is no. As we have seen, those who produce life writing in the professions are subject to regulation of another kind. Such regulation exists for good reason: life writing often entails the violation of others' privacy, and professions empower professionals over their clients. Professional life writing, then, is particularly likely to harm its subjects. To prevent this, there are systematic and procedural safeguards. One is the protection of confidentiality through anonymity or pseudonymity, though as we have seen, this fails to protect subjects against the possibility of painful self-recognition. The other is the obtaining of subjects' consent, which is ineffective in situations that are inherently coercive. My sense of such formal safeguards, then, is that, while well intentioned, they may be excessively burdensome to life writers, on the one hand, and insufficiently protective of subjects, on the other. Reliance on principles and procedures for protection may ultimately miss the point; the filling out of forms concerning the treatment of human subjects by such life writers may be more effective as an occasion for ethical reflection than as a guarantee of ethical practice. In the end, the protection of such subjects may depend as much on the ethos of particular life writers as on their application of ethical principle and their adherence to professional practices.

With regard to *lay* life writing, which is my main concern, I encourage the explicit acknowledgment of ethical issues in the hope that rehearsing such issues may induce, rather than merely delineate, ethical behavior. Lay life writers—as well as their subjects—stand to benefit from conscientious and scrupulous consideration of who might be hurt by life writing and how. Readers are likely to be more receptive to writers who face up to the ethical challenges inherent in their projects than to those who evade them; moreover, self-reflexive life writing is often aesthetically as well as ethically enriched. In any case, I encourage heightened awareness of, and vigorous debate about, the ethical issues inherent in intimate life writing; I call for self-scrutiny especially on the part of those representing vulnerable subjects. I am not calling for any formal regulation of lay life writing—not even the use of contracts between life writers and their subjects. Rather, I call for scrutiny of the sort formally applied to professional life writing to be exercised on an informal, voluntary, and self-reflexive basis. But the proof is finally in the practice, what life writers *do* rather than what they *say* they do.

To answer the third question, I do not aspire to be the czar of life writing, nor even to see such an office created. Yet it would be disingenuous of me to say that I do not want to exert what power I may have as a critic over life writing—else why write this book? But I do not consider this to be policing. While I cannot forswear whatever privilege attends my academic status, I do not consider the exercise of ethical principles and approaches in critical discourse to be policing. Policing is covert and coercive, intended to contain or constrain, rather than to expand and enrich, the range of life writing practices.

Advocating special scrutiny of the representation of vulnerable subjects leaves me open to another "p" charge: that of paternalism. I have tried to specify conditions that may entail vulnerability without claiming that they invariably lend themselves to exploitation. To say that disabled subjects are necessarily passive and vulnerable in their representation would be patronizing; I haven't claimed that. Rather, I have focused on particular instances that arguably do involve specific kinds of vulnerability. In addition, in the cases of Heidi Comfort and Shane Fistell (chapter 5) and even, perhaps, Adam Dorris (chapter 4), I have suggested that impairments that reduce social inhibition may in fact empower subjects to resist objectifying representation. Thus, I have tried to avoid an approach that some would denounce as policing (for restricting life writers) and others would denounce as paternalism (for overprotecting subjects). I have been concerned not so much to adjudicate cases and render ethical judgments as to raise pertinent questions and to model a form of inquiry. In any case, I would like my project to be judged by its explicit motives and actual effects, not its presumed politics or possible effects.

Let me conclude by proposing a different perspective on, and a different metaphor for, ethical criticism of life writing. One function of the police—in theory if not in practice—is to protect the vulnerable from harm, abuse, and exploitation. It is because that function is carried out with the entire apparatus of state power that it so often miscarries. As is often the case, then, the metaphor or analogy has a built-in bias—in this case, against policing. Although we need to acknowledge that difficult ethical dilemmas are built into life writing, what is called for is not more but rather less policing of life writing than already takes place. We may need, then, to turn to a very different arena for our metaphor—perhaps to gardening, for as a particularly vital art, life writing needs to be delicately and carefully nurtured, not coercively controlled.

Notes

PREFACE

1. I use the term in this intuitive sense, but I cannot ignore the fact that it has acquired partisan connotations in bioethics through association with the "death with dignity" movement. There are two related issues here. First, there is the danger of slippage from concern with patients' valuation of their lives to concern with the value of their lives to society. Second, "whereas 'death with dignity' first emerged as a compassionate response to the threat of overtreatment, patients now face the threat of undertreatment because of pressures to contain the escalating costs of health care" (Beauchamp and Childress 127). Thus, the idea that some lives lack dignity or are not "meaningful" can too easily be used to rationalize not treating patients or not keeping them alive.

1. CONSENSUAL RELATIONS: LIFE WRITING AND BETRAYAL

1. MacDonald's enlightenment was particularly painful and public. Having agreed to participate in prepublication promotion, he was interviewed by Mike Wallace for *60 Minutes.* Only when Wallace read him an accusatory passage did he learn of McGinniss's betrayal, and the camera recorded his visible shock (Malcolm, *Journalist* 31).

2. Some still find the verdict controversial. In 1995, Jerry Allen Potter and Fred Bost published *Fatal Justice: Reinvestigating the MacDonald Murders,* which argues that MacDonald did not receive a fair trial and is likely innocent.

3. Interestingly, in legal usage, the term "consensual" means "existing or entered into by mutual consent without formalization by document or ceremony" (*American Heritage Dictionary,* 4th ed.).

4. If the project involved only a conflict of interests, McGinniss's dilemma would have been a practical one, in which his desires were in conflict with an ethical rule, rather than an ethical one, in which two obligations or roughly equivalent values were in conflict.

5. For a more extensive probing of the ethics of life writing involving parents, see Nancy K. Miller. Miller sees such narratives as entailing betrayal, but she considers such betrayal (mostly) an enactment of a healthy relationality: "The betrayal of secrets is a requirement of the autobiographical act. To mark off your difference through betrayal—you may be the [parent], I'm the writer—is the confirmation of both separation *and* relation. For autobiography is about who we are in relation to the other, alive and dead, father and mother. That broken bond is essential to the making not only of autobiography but of history" (124).

2. AUTO/BIOGRAPHICAL, BIOMEDICAL, AND ETHNOGRAPHIC ETHICS

1. For this reason, the professional code is sometimes referred to as "physician ethics," as distinct from medical or biomedical ethics. Mary Mahowald helpfully distinguishes among various related terms:

Van Rensselaer Potter first applied the term "bioethics" to ethical issues regarding population and environment, but the term "bio" has clearly been interpreted to extend beyond biological issues to those involving health care. "Medical ethics" has a long history if the term "medical" is construed as applicable to anyone involved in health care. But its meaning may be restricted to those who are "medical" in the narrower sense, namely, physicians. [Robert M.] Veatch maintains that "medical ethics" connotes the broader view, and proposes the term "physician ethics" for the narrower perspective. The terms "health care ethics" and "clinical ethics" explicitly indicate recognition that diverse professions are involved in health care issues, and more specific terms such as "nursing ethics" and "social work ethics" are used to identify the professional perspective from which ethical questions may be addressed. If we assume the broader concept of "medicine," and wish to incorporate the biological component as well, the term "biomedical ethics" serves our purpose. (141–42)

2. They define the "common morality" as "the set of norms that all morally serious persons share" or "moral norms that bind all persons in all places," as distinct from "*moral ideals* that individuals and groups voluntarily accept" and "*communal norms* that bind only members of specific moral communities" (3).

3. The crisis of poststructuralist ethnography has also manifested itself in "confessional tales," in which the focus is not on the culture "out there" but on the processes by which that culture is investigated, written, and inevitably distorted and appropriated (Brettell 1).

4. The procedure in oral history is instructive. Interviewers are advised to transcribe interviews as accurately as possible, edit them only for clarity and readability, then return them to the interviewees for review and correction; finally, interviewees are asked to sign a legal agreement governing the use of the material. The process grants interviewees maximum control over the texts, and the process is quite visible—especially if tapes and transcripts are preserved (*How to Do Oral History* 21–33).

5. The process by which standards have been extended to federally funded research on human subjects in the social sciences and even history has not been uncontroversial; for an account exploring concern about, or resistance to, the effect of such standards on academic freedom, see Shea. One of the concerns is that the notion of "harm" has been extended from physical harm—more likely in biomedical contexts—to psychological harm. The concern is that excessive fastidiousness about causing "distress" to subjects will stifle or stunt research.

6. Some bioethicists have urged the addition of "respect for the community" to the canonical principles of biomedical ethics. Of course, biomedicine tends to define communities very differently from anthropology, for example, in terms of shared genes that create predispositions or vulnerabilities to particular diseases. How to negotiate consent for research on such communities is naturally problematic. Nevertheless, this development bids to remove a major discrepancy between the ethics of these two fields. See Weijer. I am grateful to Julie Pedroni for bringing this point to my attention.

3. MAKING, TAKING, AND FAKING LIVES

1. In a sense, *all* forms of life writing may involve collaboration to a degree rarely acknowledged. Biography—even when not authorized—is never done single-handedly, at least when living sources are consulted. And autobiography is often, perhaps almost always, a relational enterprise. Even when it is not, it may require backstage consultation with others to fill in memory's gaps. In addition, some critics have been at pains to point out that much writing—even literary writing—that we think of as having a single author is in fact the product of a number of hands. As in the case of John Stuart Mill's *Autobiography*, it may involve contributions by several individuals other than the nominal author, with some coming after that author's death (Stillinger 51–63). I confine myself here to autobiographical projects that involve conscious and active cooperation between two major contributors.

2. "Subject" is today an ambiguous, multivalent term: grammatically, it suggests agency; politically, it suggests the opposite—passivity (or worse, subjection); in poststructuralism, it suggests constructedness, fluidity, and provisionality. Here I use it in none of these senses but rather in the everyday sense of "topic"—in this case, the person the book is about.

Some critics refer to the subject of collaborative autobiography as the "dictator," others as the "speaker." In the case of ethnographic autobiography, "dictator" seems too often ironic, in view of the political meaning of that term; that is, it implies a kind of dominance not characteristic of the usual speaker; in the case of celebrity autobiography, it may be more apt, but even there it underestimates the agency of the collaborator.

The problem with using the term "speaker" for what Philippe Lejeune calls "those who do not write" is that some who do not write do not *speak* either. I am thinking here not so much of deaf people, who may use sign to communicate their narratives and who generally can read the narratives their collaborators produce, but rather those whose disability may prevent speech and sign as well as writing—such as those with severe cerebral palsy or other such disorders. In any case, "speaker" implies the ability to speak, which is not universal, and cases of disability are extremely interesting and problematic in this regard. See my discussion of Sienkiewicz-Mercer later in this chapter.

What to call the other partner is also problematic. "Author" is sometimes technically correct, but subjects can be co-authors, and even when they are not, "author" may unfairly ascribe the resulting text to one partner. Similarly, "writer" may overstate the interviewer's role, while "editor" usually understates it. For lack of a better alternative, I use "writer" for the partner more responsible for the composition of the text, because in the majority of cases one partner does most of what we usually mean by "writing"—inscribing words by hand in lasting form.

3. Philippe Lejeune has argued, provocatively, that collaborative autobiography should be seen not as an inauthentic imitation of the "real thing," but rather as a generic variant that exposes "the secrets of fabrication and functioning of the 'natural' product" (186). That is,

he argues that the interpersonal division of labor in collaborative autobiography simply exposes what is occluded, because it is intrapersonal, in solo autobiography:

> A person is always *several* people when he is writing, even all alone, even his own life. . . . By relatively isolating the roles, the collaborative autobiography calls into question again the belief in a unity that underlies, in the autobiographical genre, the notion of author and that of person. We can divide the work in this way only because it is in fact always divided in this way, even when the people who are writing fail to recognize this, because they assume the different roles themselves. Anyone who decides to write his life story acts as if he were his own ghostwriter. (188)

This raises intriguing possibilities for ethical analysis, but they are beyond the scope of my inquiry. As far as I know, Lejeune's is the first extensive analysis of the dynamics (and implicitly the ethics) of collaboration; it remains the most penetrating.

4. As it happens, those in the publishing business sometimes use the marriage analogy for collaborative writing partnerships.

5. As should become clear, I use Lejeune's term broadly. That is, I do not use it to refer only or even mainly to autobiography written by professional ethnographers (i.e., trained anthropologists). In any case, even within the field of anthropology, ethnography may be divided into sub-fields, of which academic ethnography is only one. In his useful book *Ethnography: Step by Step*, David Fetterman sketches a continuum from detached "ivory tower" ethnographers to "applied ethnographers"—"administrative," "action," and "advocate" ethnographers—the last of whom "allow participants to define their reality, consider their view about the ideal solution to their problems, and then take an active role in making social change happen" (126).

Anthropology has reckoned forthrightly, if belatedly, with the issues I address here. This process has involved much painful self-examination and self-criticism, which has both responded to and encouraged the emergence of literacy and authority among those who were once the subjects—or objects—of ethnography. The anthropologist Ruth Behar, author of an exemplary collaborative autobiography, *Translated Woman: Crossing the Border with Esperanza's Story*, has noted:

> As those who used to be "the natives" have become scholars in their own right, often studying their home communities and nations, the lines between participant and observer, friend and stranger, aboriginal and alien are no longer so easily drawn. . . . We no longer, as Clifford Geertz put it in a much-quoted phrase, strain to read the culture of others "over the shoulders of those to whom they properly belong." We now stand on the same plane with our subjects; indeed, they will only tolerate us if we are willing to confront them face to face. ("Vulnerable Observers" 28)

Behar's title, "Vulnerable Observers," refers to contemporary ethnographers who render themselves vulnerable through autobiographical exposure of their own lives and their emotional investments in their subjects; she both represents and champions this confessional trend in current ethnography. As should be obvious, such a trend can raise additional ethical questions. There is a delicate line between bringing the observer into the frame, so to speak, and allowing the observer's presence in the foreground to obscure the ethnography's nominal subject. Overreaction to a false and self-protective self-effacement may produce an equally inappropriate self-aggrandizement.

6. See my chapter "HIV/AIDS and Its Stories," in *Recovering Bodies: Illness, Disability, and Life Writing*, especially the section "Family Plots: Relational AIDS Memoirs."

7. Success as a writer can help to even the balance, however. According to his *New York Times* obituary, Gerald Frank, who ghostwrote more than a dozen celebrity autobiographies (including those of Sheilah Graham, Diana Barrymore, and Zsa Zsa Gabor), claimed that he was so good at the as-told-to form that "drunks and madmen implored" him to write their autobiographies (Smith, "Gerald Frank").

8. An example of the former would be *Cancer in Two Voices*, by Sandra Butler and Barbara Rosenblum.

9. On violations of privacy and related issues, see Paul John Eakin, "The Unseemly Profession." My work in this area is greatly indebted to his written work and to informal exchanges with him.

10. For a fuller account of this example, see my chapter *"Black Elk Speaks* with Forked Tongue," in *Altered Egos: Authority in American Autobiography,* 189–209.

11. Szanton has assisted with the memoirs of Eugene Wigner, a Hungarian-born Manhattan Project physicist, Charles Evers, a civil rights leader and brother of Medgar Evers, and Edward Brooke, a former Massachusetts senator.

12. Such stories are not always worth what publishers pay for them. For example, according to Michael Korda, although publishers love the glamour of having an ex-president as an "author," presidential memoirs usually lose money (88).

13. According to Lejeune:

The ghostwriter must first intervene and can only do so in the midst of an interpersonal relationship of dialogue; but he must next erase his intervention and take over the relationship with the reader *as if he were the model.* No doubt he will often accept this change in role with relative indifference. . . . But if he grants some value to his writing, he will live through this difficult position in the form of frustration and humiliation, of *deprivation;* or else in the lyrical form of enthusiasm, of *possession.* (190)

Strickland evidently experienced her time masquerading as Lympany as deprivation.

14. See Peter Brooks on legal confession.

15. My account of these memoirs is indebted to Gladfelder's 1997 MLA paper "'I Want to Tell You': Ghost Authors and Criminal Subjects in the Eighteenth Century." For fuller accounts of these phenomena, see his book *Criminality and Narrative in Eighteenth-Century England: Beyond the Law.*

4 ADOPTION, DISABILITY, AND SURROGACY

1. An earlier version of this chapter was published in *Biography* as "Raising Adam: Ethnicity, Disability, and the Ethics of Life Writing in Michael Dorris's *The Broken Cord"* (21.4 [autumn 1998]: 421–44).

The news of Michael Dorris's suicide in the spring of 1997 was followed almost immediately by the revelation of allegations of child abuse made against him in the course of the disintegration of his marriage to Louise Erdrich. I am concerned that, insofar as this discussion takes issue with Dorris's representation of his son in *The Broken Cord,* I may be seen as engaging in the posthumous debate over his conduct as a father. On the contrary, this chapter was first conceived and drafted in the early 1990s in response to my reaction to *The Broken Cord* when I first read it, soon after it was published. It is in no way intended to offer credence or support to any of the allegations about Dorris. Although the widely reviewed and highly praised book has attracted some criticism (see Cook-Lynn, Stange, and Vizenor), my main concern here is its relation to the discourses of disability, which no one, to my knowledge, has previously addressed.

2. The publisher's classification of the book acknowledges its fluctuating focus. On the back cover of the paperback edition, one finds the description "autobiography/child care."

3. In the case of Adam Dorris, adoption created a rupture in his life narrative. From the father's perspective—and so from Adam's—his first three years remained an impenetrable blank. This is one reason why Adam's first memory, with which his own narrative portion of the book begins, is of meeting Michael Dorris at a foster home in South Dakota. "Open" adoption, of course, helps to repair this narrative lacuna.

4. Dorris was informed before the adoption that Adam was impaired—the official diagnosis was mental retardation—but Dorris was confident that good parenting could overcome any initial developmental delays. He evidently underestimated the severity of Adam's problems.

5. For an angry critique, from a Lakota perspective, of adoption outside the tribal community, see Elizabeth Cook-Lynn's review of The Broken Cord (15–16); first published in Wicazo Sa Review, it was later reprinted in her collection Why I Can't Read Wallace Stegner.

6. Lionnet's example is Dust Tracks on a Road by Zora Neale Hurston. Michael Fischer has discussed a similar kind of autobiography, offering as examples Maxine Hong Kingston's Woman Warrior, Michael Arlen's Passage to Ararat, and Marita Golden's Migrations of the Heart.

7. The narrative thus resembles a conversion narrative insofar as Dorris's unhappy awakening to the scope of FAS in Native American life causes him to question and even to reverse some of his convictions. His anagnorisis halfway through the book involves a shift from confidence in nurture to belief in nature; from political liberalism—the idea that oppression is entirely to blame for the degradation of reservation communities—to something resembling neoconservatism; from "theoretical explanations" (102) and ivory tower detachment to political activism and crusade; from affirmation of the "politically correct right of individual choice, . . . a self-serving cultural apology that each person was beyond reproach even for destructive behavior that extended to babies" (102–3), to the idea that individual (maternal) behavior is the proximate cause that has to be addressed.

8. Gerald Vizenor has commented acerbically on this aspect of The Broken Cord. In "Firewater and Phrenology," he denounces Dorris's association of the facial characteristics of FAS children with characterological traits as a kind of twentieth-century phrenology and characterizes such "social science revelations" as "the technologies of racial politics" (315–16). But the distinction Dorris draws is explicitly not a racial one; rather, it has to do with congenital traits that cut across racial lines. The language is reminiscent of eugenicism, but the individuals it stigmatizes (quite literally) are not a racial minority but those with visible congenital impairments.

9. An irony of this aspect of the book is that the two other adopted children were also affected by maternal alcoholism, although they exhibited the less serious condition known as fetal alcohol effect (FAE). Part of the subtext of the book, then, is that Adam represents an extreme case of a condition shared by all three children Dorris and Erdrich adopted.

10. Consider Jessamyn West's ecstatic response to being diagnosed with tuberculosis early in her life: "I have never been more elated. After two years of being unable to climb stairs without panting; of pleurisy pains that made me crawl to the bathroom; of cheeks flushed to plum color in the afternoon, I now had a name for these symptoms. They were not imaginary. I was not a malingerer. I was not a hypochondriac. I was like a person who, having been living in a dream of insanity, wakes up to find himself sane. Sick, yes; but sane"

(27). Since a diagnosis of insanity obviously would not have provided this sort of relief, the passage speaks volumes about the stigma of mental illness.

11. Another interesting exception is *Deaf Like Me*, by Thomas and James Spradley, a parental memoir of a deaf child, Thomas's daughter Lynn. (Thomas's brother James, an anthropologist, helped with the writing.) It was originally published in 1978 when she was quite young. Later, one of her teachers at a school for the deaf brought the book to her attention; after reading it, she contributed an epilogue for the 1985 edition.

12. An additional complication lies in the fact that, beyond her contribution of a separate foreword, Louise Erdrich functioned as her husband's collaborator both as mother to Adam and as reconstructor, if not co-author, of the story; the book is dedicated to "Louise, who shares this story[,] who joined me in its living and telling" (v). Erdrich and Dorris generally characterized themselves as collaborators in all of their writing, but the extent of her involvement in the writing of *The Broken Cord* is not clear. Notably, however, she also assisted Adam in writing his story.

13. For the sake of consistency with the text, I call him Adam as well, except in the final short section, where I refer to an essay written after he died, in which his father uses his real name.

14. For further discussion of this mode of autobiography, see my *American Autobiography: The Prophetic Mode*.

15. In later pieces, such as "Fetal Alcohol Syndrome: A Parent's Perspective," Dorris was careful to emphasize that FAS is not a "Native American" problem but a global one.

16. Narratives by individuals with fetal alcohol syndrome are quite rare. All the more noteworthy, then, is *The Blood Runs Like a River through My Dreams*, by Nasdijj. A mixed-blood born to an alcoholic Navajo mother, Nasdijj not only has FAS but also adopted a child with it. (His son, Tommy Nothing Fancy, died at the age of six.) Here we have a very different perspective on FAS and a very different father-son relationship, for rather than coming between them, the condition bound them together.

17. In "The Broken Self," Margit Stange faults Dorris's rhetoric of "epidemic" and "race suicide." In addition, she has criticizes Dorris's writing on fetal alcohol syndrome for misogyny: "For Dorris and other writers on Native American struggles, this notion of alcoholic disease as a legacy passed on by the female bearers of children has enabled an etiology of Native American distress in which woman is both the medium of infection and, through her sexuality and fertility, an infectious agent in her own right" (127). The problem, as Stange sees it, is that pregnant women are singled out for scrutiny and blame, with too little attention to the social, cultural, and economic factors that encourage alcoholism among Native Americans. One consequence is that some of the "remedies"—sterilization of alcoholic women of childbearing age—would seem to be more truly genocidal than the "epidemic" of FAS. Stange characterizes Dorris's response to the problem as a "fantasy of the restoration of the true racial self by the excision of women from the racial body" (134). Elizabeth Cook-Lynn has voiced a related critique, arguing that Dorris did not give enough attention or credence to approaches to FAS that build on indigenous cultural values (14–15).

18. For more positive examples of parental narratives of children with disabilities, see Spradley and Spradley, which has to do with a deaf daughter; Paul West, which concerns a daughter who is deaf and brain-damaged; Bérubé, about a son with Down syndrome; and Nasdijj, which concerns a son with FAS. Only the last of these children is adopted.

19. The dangers of such distinctions between human beings and "persons" are illustrated by Peter Singer's notorious proposition that since newborn infants are not persons, it isn't always wrong to kill them—as when they are impaired and seemingly doomed to a life of

suffering. One can accept the distinction, of course, without drawing Singer's conclusion from it. He justifies his conclusion by a sort of utilitarian calculus that the sum of good in the world would be greater if a defective child were killed (and perhaps replaced by a "normal" one). A different approach (deontological, or duty-based) would grant disabled infants protection precisely because of their vulnerability, regardless of their potential.

5. BEYOND THE CLINIC

1. As broadcast in the United States by PBS, the series comprised only four episodes: "Ragin' Cajun," "Rage for Order," "Island of the Colorblind," and " 'Don't Be Shy, Mr. Sacks.'"

2. For such a view of Sacks, see Leonard Cassuto, "Oliver Sacks: The P. T. Barnum of the Postmodern World?" and "Oliver Sacks and the Medical Case Narrative." Cassuto argues that Sacks combines features of the case study and the freak show without reproducing the alienating and objectifying effects of either. My ideas about Sacks have been shaped by dialogue with Cassuto, but we reach substantially different conclusions.

3. According to his memoir *Uncle Tungsten* (2001), Sacks became familiar early on with some constituents of the freak show in the form of illustrations in medical textbooks belonging to his parents, who were both physicians:

> I would rummage through them at random, often in a state of mixed fascination and horror. Some of them I turned to again and again: there was Bland-Sutton's *Tumours Innocent and Malignant*—this was especially notable for its line drawings of monstrous teratomas and tumors, Siamese twins joined in the middle; Siamese twins with their faces fused together; two headed calves; a baby with a tiny accessory head near its ear; . . . an ovarian cyst so large it had to be carried on a handcart; and, of course, the Elephant Man. (234–35)

Further experience with the "monstrous" was less voluntary. His mother would bring home malformed fetuses: "Some of these had been stillborn, others she and the matron had quietly drowned at birth, . . . feeling that if they lived, no conscious or mental life would ever be possible for them. Eager that I should learn about anatomy and medicine, she dissected several of these for me, and then insisted, though I was only eleven, that I dissect them myself. She never perceived, I think, how distressed I became" (240–41). Perhaps Sacks's later concentration on anomalous neurological conditions has been a way of working through this early trauma by investing the "monstrous" with conscious life.

4. Of course, parental consent is not beyond ethical scrutiny. One sometimes wonders whether a kind of "stage parent" syndrome doesn't affect the parents of some disabled children, such as those who permit them to become poster children.

5. Federal Statute 45 CFR 46.102 governs "research involving human subjects." A human subject is defined as "a living individual about whom an investigator (whether professional or student) conducting research obtains (1) data through intervention or interaction with the individual, or (2) identifiable private information" (d).

6. See the book by that title by James I. Charlton.

7. See Weijer, "Protecting Communities in Research." Weijer notes that concern for communities arose first in developing countries, was refined to apply to indigenous groups in North America, and is now being extended to other sorts of groups, including ethnic groups such as Ashkenazi Jews and "disease communities" such as people with HIV/AIDS. Although disabled people do not consider themselves diseased, some disability communities

are analogous to "disease communities" in being rendered vulnerable by a shared physiological condition; others are analogous to Ashkenazi Jews in sharing a genetic condition that renders them vulnerable. As Weijer notes, problems arise when communities under consideration lack political structures empowered to review proposals and grant permission. But the acknowledgment that communities have interests distinct from, and at times in conflict with, those of individuals is an important first step.

8. See Clifford, "Partial Truths," for example.

9. For an example of a subject approaching an ethnographer, see Behar, *Translated Woman*.

10. As *Uncle Tungsten* demonstrates, Sacks found models for his medical ethic and for the idea of a humanistic clinical tale in his parents, both of whom were physicians (93, 234).

11. History provides us with examples of even more destructive forms of medicalizing, such as the "medicalization" of Jewishness as pathology by Nazi physicians (see Gilman, *Body*). There is thus no guarantee that what passes for medicalization will be demystifying, let alone de-stigmatizing.

12. The history of that account may be relevant here, insofar as it reflects Sacks's position with regard to the medical establishment. He first wrote up a number of his case histories in 1969, but he first published this material in 1970 in the form of letters to the editors (written with collaborators) of various medical journals; these letters combined scientific and humanistic discourse. One of them, published in the *Journal of the American Medical Association* (*JAMA*), explicitly warned of potentially dangerous side effects of L-dopa in this population of patients. It drew a sharply critical response attacking Sacks for undermining "the atmosphere of therapeutic optimism needed for the maximal efficiency of L-DOPA" (qtd. in Hawkins, "Myth" 10). Attributing the resistance of his colleagues to the anecdotal nature of his letters, Sacks wrote up his cases in more conventional form, replete with charts and statistics; none of these was accepted for publication. In 1972, however, Sacks was invited to publish the material as an essay in *The Listener*; encouraged by the response, he wrote up more case studies and published the book in 1973. Since its first publication, the book has gone through five editions with periodic updates. More interesting, the project became Sacks's first multimedia production, for it gave rise to a British TV documentary film directed by Duncan Dallas (1973); a one-act play by Harold Pinter, "A Kind of Alaska," which has had several productions; and, finally, a feature film starring Robin Williams in the role of Sacks (1990). What began as a kind of end run around a skeptical or hostile audience of colleagues in effect launched Sacks's career as a writer and, eventually, a kind of celebrity and neurological guru.

13. This is even more so in the film, for which Sacks served as a consultant, though he cannot be held responsible for its content. The film largely dispenses with the idea of successful accommodation. The case of the patient Leonard, which eclipses all of the others, ends with his utter regression, as evidenced by the audience's final glimpse of him being diapered by his mother and put to bed. The major beneficiary of the Sacks figure's final homily about what has been learned—to cherish life, family, and so on—is the doctor himself, who is inspired to ask a friendly and supportive nurse for a date.

14. Oddly, but perhaps accurately, the film presents Sacks as lobbying for the use of L-dopa against a benighted and economy-minded administration.

15. Kusnetz points out that Sacks seems quite oblivious at first to the extent to which his female patients, especially, may be involved in "transference-neuroses" with him (188–90).

16. Remarks made in interviews suggest that his extracurricular writing may have begun as compensation for lack of recognition in his primary field:

I remember some time ago, a former chief of mine, before I'd published much, was concerned because I wasn't on the academic register, climbing up. He said, "Sacks, I'm worried about you. You don't have any position." I said, "Oh, yes I do," and he said, "What?" And I said, "I have a position in the heart of medicine."

He said, "That's a lot of rhetoric." This has to do with being a little eccentric. My medical life is certainly different from the lives of many doctors, and yet, it may have its own center. (Interview 33)

17. Murdo McRae argues that this categorization and other features of his work reveal the "abstract and impersonal character of his own thinking," its "tendency to turn each patient into a replica of every other one" (98). McRae's article predates *An Anthropologist on Mars*; like much criticism of Sacks, McRae's may be more applicable to his early work.

18. Loss of proprioception is also the issue in "The Man Who Fell Out of Bed," which concerns a man who throws his leg out of bed because he does not recognize it as his own. The brevity and detachment of this case seem odd in view of Sacks's own similar experience of loss of proprioception—the subject of his first venture into autobiography, *A Leg to Stand On*. Sacks's lavishing of description and interpretation on his own experience contrasts sharply with his distancing account of a permanent case of the same syndrome in these two subjects.

19. The testimony of his memoir *Uncle Tungsten: Memories of a Chemical Boyhood* (2001) is interesting in this regard. The bulk of the book vividly recreates Sacks's childhood fascination with science, especially chemistry. Very little of it is overtly autobiographical, much less confessional. The exceptions are interesting precisely in that they reveal that his immersion in science served to insulate him from traumatic experiences. The most obvious of these, to which Sacks merely alludes, is the emergence of psychosis in his brother Michael after he was beaten at a boarding school. (Oliver, too, had been beaten.) Sacks acknowledges the connection between his passion for science and the anxiety that threatened to overwhelm him:

I became terrified of him, for him, of the nightmare which was becoming reality for him, the more so as I could recognize similar thoughts and feelings in myself, even though they were hidden, locked up in my own depths. What would happen to Michael, and would something similar happen to me, too? It was at this time that I set up my own lab in the house, and closed the doors, closed my ears, against Michael's madness. It was at this time that I sought for (and sometimes achieved) an intense concentration, a complete absorption in the worlds of mineralogy and chemistry and physics, in science—focusing on them, holding myself together in the chaos. It was not that I was indifferent to Michael; I felt a passionate sympathy for him, I half-knew what he was going through, but I had to keep a distance also, create my own world from the neutrality and beauty of nature, so that I would not be swept into the chaos, the madness, the seduction, of his. (186)

One could say that Sacks's whole career involves alternation between forays into unruly inner worlds and retreat into intellectual systems such as the periodic table.

20. Although this is not necessarily a culpable endeavor, Sacks had occasionally simulated neurological conditions: "'I've had to go out into the world—into their world—and share it,' Dr. Sacks says. So great is his desire for empathic experience that he has sometimes tried to induce his patients' neurological symptoms in himself. . . . 'When you take Haldol you learn how to be parkinsonian [sic], and as it wears off, mercifully, you forget'" (qtd. in Fox, "Biology," on the occasion of the publication of *Mars*). Furthermore, according to the same interview, "he plans to experience total, if temporary, color-blindness by having the area of his brain responsible for color vision 'buzzed' with a magnetic device" (30).

21. That Sacks cannot entirely transcend his medical perspective is evident in this overview of the Deaf: "Whilst I never forgot the 'medical' status of the deaf, I had now to see them in a new, 'ethnic' light, as a people with a distinctive language, sensibility, and culture of their own" (x–xi).

22. And sometimes, as here, one senses the insecurity of a man who, by his own testimony, lives an eccentric, somewhat compulsive, and quite reclusive life.

23. Of course, it is Sacks who manages our perception of this interaction; we are never able to assess the behind-the-scenes interaction between subject and life writer. And yet there is an important difference between granting even this kind of agency in representation and not doing so.

24. In the video version, Sacks notes that the islanders were converted to Congregationalism in the nineteenth century, a development that made them reluctant to marry outsiders and thus exacerbated the problem of inbreeding.

25. Obviously, Sacks is not the author of the film series in the way that he is of his written work: he is not the director of the films. But neither would I say that he is their subject; insofar as his is the only voice-over, he functions as a writer here, too. The ultimate responsibility for the films' ethics and aesthetics are the director's, as is the legal responsibility for securing consent and permission from participants. But this does not exempt Sacks from scrutiny of the ethics of the subjects' representation, most of which is produced by his interaction with them and his comments about them.

26. Another of his subjects with Tourette's syndrome, Lowell Handler, has in a sense turned the tables on Sacks. The two traveled together quite extensively to meet Touretters around the country, and in his memoir, *Twitch and Shout*, Handler offers a very interesting portrait of Sacks as an eccentric whose mannerisms of speech and gesture resemble those of Touretters. Handler acknowledges some anxiety about whether he is a friend or a specimen to Sacks; he seems to conclude that he is the former, and indeed he sometimes treats Sacks as himself a rather odd specimen. While this attests to Sacks's ability, despite his shyness, to relate easily and informally to people with neurological disorders, it also suggests the value—perhaps the necessity—of the perspective from the other side, which presents Sacks in a very different way from the way he presents himself.

6. LIFE WRITING AS DEATH WRITING

1. Ironically, among some disabled people, PAS is understood as an acronym for personal assistant services.

2. In the United States, published book-length accounts of assisted suicide are not new. For example, in 1957, the journalist Lael Tucker Wertenbaker published an account of her husband's suicide, *Death of a Man*, and in 1976, the Quaker writer Jessamyn West (best known for *The Friendly Persuasion*) published an account of her younger sister's suicide, *The Woman Said Yes*. Additional accounts have been published by Betty Rollin (*Last Wish*, 1985), Derek Humphry, a co-founder of the Hemlock Society (*Jean's Way*, 1978), and Judy Brown (*The Choice*, 1995). Although they evince awareness of both the transgressiveness of assisted suicide and the trickiness of writing about it, these accounts are not impelled by commitment to a cause. The narrators' motives are personal rather than political—to honor the decision of the deceased and to justify their own involvement in the suicide. In contrast, more recent accounts are distinguished by their awareness of being ethically and politically controversial. This reflects the increasingly urgent public debate over the ethics of euthanasia.

3. This is a somewhat ambiguous term. Here it refers not to individuals who attempt suicide and "fail" but to individuals left behind by people close to them, usually family members, who die by suicide. In "Memoirs of Assisted Suicide," which discusses accounts by Wertenbaker, West, and others, Richard K. Sanderson points out how complicated the motives of suicide assistants can be. My debt to Sanderson goes beyond his published or presented work; his comments on an early draft of this chapter helped improve it substantially.

4. A good example, as its subtitle suggests, is *My Son, My Sorrow: The Tragic Tale of Dr. Kevorkian's Youngest Patient*, by Carol Loving. Carol Loving's son Nicholas manifested symptoms of ALS (amyotrophic lateral sclerosis, also known as Lou Gehrig's disease) at a very young age—in his mid-twenties—and indicated early on that he would prefer to end his life rather than to suffer and eventually die from the effects of progressive paralysis. His mother wrote to Jack Kevorkian on his behalf, and both son and mother were greatly relieved when Kevorkian agreed to help them. The book is cast not as a memoir of, or memorial to, the son whose death Kevorkian helped bring about but as a plea for the legalization of physician-assisted suicide. Among assisted suicide narratives I have read, it is the most explicitly and single-mindedly messianic.

5. In *Seduced by Death*, Hendin critiques several such accounts, including that of the physician Timothy Quill—not, as I initially suspected, a pen name—who assisted a patient's suicide and then wrote about it, first in the *New England Journal of Medicine* and later in a book, *Death and Dignity*, and that of Andrew Solomon, whose account of assisting his mother's suicide appeared in the *New Yorker*.

6. My treatment of *Daniel* is indebted to a wide-ranging discussion with members of the NEH Summer Institute on Disability Studies, directed by Paul Longmore and Rosemarie Garland Thomson, at San Francisco State University in July 2000.

7. In a paper on memoirs by maternal survivors of suicide, Richard Sanderson notes that all of the suicides were male. Given the gendering of the expression of grief and mourning in contemporary North America, suicide survivor narratives are more likely to be written by women, as is the case with Daniel, whose mother becomes the primary caregiver, decision maker, and, posthumously, narrator and memorialist. In Jeffrey's case, it is his father who takes charge of the decision making and who writes the book—with implications to be explored later.

8. In his examination of procedures in the Netherlands, Herbert Hendin points out that Dutch physicians sometimes make the decision to end the lives of patients, without consulting them or their families, according to the physicians' own sense of whether they would want to live in the patient's condition (96). To end the life of a competent patient who has not requested euthanasia goes beyond nonvoluntary euthanasia; the act is located a significant distance down the slippery slope from "assisted suicide."

9. Although he was told at one point that he would be transferred to Craig on September 11, 1992, he hadn't been transferred by September 14, and he died days later.

10. I am grateful to Richard Sanderson for italicizing this passage for me.

11. That disability does not necessarily rule out a medical practice is illustrated by the career of the psychiatrist Arnold Beisser, but Beisser contracted polio after he graduated from medical school. (See his autobiographical book, *Flying without Wings*.) A disability as severe as Daniel's would rule out pursuit of a medical degree. Yet it could be argued that some experience of disability might be a desirable attribute in certain fields of medicine.

12. One way of reading Kafka's "The Metamorphosis" is as an account of a family's response to their contamination by such a stigma.

13. Juliet Rothman lists Darryl Stingley's *Happy to Be Alive* in her bibliography of books on spinal cord injury but does not claim to have read it.

14. Mediation—point of view—is interesting here. Although Robillard openly acknowledges the severity of his disability, his occasional descriptions of others' perceptions of him (generically) as "slumped in his wheelchair" are somewhat startling, because his prose, while not polished, is not at all slack. Similarly, being reminded of the labor-intensive collaborative process by which he "wrote" his book, using an improvised set of lip signs for individual letters, unsettles the print medium's implication of his manual dexterity. This is not to say that in this case print lies—though it masks the process by which it was composed— but rather that it renders an inside view of Robillard's condition, what it feels like to him. His paralysis is a huge inconvenience, and he would rather not be disabled, but he does not experience his condition as dehumanizing him or vitiating his essence. Indeed, as a social scientist, he is acutely aware of social attitudes toward the terminally ill: "There is something about having a fatal disease, an officially diagnosed fatal illness, that immediately renders the diagnosee less worthy, and having fewer prospects, than others. . . . It is a social text, shared by most people in society and reproduced in their remarks" (43).

15. Emily Bauer, who also had ALS, chose to end her life by having her respirator turned off, but not until she was far along in the progression of her disease (see Andrew Malcolm, *This Far and No More*). Since this was illegal in her jurisdiction at the time (1983), the act involved a degree of subterfuge; while she was on a "routine" visit home, a sympathetic physician gave her an injection of Thorazine and then turned off her respirator. Since the mid-1980s, U.S. courts have established that refusing or discontinuing life-sustaining treatment is not "suicide" but rather an act of self-determination, an exercise of the right to refuse medical treatment, even if the result is death. As Dan W. Brock points out, however, the attempt to distinguish discontinuing life support from suicide is problematic; the crux of the matter is whether the act is morally justified (343–44). In any case, it is now considered legal and medically ethical for patients like Emily Bauer and Daniel Rothman, who are physically unable to turn off their respirators, to request the cessation of their life support. Such acts are not considered physician-assisted suicide.

16. See also the passage cited from *Daniel* in which his doctor announces that he couldn't "imagine how he could want to live," and his mother responds that what matters is whether Daniel can. It also matters whether the people around him can.

17. Unfortunately, the Web site is composed entirely in the third person and seems to be, like the book, entirely his father's creation, but E-mail holds out the possibility of access to Jeffrey's point of view.

18. Compare the (relatively) reassuring accounts of the deaths of Daniel Rothman ("And, gently, Daniel touched the other shore, and he was gone" [Rothman 143]); Carmen West ("the human machine that had struggled so hard to survive intolerable punishment had ceased to function. The lungs no longer struggled to bring in air. Carmen was dead" [West, *Woman* 177–78]); Wert Wertenbaker ("I said, 'I love you I love you please die,' and he said that one first phrase, too, and went into the final struggle to die and did" [Wertenbaker 180]); and Nick Loving ("Then came the unraveling of all the pain and torment, as a very long ethereal sigh flowed from my son" [Loving 255]).

19. He acknowledges that what he had considered a "secondary" purpose of the diary, to record the predicament of the caregiver, came back to haunt him: "To that end, I was perhaps much too open about my negative feelings, feelings some of the public found unacceptable and the D.A. found useful" (135).

20. The danger of projecting a death wish onto an ill or injured child is demonstrated in *Rescuing Jeffrey;* when Jeffrey blink-spelled "IWANTTOD," his father asked, "Jeffrey, do you want to die?" (Galli 51). As it happened, that was Jeffrey's intended message, but the correct anticipation of it may seem to ratify it, even if it did not elicit it; finishing this sentence for Jeffrey is tantamount to scripting his death.

21. Nancy Mairs, another woman with MS, has recognized and indicted the proposition that disabled people "have nothing to offer to the human project, that we are, in fact, not worth taking care of. This implication breaks my heart. I am reduced to a vortex, sucking in the resources of all around me without replenishing them in kind" (76).

22. See also Alasdair MacIntyre's *Dependent Rational Animals,* in which he bases a theory of virtue on the recognition of the universality of dependency in human existence.

7. GENOME AND GENRE

1. This phrase is from the subtitle of Matt Ridley's lively and sensible *Genome: The Autobiography of a Species in Twenty-three Chapters.* Ridley explores various ways in which the genome offers a record of human history and evolution, but given the complexity of the genome and the problem of the idea of the "autobiography" of an unself-conscious biological unit such as a species, he wisely does not develop this conceit.

2. Although not common, this has already been reported. According to McGee, "Already there are several well-known cases in which women's genetic tests were used to deny insurance for fetuses (as unborn members of the insured's family) on the basis of a fetal 'pre-existing' condition" (84).

3. As Alison Jolly explains, a gene *for* something may better be understood as a gene *against* something. That is, while it may take a subtle combination and interaction of genes to create a particular trait such as intelligence, it may take only one gene to undermine or destroy the effect of the other genes; that gene is the gene "for" the effect it produces (270). Matt Ridley puts it another way. In his account, the "gene for X" is actually a mutation of a gene that everyone has; thus, those who develop condition "X" either have a mutation of a common gene or else lack that gene. In any case, as Ridley intentionally reiterates: "GENES ARE NOT THERE TO CAUSE DISEASE" (passim).

4. See my *Recovering Bodies* for a further account of this trend in biomedicine (21–23).

5. For a provocative autobiographical/critical look at the implications of medical imaging, including DNA analysis (in the case of breast cancer), see Kay Cook's "Medical Identity: My DNA/Myself."

6. One of the ironies of DNA as unique identifier is that even though our genes may mark each of us (excepting identical twins) as unique, they are not uniquely ours; thus, although courts have ruled that genes may be patented by those who can successfully isolate them (Eisenberg 227–28), individuals may not patent their own genes. We may not commodify ourselves in this way or to this extent.

7. A recent example of the application of DNA evidence to the biography of European royalty was the determination that it was Louis XVII, the French dauphin—and not an impostor replacing him—who died in prison in France in 1795. (The determination of the identity of the dead prisoner involved matching DNA from surviving locks of Marie Antoinette's hair with DNA from the dead boy's heart, taken as a souvenir by one of the doctors who performed the initial autopsy.) The notion that the dauphin had survived led to various claims to his identity. One impostor had been "convincing enough to get the government of Nether-

lands [sic] to bury him under a tombstone indicating that he was the true heir to the French throne." The definitive identification of the real dauphin not only "completes" his biography but also drastically revises those of claimants to his identity. "The Bourbon family is now asking for a proper burial for the boy," though they have not, apparently, asked for the exhumation of the pretender (Daley 2).

8. Since DNA can be planted by police, its presence at a crime scene is subject to some doubt. Ironically, because it is almost impossible to remove from a crime scene, the utter absence of a suspect's DNA is more compelling than its presence. The typical scenario of exoneration, however, involves the freeing of a convict when tests not available at the time of conviction reveal that hair or semen thought to be the perpetrator's does not match the DNA of the convicted suspect.

9. The effect goes well beyond the life of the suspect to those of the suspect's family members and that of the crime victim, all of which may be changed by identification of a perpetrator.

10. An American writer, Blake Eskin, has also written an exposé, *A Life in Pieces*.

11. DNA might be invoked as a test of many narratives of contested identity, such as some recent supposedly Aboriginal autobiographies in Australia. Such an approach, though it promises definitive results, when the circumstances are right, also tends to reify and essentialize a blood-based notion of "authenticity."

12. See Mark Twain's "Jim Blaine and His Grandfather's Old Ram" and the section "Transports" in Sacks's *Man Who Mistook His Wife for a Hat*.

13. Richard Berendzen, who was fired for making obscene phone calls from his office when he was president of American University, was defended by his lawyers on the grounds that he had a genetic predisposition to act abnormally under stress. In his post-therapeutic autobiography, *Come Here*, however, Berendzen attributed his actions to childhood sexual abuse, an exculpatory schema now so common in apologia that it has been denounced as the abuse excuse (Nelkin and Lindee 144).

14. It should be noted that gene therapy in this instance is not as promising as it may seem. SCID is an obvious candidate for gene therapy—"a perfect target"—because it involves bone marrow cells, which are easily accessible and which rapidly reproduce themselves. Although its success does not guarantee that other conditions will be easily treatable, its failure would have been considered a very bad sign; according to an American physician, W. French Anderson, a member of the team that first attempted gene therapy in 1990, "because you can correct SCID doesn't mean you can correct any other disease . . . [but] if you can't correct SCID, you can't correct anything else" (Kolata A16). In addition, the experiment may not have been as successful as it first seemed: it was halted in September 2002 for fear that it had given one of the subjects, a three-year-old boy, a leukemia-like illness (Stolberg).

15. It is often the case, however, that even when genes can be identified, the first effective therapies to be devised intervene much later in the causal sequence. For example, the treatment of the genetic condition phenylketonuria (PKU) in children involves controlling diet rather than altering genes.

16. This tendency has been parodied and the determinism underlying it debunked in John J. Medina, *The Genetic Inferno: Inside the Seven Deadly Sins*.

17. One of the differences between the government-funded, not-for-profit Human Genome Project and the commercial Celera Genomics project is that the latter works from an even more limited sample; according to J. Craig Venter, the scientist who headed the private venture, Celera used DNA from "three females and two males who have identified themselves as Hispanic, Asian, Caucasian or African-American" (Recer 9A). Indeed, in April

2002, Venter revealed that the DNA decoded by Celera was mostly his; he apparently bypassed or subverted what was intended to be an anonymous selection process. Thus, the private project was revealed to have an autobiographical dimension and to be a hitherto unprecedented capitalization of the "I": call it Venter Capital. Some ethicists and genetic researchers expressed disappointment with Venter, but his revelation reminds us that "the human genome" is really not definitive.

18. See Diane Paul, "Eugenic Anxieties," for a discussion of the various understandings of the term.

19. See my chapter "Signs of Life: Deafness and Personal Narrative," in *Recovering Bodies*, 221–87.

20. I am grateful to Carrie Sandahl for alerting me to this phenomenon.

21. An extreme response to a family's susceptibility to HD occurred in 2002, when Carol Carr, who had lost her husband to it, shot to death both of her sons, who also had the disease, in a nursing home in Georgia (Rimer).

22. In view of the fact that the risk of carrying the Huntington's gene cast a pall over both sisters during their potential childbearing years—compromising their sense of their womanliness (72)—Wexler does not much explore what it must have been like for her mother to conceive and bear two children.

23. Indeed, Wexler felt that to render fully the dynamics of her family, she had to tell the story of her father's long-term affair with a colleague and close family friend against the woman's wishes. Although this friend later relented, Wexler's decision caused them to become estranged.

24. Her response is not atypical. According to Kimberly A. Quaid, when testing for the HD gene is offered free of charge, only about 12 percent of those eligible take the test. As of 1992, out of an estimated 125,000 people at risk for HD, only some 225 had been tested (5).

EPILOGUE

1. Despite academics' concern with underrepresentation of the marginalized in life writing, the dynamics of this sort of control have not been much examined. One reason may be that compared to other literary genres, life writing genres are quite accessible, even to the marginalized. (Indeed, what accounts in part for periodic backlashes against life writing—such as that against the "memoir boom" of the 1990s—is precisely its accessibility to new groups.) A 2002 essay on life writing by Lorraine Adams distinguishes somewhat prejudicially between life writing by "somebodies" (i.e., people already publicly known) and that by "nobodies" (i.e., people hitherto relatively anonymous). But historically, life writing, especially autobiography, has functioned as a point of entry into literary culture for disempowered others, such as slaves, Native Americans, and people with various illnesses and disabilities. In any case, my recent work has focused on, and advocated on behalf of, life writing by "nobodies."

Works Cited

Adams, Henry. *The Education of Henry Adams*. 1918. Ed. Ernest Samuels. Boston: Houghton Mifflin, 1973.

Adams, Lorraine. "Almost Famous: The Rise of the 'Nobody' Memoir." *Washington Monthly* (April 2002). http://www.washingtonmonthly.com/features/2001/0204.adams.html.

Albom, Mitch. *Tuesdays with Morrie: An Old Man, a Young Man, and Life's Greatest Lesson*. New York: Doubleday, 1997.

Annas, George J. "Rules for Gene Banks: Protecting Privacy in the Genetics Age." In Murphy and Lappé. 75–90.

——, and Sherman Elias, eds. *Gene Mapping: Using Law and Ethics as Guides*. New York: Oxford UP, 1992.

——. "Social Policy Research Priorities for the Human Genome Project." In Annas and Elias. 269–75.

Apter, Terri. "Expert Witness: Who Controls the Psychologist's Narrative?" In Josselson, *Ethics and Process*. 22–44.

Baier, Annette. "Trust and Anti-trust." *Ethics* 96.2 (January 1986): 231–60.

Battin, Margaret Pabst. "Manipulated Suicide." In *The Least Worst Death: Essays in Bioethics on the End of Life*. New York: Oxford UP, 1994. 195–204.

Bauby, Jean-Dominique. *The Diving Bell and the Butterfly*. Trans. Jeremy Leggatt. New York: Knopf, 1997.

Bayley, John. *Elegy for Iris*. New York: St. Martin's, 1999.

Beauchamp, Tom L., and James F. Childress. *Principles of Biomedical Ethics*. 5th ed. New York: Oxford UP, 2001.

Behar, Ruth. *Translated Woman: Crossing the Border with Esperanza's Story*. Boston: Beacon, 1993.

——. "The Vulnerable Observer." In *The Vulnerable Observer: Anthropology That Breaks Your Heart*. Boston: Beacon, 1996. 1–33.

Beisser, Arnold. *Flying without Wings: Personal Reflections on Loss, Disability, and Healing*. New York: Bantam, 1988.

Benjamin, Jessica. *Shadow of the Other: Intersubjectivity and Gender in Psychoanalysis*. New York: Routledge, 1998.

Berendzen, Richard, and Laura Palmer. *Come Here*. New York: Villard, 1993.

Bergmann, Linda S. "Widows, Hacks, and Biographers: The Voice of Professionalism in Elizabeth Agassiz's *Louis Agassiz: His Life and Correspondence*." *a/b: Auto/Biography Studies* 12.1 (spring 1997): 1–21.

Bérubé, Michael. *Life as We Know It: A Father, a Family, and an Exceptional Child*. New York: Pantheon, 1996.

Biklen, Douglas. *Communication Unbound: How Facilitated Communication Is Challenging Traditional Views of Autism and Ability/Disability*. New York: Teachers College P, 1993.

Bok, Sissela. *Secrets: On the Ethics of Concealment and Revelation*. New York: Pantheon, 1982.

Booth, Wayne C. *The Company We Keep: An Ethics of Fiction*. Berkeley: U of California P, 1988.

Brettell, Caroline B. "Introduction: Fieldwork, Text, and Audience." In *When They Read What We Write: The Politics of Ethnography*. Ed. Caroline B. Brettell. Westport, Conn.: Bergin and Garvey, 1993. 1–24.

Brock, Dan W. "Death and Dying." In Veatch. 329–56.

Broeker, Beth. "Stalked by My Birth Mother." *Salon.* http://www.salon.com/mwt/feature/2000/05/08/stalked/print.html.

Brooks, Peter. *Troubling Confessions: Speaking Guilt in Law and Literature*. Chicago: U of Chicago P, 2000.

Brown, Judy. *The Choice: Seasons of Loss and Renewal after a Father's Decision to Die*. Berkeley: Conari, 1995.

Butler, Sandra, and Barbara Rosenblum. *Cancer in Two Voices*. San Francisco: Spinsters Ink, 1991.

Campbell, Courtney. "Give Me Liberty and Give Me Death: Assisted Suicide in Oregon." In David Smith. *Alternatives to Physician-Assisted Suicide*. 40–62.

Caplan, Arthur L. "The Concepts of Health and Disease." In Veatch. 49–62.

Cassell, Eric J. *The Nature of Suffering and the Goals of Medicine*. New York: Oxford UP, 1991.

Cassuto, Leonard. "Oliver Sacks: The P. T. Barnum of the Postmodern World?" *American Quarterly* 52.2 (June 2000): 326–33.

——. "Oliver Sacks and the Medical Case Narrative." In *Disability Studies: Enabling the Humanities*. Ed. Sharon L. Snyder, Brenda Jo Brueggemann, and Rosemarie Garland-Thomson. New York: MLA, 2002. 118–30.

Charlton, James I. *Nothing about Us without Us: Disability Oppression and Empowerment*. Berkeley: U of California P, 1998.

Clifford, James. "On Ethnographic Allegory." In Clifford and Marcus. 98–119.

——. "On Ethnographic Authority." In *The Predicament of Culture: Twentieth-Century Ethnography, Literature, and Art*. Cambridge: Harvard UP, 1988. 21–54.

——. "Introduction: Partial Truths." In Clifford and Marcus. 1–26.

——, and George E. Marcus, eds. *Writing Culture: The Poetics and Politics of Ethnography*. Berkeley: U of California P, 1986.

Cockburn, Alexander. "Wonders in Barmy Land." *Nation*, 14 June 1993: 822.

Cohen, Randy. "Case Study Study." *New York Times Magazine*, 11 November 2001: 50.

——. "A Novel Solution." *New York Times Magazine*, 9 May 1999: 28.

Condit, Celeste Michelle. *The Meanings of the Gene: Public Debates about Human Heredity*. Madison: U of Wisconsin P, 1999.

Cook, Kay K. "Medical Identity: My DNA / Myself." In *Getting a Life: Everyday Uses of Autobiography*. Ed. Sidonie Smith and Julia Watson. Minneapolis: U of Minnesota P, 1996. 63–83.

Cook-Lynn, Elizabeth. "*The Broken Cord*" (review). In *Why I Can't Read Wallace Stegner and Other Essays: A Tribal Voice*. Madison: U of Wisconsin P, 1996. 11–16.

Cooke, Maeve. "Questioning Autonomy: The Feminist Challenge and the Challenge for Feminism." In *Questioning Ethics: Contemporary Debates in Philosophy*. Ed. Richard Kearney and Mark Dooley. New York: Routledge, 1999. 258–82.

Coombe, Rosemary J. "Author / izing the Celebrity: Publicity Rights, Postmodern Politics, and Unauthorized Genders." In Woodmansee and Jaszi. 101–31.

Couser, G. Thomas. *Altered Egos: Authority in American Autobiography*. New York: Oxford UP, 1989.

——. *American Autobiography: The Prophetic Mode*. Amherst: U of Massachusetts P, 1979.

——. *Recovering Bodies: Illness, Disability, and Life Writing*. Madison: U of Wisconsin P, 1997.

Cranor, Carl F., ed. *Are Genes Us? The Social Consequences of the New Genetics*. New Brunswick: Rutgers UP, 1994.

Crossley, Rosemary, and Anne McDonald. 1980. *Annie's Coming Out*. New York: Viking, 1984.

Daley, Suzanne. "Solving a Royal Mystery." *New York Times*, 23 April 2000, sec. 4:2.

Davidson, Elsa. "Size Matters." 20 October 1999. www.feedmag.com/deepread/dr26llofi.html.

Davis, Lennard J. *My Sense of Silence: Memoirs of a Childhood with Deafness*. Urbana: U of Illinois P, 2000.

——, ed. *Shall I Say a Kiss? Courtship Letters of a Deaf Couple*. Washington, D.C.: Gallaudet UP, 1999.

Davis, Miles, with Quincy Troupe. *Miles: The Autobiography*. New York: Simon and Schuster, 1989.

Davis, Todd F., and Kenneth Womack, eds. *Mapping the Ethical Turn: A Reader in Ethics, Culture, and Literary Theory*. Charlottesville: U of Virginia P, 2001.

Dawkins, Richard. *The Selfish Gene.* New York: Oxford UP, 1989.

deGrazia, Margreta. "Sanctioning Voice: Quotation Marks, the Abolition of Torture, and the Fifth Amendment." In Woodmansee and Jaszi. 281–302.

DeLury, George E. *But What If She Wants to Die? A Husband's Diary.* Secaucus, N.J.: Birch Lane, 1997.

DeMallie, Raymond J. Introduction to *The Sixth Grandfather: Black Elk's Teachings as Given to John G. Neihardt.* Ed. Raymond J. DeMallie. Lincoln: U of Nebraska P, 1984. 1–74.

Donchin, Anne. "Autonomy and Interdependence: Quandaries in Decision Making." In Mackenzie and Stoljar. 236–58.

"'Don't Be Shy, Mr. Sacks': Williams Syndrome." *The Mind Traveller: Oliver Sacks.* BBC. 1998.

Dorris, Michael. *The Broken Cord.* New York: Harper and Row, 1989.

———. "Fetal Alcohol Syndrome: A Parent's Perspective." In *Paper Trail.* 82–102.

———. *Paper Trail: Essays.* New York: HarperCollins, 1994.

———. "The Power of Love." In *Paper Trail.* 111–17.

Doyle, Richard. "Vital Language." In Cranor. 52–68.

Eakin, Paul John. "Relational Selves, Relational Lives: The Story of the Story." In *True Relations: Essays on Autobiography and the Postmodern.* Ed. G. Thomas Couser and Joseph Fichtelberg. Westport, Conn.: Greenwood, 1998. 63–81.

———. "The Unseemly Profession: Privacy, Inviolate Personality, and the Ethics of Life Writing." In *Renegotiating Ethics in Literature, Philosophy, and Theory.* Ed. Jane Adamson, Richard Freadman, and David Parker. Cambridge: Cambridge UP, 1998. 161–80.

Egan, Susanna. *Mirror Talk: Genres of Crisis in Contemporary Autobiography.* Chapel Hill: U of North Carolina P, 1999.

Eisenberg, Rebecca S. "Patent Rights in the Humane Genome Project." In Annas and Elias. 226–45.

Ells, Carolyn. "Lessons about Autonomy from the Experience of Disability." *Social Theory and Practice.* 27. 4 (October 2001): 599–615.

Erdrich, Louise. Foreword to Dorris, *The Broken Cord.* xi–xx.

Eskin, Blake. *A Life in Pieces: The Making and Unmaking of Benjamin Wilkomirski.* New York: Norton, 2002.

Federal Statute. Title 45 (Public Welfare), pt. 46 (Protection of Human Subjects). http://ohrp.osophs.dhhs.gov/humansubjects/guidance/45cfr46.htm.

Feinberg, Joel. "Autonomy." In *The Inner Citadel: Essays on Individual Autonomy.* Ed. John Christman. New York: Oxford UP, 1989. 27–53.

———. *Harm to Self.* New York: Oxford UP, 1986. Vol. 3 of *The Moral Limits of the Criminal Law.* 4 vols. 1984–87.

Fetterman, David M. *Ethnography: Step by Step.* Newbury Park, Calif.: Sage, 1989.

Fischer, Michael M. J. "Ethnicity and the Postmodern Arts of Memory." In Clifford and Marcus. 194–223.

Foucault, Michel. *The Birth of the Clinic: An Archaeology of Medical Perception.* Trans. A. M. Sheridan Smith. New York: Vintage, 1973.

Fox, Elaine, Jeffrey J. Kamakahi, and Stella M. Čapek. *Come Lovely and Soothing Death: The Right to Die Movement in the United States*. New York: Twayne, 1999.

Frank, Arthur W. *The Wounded Storyteller: Body, Illness, and Ethics*. Chicago: U of Chicago P, 1995.

Galli, Richard. *Rescuing Jeffrey*. Chapel Hill: Algonquin, 2000.

Gilligan, Carol. *In a Different Voice: Psychological Theory and Women's Development*. Cambridge: Harvard UP, 1982.

Gilman, Sander L. *The Jew's Body*. New York: Routledge, 1991.

——. "Private Knowledge." *Patterns of Prejudice* 36.1 (January 2002): 5–16.

Gladfelder, Hal. *Criminality and Narrative in Eighteenth-Century England: Beyond the Law*. Baltimore: Johns Hopkins UP, 2001.

——. "'I Want to Tell You': Ghost Authors and Criminal Subjects in the Eighteenth Century." Unpublished paper. MLA, 1997.

Goffman, Erving. *Stigma: Notes on the Management of Spoiled Identity*. Englewood Cliffs, N.J.: Prentice-Hall, 1963.

Goldberg, Carey. "DNA Offers Link to Black History." http://www.nytimes.com/library/national/082800black-dna.html.

Haley, Alex. "Epilogue." In *The Autobiography of Malcolm X*, by Malcolm X, with Alex Haley. New York: Grove, 1965. 383–456.

Hampl, Patricia. "Other People's Secrets." In *I Could Tell You Stories*. New York: Norton, 1999. 208–29.

Hanlan, Archie J. *Autobiography of Dying*. Ed. Muriel E. Nelson. Garden City, N.Y.: Doubleday, 1979.

Harpham, Geoffrey Galt. *Getting It Right: Language, Literature, and Ethics*. Chicago: U of Chicago P, 1992.

Hawkins, Anne Hunsaker. "The Myth of Cure and the Process of Accommodation: *Awakenings* Revisited." *Medical Humanities Review* 8.1 (spring 1994): 9–21.

——. "Oliver Sacks's *Awakenings*: Reshaping Clinical Discourse." *Configurations* 1.2 (1993): 229–45.

Hay, Louise L. *You Can Heal Your Life*. Santa Monica, Calif.: Hay House, 1984.

Hendin, Herbert, M.D. *Seduced by Death: Doctors, Patients, and Assisted Suicide*. Rev. ed. New York: Norton, 1998.

Hillman, James. *Suicide and the Soul*. 1964. New York: Harper, 1973.

Hoge, Warren. "Now It Can Be Told: 1992 Tell-All Book's Source Was Diana." *New York Times*, 30 September 1997: A7.

Hood, Leroy. "Biology and Medicine in the Twenty-first Century." In Kevles and Hood, *Code*. 136–63.

How to Do Oral History. 2nd ed. Honolulu: Center for Oral History, U of Hawaii, 1989.

Humphry, Derek. *Jean's Way*. New York: Quartet, 1978.

Hunter, Kathryn Montgomery. *Doctors' Stories: The Narrative Structure of Medicine*. Princeton: Princeton UP, 1991.

"Island of the Colorblind: Monochromatism." *The Mind Traveller: Oliver Sacks*. BBC. 1998.

Jolly, Alison. *Lucy's Legacy: Sex and Intelligence in Human Evolution.* Cambridge: Harvard UP, 1999.

Jones, Maggie. "The Genetic Report Card That Will Tell You If Your Embryo Will Get Prostate Cancer." *New York Times Magazine,* 11 June 2000: 80.

Josselson, Ruthellen, ed. *Ethics and Process in the Narrative Study of Lives.* Thousand Oaks, Calif.: Sage, 1996. Vol. 4 of *The Narrative Study of Lives.* 4 vols. 1993–96.

——. "On Writing Other People's Lives: Self-Analytic Reflections of a Narrative Researcher." In Josselson, *Ethics and Process.* 60–71.

Kafka, Franz. "The Metamorphosis." In *The Metamorphosis and Other Stories.* Trans. Joachim Neugroschel. New York: Scribner's, 1993. 117–41.

Karr, Mary. *The Liar's Club: A Memoir.* New York: Penguin, 1995.

Kavka, Gregory S. "Upside Risks: Social Consequences of Beneficial Biotechnology." In Cranor. 155–79.

Keller, Evelyn Fox. "Nature, Nurture, and the Human Genome Project." In Kevles and Hood, *Code.* 281–99.

Kerby, Anthony Paul. *Narrative and the Self.* Bloomington: Indiana UP, 1991.

Kevles, Daniel J., and Leroy Hood, eds. *The Code of Codes: Scientific and Social Issues in the Human Genome Project.* Cambridge: Harvard UP, 1992.

——. "Reflections." In Kevles and Hood, *Code.* 300–28.

Kingsley, Jason, and Mitchell Levitz. *Count Us In: Growing Up with Down Syndrome.* New York: Harcourt Brace, 1994.

Kolata, Gina. "Scientists Report the First Success of Gene Therapy." *New York Times,* 28 April 2000: A1, A16.

Korda, Michael. "Prompting the President." *New Yorker,* 6 October 1997: 88–95.

Krupat, Arnold. *For Those Who Come After: A Study of Native American Autobiography.* Berkeley: U of California P, 1985.

Kusnetz, Ella. "The Soul of Oliver Sacks." *Massachusetts Review* 33.2 (1992): 175–98.

Lander, Eric. "DNA Fingerprinting: Science, Law, and the Ultimate Identifier." In Kevles and Hood, *Code.* 191–210.

Lappin, Elena. "The Man with Two Heads." *Granta* 66 (summer 1999): 7–65.

Lejeune, Philippe. "The Autobiography of Those Who Do Not Write." In *On Autobiography.* Ed. Paul John Eakin. Trans. Katherine Leary. Minneapolis: U of Minnesota P, 1989. 185–215.

Lesser, Wendy. "Seeing *Awakenings* with Its Real-life Cast." *New York Times,* 21 January 2001. http://nytimes.com/2001/01/21/arts/21LESS.html.

Lewontin, Richard C. "Sex, Lies, and Social Science." In *It Ain't Necessarily So: The Dream of the Human Genome and Other Illusions.* New York: New York Review of Books, 2000. 227–69.

Lionnet, Françoise. *Autobiographical Voices: Race, Gender, Self-Portraiture.* Ithaca: Cornell UP, 1989.

Lloyd, Elisabeth A. "Normality and Variation: The Human Genome Project and the Ideal Human Type." In Cranor. 99–112.

Loving, Carol. *My Son, My Sorrow: The Tragic Tale of Dr. Kevorkian's Youngest Patient.* Far Hills, N.J.: New Horizon, 1998.

Luria, A. R. *The Man with a Shattered World: The History of a Brain Wound*. Trans. Lynn Solotaroff. New York: Basic, 1972.

Mächler, Stefan. *The Wilkomirski Affair: A Study in Biographical Truth*. Trans. John E. Woods. New York: Schocken, 2001.

MacIntyre, Alasdair. *Dependent Rational Animals: Or, Why Human Beings Need the Virtues*. Lasalle, Ill.: Open Court, 1999.

Mackenzie, Catriona, and Natalie Stoljar, eds. *Relational Autonomy: Feminist Perspectives on Autonomy, Agency, and the Social Self*. New York: Oxford UP, 2000.

Mahowald, Mary B. "Biomedical Ethics: A Precocious Youth." In *New Directions in Ethics: The Challenge of Applied Ethics*. Ed. Joseph P. DeMarco and Richard M. Fox. New York: Routledge, 1986. 141–57.

Mairs, Nancy. "Taking Care." In *Waist-High in the World: A Life among the Disabled*. Boston: Beacon, 1996. 64–84.

Malcolm, Andrew H. *This Far and No More: A True Story*. New York: Times Books, 1987.

Malcolm, Janet. *The Journalist and the Murderer*. New York: Vintage, 1990.

The Man Who. By Peter Brook. Dir. Peter Brook. Royal National Theatre. June 1994.

Mappes, Thomas A., and David DeGrazia. *Biomedical Ethics*. 4th ed. New York: McGraw-Hill, 1996.

Marion, Robert. *Was George Washington Really the Father of Our Country? A Clinical Geneticist Looks at World History*. Reading, Mass.: Addison-Wesley, 1994.

McBeth, Sally. "Myths of Objectivity and the Collaborative Process in Life History Research." In *When They Read What We Write: The Politics of Ethnography*. Westport, Conn.: Bergin and Garvey, 1993. 145–62.

McGee, Glenn. *The Perfect Baby: A Pragmatic Approach to Genetics*. New York: Rowan and Littlefield, 1997.

McGinniss, Joe. *Fatal Vision*. New York: Putnam, 1983.

McLeod, Carolyn, and Susan Sherwin. "Relational Autonomy, Self-Trust, and Health Care for Patients Who Are Oppressed." In Mackenzie and Stoljar. 259–79.

McRae, Murdo William. "Oliver Sacks's Neurology of Identity." In *The Literature of Science: Perspectives on Popular Scientific Writings*. Ed. Murdo William McRae. Athens: U of Georgia P, 1993. 97–110.

Medina, John J. *The Genetic Inferno: Inside the Seven Deadly Sins*. New York: Cambridge UP, 2000.

Mehlman, Maxwell J. "Dying to Save Money: Economic Motives for Physician-Assisted Suicide." In David Smith. 22–39.

Miller, Nancy K. *Bequest and Betrayal: Memoirs of a Parent's Death*. New York: Oxford UP, 1996.

Mitchell, David T., and Sharon L. Snyder. "Introduction: Disability Studies and the Double Bind of Representation." In *The Body and Physical Difference: Discourses of Disability*. Ed. David T. Mitchell and Sharon L. Snyder. Ann Arbor: U of Michigan P, 1997. 1–31.

Morton, Andrew. *Diana: Her True Story*. New York: Simon and Schuster, 1992.

——. *Diana: Her True Story in Her Own Words*. Rev. ed. New York: Pocket, 1998.

Murphy, Robert. *The Body Silent.* New York: Henry Holt, 1987.

Murphy, Timothy F. "The Genome Project and the Meaning of Difference." In Murphy and Lappé. 1–13.

——, and Marc A. Lappé, eds. *Justice and the Human Genome Project.* Berkeley: U of California P, 1994.

Nasdijj. *The Blood Runs Like a River through My Dreams: A Memoir.* Boston: Houghton Mifflin, 2000.

Neihardt, John G. *Black Elk Speaks, Being the Life Story of a Holy Man of the Oglala Sioux.* 1932. Lincoln: U of Nebraska P, 1979.

Nelkin, Dorothy. "The Social Power of Genetic Information." In Kevles and Hood, *Code.* 177–90.

——, and M. Susan Lindee. *The DNA Mystique: The Gene as a Cultural Icon.* New York: W. H. Freeman, 1995.

Newton, Adam Zachary. *Narrative Ethics.* Cambridge: Harvard UP, 1995.

Orlean, Susan. *The Bullfighter Checks Her Makeup: My Encounters with Extraordinary People.* New York: Random House, 2001.

——. Interview. Public Radio International. 3 May 2001.

Ozick, Cynthia. "Who Owns Anne Frank?" *New Yorker,* 6 October 1997: 76–87.

Park, Clara Claiborne. *Exiting Nirvana: A Daughter's Life with Autism.* Boston: Little, Brown, 2001.

——. *The Siege: The First Eight Years of an Autistic Child.* 1967. Boston: Little, Brown, 1982.

Paul, Diane B. "Eugenic Anxieties, Social Realities, and Political Choices." In Cranor. 142–54.

Pellegrino, Edmund D., and David C. Thomasma. *The Virtues in Medical Practice.* New York: Oxford UP, 1993.

Peterson, Peter. "Postscript from Daniel's Physician." In Rothman, *Saying Goodbye to Daniel.* 165–67.

"Poison in Paradise: Guam Disease." *The Mind Traveller: Oliver Sacks.* BBC. 1998.

Potter, Jerry Allen, with Fred Bost. *Fatal Justice: Reinvestigating the MacDonald Murders.* 1995. New York: Norton, 1997.

Quaid, Kimberly A. "A Few Words from a 'Wise' Woman." In *Genes and Human Self-Knowledge.* Ed. Robert F. Weir, Susan C. Lawrence, and Evan Fales. Iowa City: U of Iowa P, 1994. 3–17.

Quill, Timothy. *Death and Dignity: Making Choices and Taking Charge.* New York: Norton, 1993.

"Rage for Order: Autism." *The Mind Traveller: Oliver Sacks.* BBC. 1998.

"The Ragin' Cajun: Usher Syndrome." *The Mind Traveller: Oliver Sacks.* BBC. 1998.

Rapp, Rayna, and Faye Ginsburg. "Enabling Disability: Rewriting Kinship, Reimagining Citizenship." *Public Culture* 13.3 (n.d.): 533–56.

Recer, Paul. "Genetic Code Mostly Mapped." *Boulder Daily Camera,* 27 June 2000: 1A, 9A.

Reeve, Christopher. *Still Me.* New York: Random House, 1998.

Ridley, Matt. *Genome: The Autobiography of a Species in Twenty-three Chapters.* New York: HarperCollins, 1999.

Rimer, Sara. "A Deadly Disease Destroys Families as Well as Patients." *New York Times*, 24 June 2002: A14.

Robillard, Albert B. *Meaning of a Disability: The Lived Experience of Paralysis.* Philadelphia: Temple UP, 1999.

Rollin, Betty. *Last Wish.* 1985. New York: Public Affairs, 1996.

Rosenwald, George C. "Making Whole: Method and Ethics in Mainstream and Narrative Psychology." In Josselson, *Ethics and Process.* 245–74.

Rothman, Barbara Katz. *Genetic Maps and Human Imaginations: The Limits of Science in Understanding Who We Are.* New York: Norton, 1998.

Rothman, Juliet Cassuto. *Saying Goodbye to Daniel: When Death Is the Best Choice.* New York: Continuum, 1995.

Roy, Travis, with E. M. Swift. *Eleven Seconds: A Story of Tragedy, Courage, and Triumph.* New York: Warner, 1998.

Sacks, Oliver. *An Anthropologist on Mars: Seven Paradoxical Tales.* New York: Knopf, 1995.

——. *Awakenings.* 1973. Rev. ed. New York: Dutton, 1983.

——. Interview. "The Man Who Mistook His Life for a What?" *Psychology Today* (May–June 1995): 28–33.

——. *The Island of the Colorblind and Cycad Island.* New York: Knopf, 1997.

——. *A Leg to Stand On.* New York: Summit, 1984.

——. *The Man Who Mistook His Wife for a Hat, and Other Clinical Tales.* New York: Summit, 1985.

——, M.D. *Migraine: Understanding a Common Disorder.* 1970. Rev. ed. Berkeley: U of California P, 1985.

——. *Seeing Voices: A Journey into the Land of the Deaf.* Berkeley: U of California P, 1989.

——. *Uncle Tungsten: Memories of a Chemical Boyhood.* New York: Knopf, 2001.

——. "Where Biology Meets Biography." Interview with Margalit Fox. *New York Times Book Review*, 19 February 1995: 30.

Sanderson, Richard K. "Memoirs of Assisted Suicide." Unpublished essay.

——. "Relational Deaths: Narratives of Suicide Survivorship." In *True Relations: Essays on Autobiography and the Postmodern.* Ed. G. Thomas Couser and Joseph Fichtelberg. Westport, Conn.: Greenwood, 1998. 33–50.

Sandomir, Richard. "Co-author Sues to Publish Vincent Book." *New York Times*, 11 August 1997: 21, 25 (Sports).

Severo, Richard. "Hedy Lamarr, Sultry Star Who Reigned in Hollywood of 30's and 40's, Dies at 86." *New York Times*, 20 January 2000. http://www.nytimes.com/yr/mo/day/news/national/obit-h-lamarr.html.

Shakespeare, Tom. Review of Oliver Sacks, *An Anthropologist on Mars. Disability and Society* 11.1 (1996): 137–42.

"Shane: Tourette's Syndrome." *The Mind Traveller: Oliver Sacks.* BBC. 1998.

Shea, Christopher. "Don't Talk to the Humans." *Lingua Franca* (September 2000): 27–34.

Sherwin, Susan. *No Longer Patient: Feminist Ethics and Health Care.* Philadelphia: Temple UP, 1992.

Shuffleton, Frank. "Being Definitive: Jefferson Biography under the Shadow of Dumas Malone." *Biography* 18.4 (fall 1995): 291–304.

Singer, Peter, and Helga Kuhse. *Should the Baby Live? The Problem of Handicapped Infants.* New York: Oxford UP, 1985.

Sienkiewicz-Mercer, Ruth, and Steven B. Kaplan. *I Raise My Eyes to Say Yes.* Boston: Houghton Mifflin, 1989.

Smith, David, ed. *Alternatives to Physician-Assisted Suicide.* Bloomington: Poynter Center, 2000.

Smith, Dinitia. "Gerald Frank Is Dead at 91; Author of Celebrity Memoirs." *New York Times,* 19 September 1998: A12.

Smith, Sidonie. "Taking It to a Limit One More Time: Autobiography and Autism." In *Getting a Life: Everyday Uses of Autobiography.* Ed. Sidonie Smith and Julia Watson. Minneapolis: U of Minnesota P, 1996. 226–46.

Smith, Wesley J. *The Culture of Death: The Assault on Medical Ethics in America.* San Francisco: Encounter, 2000.

——. *Forced Exit: The Slippery Slope from Assisted Suicide to Legalized Murder.* New York: Times, 1997.

Solomon, Andrew. "A Death of One's Own." *New Yorker,* 22 May 1995: 54–69.

Spiegelman, Art. *Maus I: A Survivor's Tale; My Father Bleeds History.* New York: Pantheon, 1986.

——. *Maus II: A Survivor's Tale; And Here My Troubles Began.* New York: Pantheon, 1991.

Spradley, Thomas S., and James P. Spradley. *Deaf Like Me.* 1978. Rpt. Washington, D.C.: Gallaudet UP, 1985. Epilogue by Lynn Spradley.

Stange, Margit. "The Broken Self: Fetal Alcohol Syndrome." In *Body Politics: Disease, Desire, and the Family.* Ed. Michael Ryan and Avery Gordon. Boulder, Colo.: Westview, 1994. 126–36.

Steiner, Peter. Cartoon. *New Yorker,* 15 September 1997: 72.

Stillinger, Jack. *Multiple Authorship and the Myth of Solitary Genius.* New York: Oxford UP, 1991.

Stingley, Darryl, with Mark Mulvoy. *Happy to Be Alive.* New York: Beaufort, 1983.

Stolberg, Sheryl Gay. "Trials Are Halted on a Gene Therapy." *New York Times,* 4 October 2002: A1.

Strickland, Margot. "Ghosting an Autobiography." *Biography* 18.1 (winter 1995): 65–68.

——, and Moura Lympany. *Moura Lympany: Her Autobiography.* London: Dufour, 1991.

Szanton, Andrew. *The Recollections of Eugene P. Wigner as Told to Andrew Szanton.* New York: Plenum, 1992.

——. Telephone interview, 11 November 1997.

——, and Charles Evers. *Have No Fear: The Charles Evers Story.* New York: Wiley, 1997.

Thomas, Carol. *Female Forms: Experiencing and Understanding Disability.* Philadelphia: Open UP, 1999.

Thompson, Mike. "Genome Outcome." Cartoon. *Detroit Free Press,* 27 June 2000. cagle.slate.msn.com/news/gene/gene5.asp.

Thomson, Rosemarie Garland. "Introduction: From Wonder to Error—A Genealogy of Freak Discourse in Modernity." In *Freakery: Cultural Spectacles of the Extraordinary Body*. Ed. Rosemarie Garland Thomson. New York: New York UP, 1996. 1–19.

Thoreau, Henry David. *Walden*. 1854. Ed. J. Lyndon Shanley. Princeton: Princeton UP, 1971.

Troupe, Quincy. *Miles and Me*. Berkeley: U of California P, 2000.

Twachtman-Cullen, Diane. *A Passion to Believe: Autism and the Facilitated Communication Phenomenon*. Boulder, Colo.: Westview, 1997.

Twain, Mark. "Jim Blaine and His Grandfather's Old Ram." In *Selected Shorter Writings of Mark Twain*. Ed. Walter Blair. Boston: Houghton Mifflin, 1962. 40–44.

Veatch, Robert M., ed. *Medical Ethics*. Boston: Jones and Bartlett, 1989.

Vizenor, Gerald. "Firewater and Phrenology." In *Crossbloods: Bone Courts, Bingo, and Other Reports*. Minneapolis: U of Minnesota P, 1990. 300–19.

——. "Postindian Warriors." *Manifest Manners: Postindian Warriors of Survivance*. Middletown, Conn.: Wesleyan UP, 1994. 1–44.

Wade, Nicholas. "After 10 Years' Effort, Genome Mapping Team Achieves Sequence of a Human Chromosome." *New York Times*, 2 December 1999. http://www.nytimes.com/library/national/science/120299sci-genome.html.

——. "The Hidden Traps in Fooling Mother Nature." *New York Times*, 5 September 1999: sec. 4:1, 4.

——. "The Human Family Tree: 10 Adams and 18 Eves." *New York Times*, 2 May 2000. http://www.nytimes.com/library/national/science/050200sci-genetics-evoluion.html.

Weijer, Charles. "Protecting Communities in Research: Philosophical and Pragmatic Challenges." *Cambridge Quarterly of Healthcare Ethics* 8 (1999): 501–13.

Wertenbaker, Lael Tucker. *Death of a Man*. New York: Random House, 1957.

Wendell, Susan. *The Rejected Body: Feminist Philosophical Reflections on Disability*. New York: Routledge, 1996

West, Jessamyn. *The Woman Said Yes: Encounters with Life and Death*. New York: Harcourt, 1976.

West, Paul. *Words for a Deaf Daughter*. New York: Harper and Row, 1970.

Wexler, Alice. *Emma Goldman: An Intimate Life*. New York: Pantheon, 1984.

——. *Mapping Fate: A Memoir of Family, Risk, and Genetic Research*. New York: Times Books, 1995.

Wexler, Nancy. "Clairvoyance and Caution: Repercussions from the Human Genome Project." In Kevles and Hood, *Code*. 211–43.

Wilgoren, Jodi. "Confession Had His Signature; DNA Did Not." *New York Times*, 26 August 2002: A1.

Wilkomirski, Binjamin. *Fragments: Memories of a Wartime Childhood*. Trans. Carol Brown Janeway. New York: Schocken Books, 1996.

Willett, Jeffrey, and Mary Jo Deegan. "Liminality and Disability: Rites of Passage and Community in Hypermodern Society." *Disability Studies Quarterly* 21.3 (summer 2001): 137–52.

Wilson, James C. "(Re)Writing the Genetic Body-Text: Disability, Textuality, and the Human Genome Project." *Cultural Critique* 50 (2002): 23–39.

Wiltshire, John. "Deficits and Enhancements: Reflections on the Writing of Oliver Sacks." *Cambridge Quarterly* 20.4 (1991): 304–21.

Woodmansee, Martha, and Peter Jaszi, eds. *The Construction of Authorship: Textual Appropriation in Law and Literature.* Durham: Duke UP, 1994.

Wright, William. *Born That Way: Genes, Behavior, Personality.* New York: Routledge, 1998.

Wyden, Peter. "The Blockbustering of Lee Iacocca." *New York Times Book Review,* 13 September 1987: 1, 54–55.

Index

abortion, 168, 183–89
Adams, Henry, 126
adoption, 56–77, 177–78, 208n3
Annas, George J., 169
Annas, George J., and Sherman Elias, 187–88
anonymity, as protection of subject, 20, 77
Apter, Terri, 20
as-told-to autobiography, 35–39, 54–55. *See also* collaborative life writing
authorized biography, 56–57
autism, 52, 96, 106–7, 109–12, 116, 118
auto/bio/ethics, defined, ix
autobiographical pact, 46, 174
auto/biography, ix, 40, 56, 63
autoethnography, 59
autonomy, 18–23, 25–26, 65, 76, 82–83, 88, 125–26, 130, 133–43, 145, 153–63, 175; as capacity versus as condition, 18, 65, 83; feminist critique of, 18. *See also* surrogacy
autoradiography, 169–70, 172

Battin, Margaret Pabst, 125
Bayley, John, ix–x, 23
Beauchamp, Tom L., and James F. Childress, 15, 17–19, 22–30, 36, 76, 83–84, 88, 145, 203n1
Bedlamites, 76–79
Behar, Ruth, 206n5
beneficence, 20, 26–28, 133–34
benefits of life writing, 24, 82. *See also* proceeds of life writing
Berendzen, Richard, 217n13
Bérubé, Michael, 195–96
Beth Abraham Hospital ("Mount Carmel"), 90, 93–94

Biklen, Douglas, 52–53
bioethics. *See* biomedical ethics
biomedical ethics, ix–x, 14–31, 204n1
Black Elk. See *Black Elk Speaks*
Black Elk Speaks, 42–43, 48–49, 54–55
Bok, Sissela, 116
Booth, Wayne C., 34
Brettell, Caroline B., 32
Broeker, Beth, 178

Campbell, Courtney, 130
case history, medical. *See* Sacks, Oliver
Cassell, Eric J., 156
Cassuto, Leonard, 210n2
celebrity autobiography, 39–40, 44–50. *See also* as-told-to autobiography
children, as subjects of life writing, 79–81. *See also* Dorris, Adam; parental life writing
Clifford, James, 32, 63, 65–66, 74
Cockburn, Andrew, 75–78, 82
Cohen, Randy, xi–xii
collaborative life writing, 34–55
color-blindness, 116–17
Comfort, Heidi, 80–81, 202
common morality, 204n2
competence. *See* autonomy
Condit, Celeste Michelle, 167
confession, legal, 51–53, 158
consequentialist ethics, 10–11, 19–20, 140, 209n19
conversion narrative, 208n7
Cooke, Maeve, 18
Coombe, Rosemary J., 40
Crossley, Rosemary, 53
cystic fibrosis, 168, 183